The Dark Side
of Humanity

The Dark Side of Humanity

The Work of Robert Hertz and its Legacy

Robert Parkin

harwood academic publishers
Australia • Canada • China • France • Germany • India • Japan
Luxembourg • Malaysia • The Netherlands • Russia • Singapore
Switzerland • Thailand • United Kingdom

Copyright © 1996 by OPA (Overseas Publishers Association) Amsterdam B.V.
Published in The Netherlands by Harwood Academic Publishers GmbH.

Emmaplein 5
1075 AW Amsterdam
The Netherlands

British Library Cataloguing in Publication Data

Parkin, Robert
    The dark side of humanity: the work of Robert Hertz and its legacy
    1. Hertz, Robert — Criticism and interpretation
    2. Anthropologists — France   3. Anthropologists' writings —
    History and criticism   4. Anthropology   5. Ethnology
    6. Ethnologists — France
    I. Title
    301'.092

    ISBN   3-7186-5861-5

Contents

Preface

Robert Hertz was born in 1881 and killed in action on the Meuse in April 1915, at the age of 33, after a relatively uneventful life devoted to sociology and socialism. He has come to exemplify perhaps more than anyone else the tragedy of the Durkheimians, many of whom, including the master himself, died during, though not necessarily as a result of, the First World War. Although nominally a sociologist of religion, he has certainly had more influence in anthropology than in sociology or any other related discipline. Most anthropologists today would probably place him third in any league table of the Durkheimians, next only to the master and Mauss in terms of the quality, influence and relevance of his work.

Hertz seems to have been aiming to carve out a specific niche for himself in respect of what the Durkheimians were trying to achieve — not so much thematically as with regard to the particular angle from which he approached the collective effort. Though probably less intended at the time, his works have also proved, in different ways, to have had relevance for most of the major subsequent anthropological approaches to ritual, itself a key explanandum for the Durkheimians. The degree of admiration he excited in both contemporaries and latter-day followers has become almost adulation at times, as the warmth of Durkheim's and Mauss's memorials for him show. Given the circumstances of his death and the subsequent regret at the truncated promise of his life, he has become the nearest thing anthropology has to a sort of Chatterton figure, or to those legendary popular entertainers who have won enduring fame by showing promise before dying tragically young. There is no doubt that he was gifted and diligent, as well as being socially concerned, and as a consequence much admired by his colleagues. However, thanks to the efforts of Evans-Pritchard and Rodney Needham in particular, his academic reputation and memory are now secure, and we can begin to put his work in its proper context as regards not only the *Année* and anthropology generally but also his own life and personality.

The present book is thus not a conventional biography — though biographical details are included — nor even entirely an intellectual one. Certainly it is in part an attempt to situate Hertz's work in the history of anthropology by discussing his ideas and showing how they were related to those of his contemporaries — especially but not entirely those in the *Année*.

But a considerable amount of effort has also gone into discussing the ways in which they have been utilized and developed by later scholars, who have almost uniformly found them an inspiration, though often in unexpected ways. This is true of all his major works, mainly those on death and on right and left, but also those on sin and on the cult of St. Besse, which are at last beginning to be recognized after a long period of neglect.

In the course of writing this book, Maurice Godelier and Serge Tcherkézoff gave me invaluable help and support in arranging two research trips to Paris, in spring 1992 and early summer 1993, for which they are duly thanked here. These trips were funded by the Centre National de la Recherche Scientifique, and I also acknowledge the help of Hinnerck Bruhns of CNRS in this regard. I would also like to thank Françoise Héritier for giving me permission to examine the archive of Hertz's letters and other papers, including manuscripts, in the Laboratoire d'Anthropologie Sociale. This archive was presented to the Laboratoire by members of Hertz's family in the 1960s, with further additions in the 1980s, and it includes Hertz's personal library. It is listed under the title of the Fonds Robert Hertz (abbreviated to FRH in the present book). Citations of and from Hertz's and others' letters are from it, except where otherwise stated. Marion Abelès and her staff are thanked for their unfailing help during my sojourns in the Laboratoire library; and Marion Abelès and Marie Mauzé for helping me decipher late nineteenth- and early twentieth-century French handwriting on occasion. Philippe Besnard drew my attention to a handful of letters from Durkheim to Mauss which discuss Hertz after his death.

Finally, special words of gratitude go to Margaret Gardiner, whose father Sir Alan Gardiner was a close friend of Hertz in his youth and who allowed me to peruse reminiscences of Hertz that he had later written down for the benefit of his family; and to Antoine Hertz, who welcomed me most warmly at his home in the Dordogne and clarified a number of uncertainties concerning details of his father's life. The willing help of all these named individuals and institutions does not in any way diminish the full responsibility for the contents of the present work from being mine and mine alone.

The translations of quotations from works in French are by myself where a published translation does not already exist.

Table of Main Events in Hertz's Life

22 June 1881	Born at Saint-Cloud, near Paris
1889	Entered Lycée Janson de Sailly
1898	Entered Lycée Henri IV
1900	Accepted for Ecole Normale Supérieure
12 Nov 1900	Started military service (approx. 1 year)
About 1900	Met Durkheim
1901	Matriculated at Ecole Normale Supérieure
July 1903	Further military training
24 August 1904	Married Alice Bauer
29 August 1904	Graduated from Ecole Normale Supérieure; joined Durkheim's research group
Oct 1904–July 1905	In England (mainly reading in British Museum)
Autumn 1905–Summer 1906	Teaching in lycée, Douai
July–August 1906	At British Museum
Sept 1906	Further military training
1907	'La représentation collective de la mort' published
1908–1912	Lecturing at Ecole Pratique des Hautes Etudes
March 1908	Groupe d'Etudes Socialistes founded; Cahiers du Socialiste launched
1909	'La prééminence de la main droite' published
6 January 1909	Birth of Antoine Hertz, son
May 1909	Further military training
Autumn 1910	At British Museum
1911	Working on thesis on sin
20 July–1 Sept 1912	Fieldwork on St. Besse cult
1913	'Saint Besse' published; work on rocks and mountains
1914	Called up into army (2nd Company, 44th Territorial Infantry Regiment)
November 1914	Transfer to 17th Company, 330th Regiment
13 April 1915	Killed in action on plain of Wöevre
1917	'Contes et dictons' published
1922	'Le peché et l'expiation' published
16 November 1927	Death of Alice Hertz
1928	*Mélanges* published
1960	English translations of 'Mort' and 'La main droite' published
1983	English translation of 'Saint Besse' published
1994	English translation of 'Le peché et l'expiation' published

List of Illustrations

Between pages 152 and 153

All photographs by Robert Parkin 1990

CHAPTER ONE

Life and Career

Robert Walter Hertz was born at Saint Cloud near Paris on 22nd June 1881, into a relatively well-off Jewish family, the fourth of five children born to Adolphe Hertz, merchant, and Josephine Strahlheim. His father was then forty years old and came from a German-Jewish family who in former times had been bankers to a local prince somewhere in Germany. He came to France as a young man and obtained naturalization in 1880 but died in a climbing accident in the Alps in 1899, while Hertz was still a teenager. At the time of Robert's birth, his mother was 25 years old. She came from a British or American family and survived Robert, dying in 1927. Robert had three elder sisters, Fanny, Cécile and Dora, and a younger brother Jacques, who between them provided him with a number of nephews and nieces. He himself had only one child, Antoine, born in Paris on 6/1/1909.[1]

Hertz attended the Lycée Janson de Sailly between 1889 and entering Henri IV in 1898 to prepare for the Ecole Normale Supérieure (ENS). At both schools, he showed himself to be a precocious student, and he left Henri IV second in his year.[2] A year of military service intervened between his acceptance for the ENS in 1900 and his matriculation in 1901, a period he regarded as time wasted.[3] He graduated from the ENS on 29th August 1904 with first place in the *agrégation de philosophie*, which was normally intended as a qualification to teach in secondary education.[4]

But Hertz did not follow this path directly, nor was it to be his ultimate career. Indeed, deciding what to do in life did not come easily to him. At school, he had been attracted for a time by politics, but soon came to feel that as a Jew in contemporary France — then at the height of the Dreyfus Affair — he would be able to achieve nothing. Science was already another possibility, perhaps medicine, but more likely philosophy of a scientific sort, i.e. science that was 'grounded in facts'.[5] His mind already seemed to be receptive to Durkheimianism, though it was a few years yet before he would meet Durkheim himself.

That meeting took place around the time of his acceptance into the ENS,[6] which was now becoming, with Durkheim ensconced in the Sorbonne (from 1902), a major recruiting ground for the *Année*. Hertz joined the *Année* soon after graduating, making him one of those who entered in the first decade of this century, along with such figures as Bianconi, Gelly and Reynier.[7] He was therefore of a later generation than Mauss, Hubert, Bouglé, Simiand and Halbwachs, who had all joined in the 1890s, though he clearly outshone his own contemporaries. Durkheim tells us that Hertz's main interest at this time was in social and economic questions, and that he was disturbed at the threat to order from what he saw as the anarchy of the contemporary economic system. Given that he saw that system as being driven essentially by individual interests, Hertz's fears fell entirely into line with a very widespread nineteenth-century French attitude towards individualism.[8] Durkheim must have sympathized,[9] but he was evidently able to impress upon Hertz that one could not study such matters effectively without examining 'the psychological nature of man in society, the way in which the ideas that guide him are formed and developed, religious and moral ideas, juridicial concepts, etc.'[10]

In short, Durkheim rapidly made a convert of this bright and somewhat ernest 19-year-old. Hertz's relations with both Durkheim and Mauss were close: they both came to speak of him as a friend as well as a pupil, and Mauss's obituary of him is perhaps the warmest of all those he wrote on his late colleagues after the war.[11] As a student, Hertz enjoyed direct contact with them both rather than through one of the master's lieutenants, such as Hubert, Simiand or Bouglé, who were each responsible for particular subgroups, according to topic.[12] To what extent this was a privilege arising out of Hertz's particular potential, or out of the Jewishness he shared with Durkheim and his nephew, is no longer clear.[13] Yet he was certainly noticed by the others and was counted among the inner group for the purposes of contributing to Durkheim's *Festschrift* (along with Simiand, Mauss, Hubert, Bouglé, Fauconnet and Huvelin), a project that never got beyond the planning sta*;e.[14] And as one of the sociologists of religion in the group, he does seem to have had some influence on Mauss, who was seven years his senior, though perhaps not on Hubert, who was later to indicate his misgivings with some of Hertz's work.[15]

The hesitation Hertz felt at the ENS between taking up sociology pure and simple and concentrating on its various 'branches' — religious and economic on the one hand, moral and political on the other — imposed a choice on him that he never really made, according to Mauss. This led him, after his *agrégation*, to choose subjects for study in which 'the moral jousted with the religious' — especially the work on sin, which was to have been his doctoral thesis.[16] Mauss is perhaps justified in identifying in Hertz an interest in 'the dark side of humanity', or what he elsewhere calls 'the dark and sinister sides of human mentality', but he restricts himself to linking this with a certain strain of pessimism in his character.[17] Hubert Bourgin, however, who seems to have known Hertz well at this time, hints strongly that Hertz's choice of academic topics was directly influenced by his concern over what he perceived as the growing anarchy and social breakdown of contemporary France.[18] He does not link this to any specific works of Hertz's, nor does Hertz express these feelings directly in his academic writings. Nonetheless, it is easy to see them reflected in his study on sin, which deals not only with the transgression of social rules, but with how the social breach it brings about is repaired (Hertz is as concerned with the sinner's response, activated by his or her conscience, as with the operation of social sanctions). The long essay on death, similarly, is all about the breach in the social fabric brought about by the loss of one of its members, which is often seen not as an act of God or nature but as the outcome of another person's moral transgression. With the paper on right and left, the matter is not immediately so clear. Hertz's wife Alice tells us that his interest here was stimulated originally by a problem in education, the encouragment of ambidexterity in children, and she suggests that only subsequently did he see in it a 'sociological problem', which she identifies as the social representation of space.[19] Certainly the article ends with Hertz approving the encouragement being given to ambidexterity in the modern world. But in that Hertz treats the left hand itself as a sociological problem, one might say that the article is also concerned with how the negative aspects of social life may be symbolized. Even the monograph on St Besse, in that it became a disquisition on the competitiveness between classes and communities over a single rite, could be interpreted as reflecting this concern. At all events, there can be little doubt that Hertz intended much of his work as showing how a postivist, scientific sociology could be applied to intellectualist thinking on contemporary problems, a point we shall return to.

Hertz's doctoral supervisor was, of course, Durkheim, and what is left to us of the thesis certainly reflects his influence. Hertz's letters to his friend Pierre Roussel show clearly that the choice was not made immediately. Death seems to have been the first option, though in the event this topic was treated in a separate article.[20] He then thought of mourning as a subject, but rejected it, having had enough of anything to do with death by this time.[21] Next, he mentions the desire for a more narrowly defined topic, whether thematically or geographically, one idea being something 'half-religious, half-moral' on Greece. This would have been linguistically easy for him (cf. n. 2, above), as well as bringing him academically closer to his friend. Sin and expiation, especially the phenomenon of confession, receive mention as a possible topic in the same letter,[22] though even a year later (July 1908) there is still doubt as to whether this will be the thesis.[23] There is evidence that Hertz did not find writing congenial, preferring the thrill of discovering new facts in the library to the drudgery of putting it all together.[24] Nonetheless, his first article, on death (1907a), proved too long to publish without considerable cuts having to be made. In the words of his wife: 'His teachers, having received his work, set about reducing it to proper proportions. They had to prune it, cut it down, make the canvas, painted with a little too much fantasy, fit the *Année's* scientific frame.'[25] One gets a glimpse here of how fresh the work must have seemed to all the group, how much they must have felt themselves to be pioneers, on the threshold of new discoveries, new perspectives, developing a new science together.

After graduating, getting married and joining the *Année*, Hertz was immediately given a scholarship to study ethnographic materials in England, possibly a prize for coming first in his *agrégation*.[26] He reports being more attracted to England than to Germany, unlike Durkheim, who spent the academic year 1885-6 in Germany and returned both impressed and influenced by much of what he learnt.[27] Hertz's own post-graduation academic year, between October 1904 and July 1905, was spent mainly at the British Museum, working through ethnographic documents for his study on death.[28] Much of this material would eventually have found its way into his thesis on sin had he lived to complete it, though as we have seen, a final decision on the topic still had not been taken.[29]

A number of friends — Mauss, Maurice Halbwachs and Jean Chevalier — visited Hertz in England.[30] In between studying, there were trips to Cambridge, Oxford, Canterbury, Wales and northwest England. His letters to Roussel tell us much about his activities and his impressions of his English colleagues.[31] Thus he reported meeting Hartland at the Folklore Society, which he had been attending along with the Anthropology Institute, though not the Sociology Institute, which he regarded as a farce. He also followed Westermarck's lectures, but found them unsatisfactory, despite Westermarck's erudition. He found too that in general the English regarded Durkheim's work as 'fanciful', while Hertz in his turn felt English scholarship to be fundamentally unscientific, consisting too much in the mere collection of facts.[32] A prime example was the work of Frazer, whom Hertz met in Cambridge in 1905. He describes him as erudite but untheoretical, personally shy but also vain and proud, 'passionately irreligious and anti-Christian', this being 'certainly one of the motives of his research'. Hertz also related university gossip to the effect that Frazer lived and worked practically the whole time in his college, Trinity, only visiting his wife once a week to dine, and he was able to report directly Frazer's own admission that he had never once stepped inside the university museum (which Hertz considered a good one): 'I work only in books'.[33]

But it was the reading and collection of ethnographic data that was the main purpose of Hertz's being in England. His wife Alice gives us a picture of him pacing up and down his room in his lodgings in Highgate, reflecting on his theme, developing his ideas, and virtually living, as far as he could, with the Dayaks who were his favourite ethnic group at that time, learning their language, etc.[34] Later, when researching the question of sin, it would be the Maori that particularly interested him. By the middle of 1906, Durkheim was evidently pressing him to write something on death, and this led to a further short trip to the British Museum.[35]

Yet as we have seen, Hertz was by no means an ivory-tower academic but took what Mauss calls the moral side of his work equally seriously. This led him, like many of his colleagues, into a type of political activism which was at once intellectual and practical. The sympathies of virtually all the Durkheimians with the socialism of Jean Jaurès are well known, as is their opposition both to revolutionary Marxism, including its local Guesdist variant, and to the republican individualism of Georges Clemenceau. The former promoted unrelenting class hostility, and Clemenceau's personal belief in the inevitability of conflict and of the selfishness of individuals was in its way equally the antithesis of Durkheimian collectivism.[36] Indeed, the new sociology was envisaged as a science *for* society as much as *of* society. Durkheim saw himself as an educator as much as a sociologist, in accordance with his professional status as *chargé de cours* in both social science and pedagogy at Bordeaux. For many of the acolytes, though not for himself, this commitment extended to a more literal activism, organizing strikes, lecturing to workers and running campaigns connected with the Dreyfus affair and other issues. Mauss, for instance, was involved in organizing co-operatives, and he, Simiand and Lévy-Bruhl all took part in the launch of the newspaper *L'Humanité*, along with Lucien Herr and Jaurès. Three certificates in the FRH, all dated 25/3/1912, indicate that Hertz was also a member of the Société Nouvelle de l'Humanité that was formed to undertake the launch.[37]

Hertz had been attracted to socialism at least from his entry into the ENS,[38] where he encountered Lucien Herr, its librarian from 1888 to 1916 and socialist *eminence grise* of the period. Herr is credited with converting both Jean Jaurès and Léon Blum, as well as numerous Normalians, to social-ism.[39] Hertz himself was evidently a not uncritical adherent.[40] Indeed, to begin with he rather suspected both the collectivism of the socialists and their desire for a new society.[41] His socialism was always distinctly Fabian in kind, something for which his friendship from school days with Frederick Lawson Dodd, a leading British Fabian, must have been partly responsible.[42] Indeed, his personal experience of England, which consisted of occasional visits to Fabian summer schools as well as research in the British Museum, made him view the country increasingly as the model for French social and political reform, though for the moment the weakness of the French state was preventing much progress.[43]

Hubert Bourgin makes it clear that Hertz eventually came to agree fully with Durkheim's scientific approach and the place of the new sociology within it, in contrast to the more romantic and utopian socialism of the past: 'he understood socialism as a method of studying and solving social problems', one which entailed bringing the lessons acquired from the study of non-European societies critically to bear on all manner of contemporary social, economic and political problems.[44] For Hertz, the science was in the method of the research rather than in its aims. In Bourgin's words, that method was to be applied

> not to historical problems, chosen for their interest, for their scientific significance, but to the practical, current problems which the conditions of our life in contemporary society present, and which ... must be approached and solved using all the precautions and scruples that the learned bring to the examination of ancient and defunct societies.[45]

In Hertz's own words, taken from an unpublished lecture: 'Socialism must maintain contact with the developing social science, since it is nothing less than sociology in action, applying itself to the social problems of the time.'[46] Behind this, once again, is clearly the fear that the strains engendered by the contemporary capitalist system might lead to social breakdown. Indeed, this triple nexus — social anarchy as the problem, sociology and socialism as the solutions — seems to have dominated his own commitment in life, even though it does not appear explicitly in his academic writings.[47] As Mauss hinted (see above), there rapidly arose for Hertz a certain tension between the demands of science and the pressure of contemporary problems, one which he was never entirely able to resolve to his own satisfaction.

Hertz wrote a number of reviews and papers on social problems and the socialist response to them, not all of which were published. His earliest contributions of this sort, indeed his earliest publications, were two reviews (see Hertz 1902, 1903) for the academic-cum-socialist journal *Notes Critiques — Sciences Sociales,* published between 1900 and 1906 and edited by François Simiand. The background to this venture reflects the collectivism of the times in the circles in which Hertz moved. Many of the Durkheimians were members of the Société Nouvelle de Librairie et d'Edition, which Herr had helped found with other like-minded souls in 1899 to take over the ailing Péguist bookshop, the Librairie Georges Bellais. Hertz, along with Mauss, Hubert, Halbwachs, Simiand, Fauconnet and Hubert Bourgin, was a shareholder, and he also belonged to the Groupe de l'Unité Socialiste, its activist wing. Another of the Société's ventures was this initially twice-monthly, then monthly journal, which was intended to complement the *Année Sociologique* by reviewing books on contemporary social problems, as well as ethnology, history and general philosophy. Like the *Année Sociologique,* it was seen as a collective effort, something reflected in the anonymity of reviewers in the first year of publication, a policy thereafter abandoned. Another of its rationales was the need to separate politics from academic writings, the *Année Sociologique* representing the latter.[48] Most of the Durkheimians contributed reviews, including the master and Hertz. Despite the common personnel and intended complementarity, the two journals began as separate ventures and remained so. The appearance of *Notes Critiques* even seems to have triggered a minor crisis in the *Année,* through fear of its being supplanted, and the issue of a fourth volume of the latter was in doubt for a while.[49] Nonetheless it was the *Année Sociologique* that survived, *Notes Critiques* ceasing publication in 1906.

Possibly its demise had something to do with the setting up of the Groupe d'Etudes Socialistes (GES) in March 1908, apparently largely on Hertz's initiative. In essence, the GES was a small debating society which aimed to support the socialist movement in France from an academic or at least intellectual standpoint. It was based on the idea of Sidney and Beatrice Webbs' Fabian Society in Britain, although Hertz always resisted the setting up of a distinct Fabian movement in France along British lines, for fear of it competing with the existing Parti Socialiste.[50] Normally, at least in the years for which we have detailed records, it consisted of between forty and sixty members, who met every month in the academic year to hear and discuss a paper by one of them on a particular topical problem that socialists were or should be concerned with. Many Durkheimians were members, including Mauss, though not Durkheim himself. Hertz was continually active as its treasurer and one of its secretaries, and François Simiand was also regularly a committee member, as, at least latterly, was Henri Lévy-Bruhl.

Hertz, Simiand and Hubert Bourgin also founded the series Cahiers du Socialiste as a vehicle for publishing revised versions of the talks given at the GES's meetings.[51] This was in line with the Groupe's goal of establishing and disseminating information that might be useful in socialist campaigns, and although it came in for some criticism for being too academic and remote from real conditions, its publications were often used as a source of propaganda by socialist candidates in elections. Hertz himself contributed a pamphlet on depopulation in France to the series (1910a; see pp. 51–5), and others who published in it included Bianconi, Halbwachs, Granet, Henri Lévy-Bruhl and, via translation, Sidney and Beatrice Webb.[52] Although the GES went through something of a bad patch in 1913, with income from the sales of its brochures declining — aggravated by the fact that speakers were

tardy in revising their talks for publication – the general election the following year gave it a new lease of life, and it was the war which finally killed it
off.[53] The papers Hertz gave at the Ecole Socialiste,[54] on Saint-Simonism, on
the Fabian Society and on the prevention of destitution, are also representa-
tive of his academic and educational activities in support of the socialist
movement.[55]

Lukes mentions a letter from Durkheim to Hamelin from as early as
11th September 1904,[56] shortly after Hertz joined the *Année,* expressing the
fear that Hertz's political activities might lead him away from academia. We
have already seen that there was considerable competition for Hertz's attention between these two sorts of activity. Yet despite these fears, he was not
lost to academic scholarship. He became an equally active member of the
Institut Française d'Anthropologie, founded in 1911, as were Durkheim,
Mauss, Hubert and Lévy-Bruhl.[57] Mauss mentions his collaboration in a
posthumous book of Félix Rauh's lectures as something also arising out of
this moral concern,[58] though in a letter to his mother, Hertz himself expected
the task to be 'tiresome' and 'thankless'.[59] Nonetheless, he must have
attended Rauh's lectures at some time or have been otherwise familiar with
his work to have been enlisted into this venture. He certainly lectured on 'la
morale' at or shortly after this time himself,[60] and it was evidently a key interest of his, given its importance in the Durkheimian view of social solidarity
which was of so much concern to Hertz for pragmatic as well as intellectual
reasons.

Yet another aspect of this moral concern was the year he spent teaching philosophy at the *lycée* in Douai between 1905 and 1906, after his year in
England. Durkheim hints that this was financially unnecessary, and it is clear
that he and others would have preferred Hertz to have devoted himself
entirely to research in Paris.[61] This suggests that the undertaking to teach in
state schools for at least ten years that Normalians were supposed to give[62]
could be circumvented or postponed in some circumstances. But Hertz
himself evidently had both the desire to teach and the sense of duty to do
some useful social task. Mauss tells us that he enjoyed teaching greatly,
regarding it at least in part as a means of moral instruction - at any rate, this is
what Hertz himself had told him.[63] This is not entirely borne out by some of
his letters to Roussel, in which he describes Douai as a 'tomb' (an explicit
allusion to his work on death) and his pupils as 'a dozen petit-bourgeois', and
complains of feeling 'sad at teaching things I scarcely believe in to children I
don't believe in'. He also found that his attempts to treat his pupils as individuals merely led to breaches of discipline. But one or two were more dedicated, and in general he was pleased to have opted for the role of teacher as
what he called his *métier*. After leaving Douai he felt somewhat adrift, saying

that he yearned for 'a regular and engaging activity, of a function, and [I] desire to teach.'[64]

This feeling persisted into later years. In a letter to Dodd of 23rd February 1909, he says: '[I] have had such an easy life in all respects. Sometimes I look forward to a trial which will test my faith.' He was only to find this in the war which took his life. Two and a half years later, in autumn 1911, he told Dodd that although he was working on his thesis on sin, it was not without some difficulty:

> ... a hard and complex bit of work. I long for a more definite *métier* than I have at present, and I hope that this thesis will soon give me an opportunity of entering a good university.[65]

And eighteen months later, he was still complaining:

> I have the feeling of living in artificial and unwholesome conditions because I have money and no regular profession. Free intellectual work is tiring but has not the regularity of a *métier*.[66]

This seems to have lay behind the distaste he sometimes felt for writing (as distinct from actually discovering new facts). In a letter of late 1913, he tells Dodd that he is writing up his 'book ... about the cults and legends of the mounts [i.e. mountains] and the rocks', saying that he finds it difficult to assess the value of all the effort involved, though this does not affect him when he is actually working:

> Sometimes I think all that is rubbish – fanciful theories with no touch with reality – just the kind of thing to give the illusion of activity to an ordinary *rentier*.[67]

Hertz's decision to take what appears to have been the first of many year's leave from Douai in 1906–07 was prompted by his promise to Durkheim – who had 'almost imposed it on me' – to write up his article on death for publication, which he felt would otherwise be impossible for him.[68]

Hertz's wife shared his interest in education and indeed made it her own *métier*.[69] She was older than Hertz, born Alice Sarah Bauer in 1877.[70] They became engaged during his years at the ENS and were married on 24th August 1904, five days before his *agrégation*. A honeymoon at Belle-Isle-en-Mer intervened before their going to England for Hertz's study trip.[71] In her own education, Alice had concentrated particularly on biology and the natural sciences, but she then developed a special interest in problems of education for the very young. She decided on this as a career while with her husband in London, where she taught in a school in Hampstead, studied child pedagogy, and took a London County Council certificate in the subject. This was exactly the time when the kindergarten movement, which had originated in Switzerland and Holland, was establishing itself in the better-off parts of London. She also became involved in the Froebel Society, which had been founded in England in 1874 to promote the kindergarten idea, and at some point was its secretary. The Montesori movement also influenced her ideas, though her own main concern was in teacher-training rather than in actually teaching herself.[72] Later, while she and her husband were living in Douai, she worked out how to adapt these methods to French education, and she opened the first kindergartens in Paris in 1909. She produced books of songs and games for young children (e.g. Hertz and Trouillon 1920, written 1913), and wrote articles for *L'Education joyeuse* and the *Revue Moulin Vert*; a work entitled *Minou à la montagne* is also credited to her.[73]

After Douai, Hertz enrolled as a student at the Ecole Pratique des Hautes Etudes in Paris for the academic year 1906–7, where he followed in particular Mauss's courses on African ethnography. From 1908 until 1912 he himself lectured there, initially as a replacement for Mauss. According to Alphandéry, his subjects were 'religious sociology, rites eliminating sin [1908-9], the religious element in penal law [1910-11], etc.' He apparently also lectured on morality, perhaps later.[74] From Karady, it is pretty clear that this would not have been a secure teaching post but more of a research appointment, and more marginal. Similar posts were found for Mauss, Hubert and Simiand, which enabled them to avoid heavy teaching loads and administrative duties at the price of relative insecurity.[75] Apart from his teaching and his work on his thesis and other papers, Hertz also contributed several reviews to the last five volumes of the *Année Sociologique*.[76] This journal, whose name has since come to be attached informally to the group which collected around Durkheim, was the vehicle he founded for their researches, a big part of which, especially in the early days, was devoted to reviews of others' work. It took up a great deal of Durkheim's time, especially given his perfectionism.[77] Leading colleagues helped with particular sections and Hertz's name appeared with others in this context, but he never seems to have enjoyed the editorial influence of Hubert, Mauss or Simiand.[78]

By 1912, Hertz had collected sufficient data for his thesis on sin and expiation, and had sketched out his ideas on the subject, but apparently baulked at the task of actually writing it, for reasons already given. Indeed, Mauss, who apparently also had difficulties with writing, seems to have felt that the task would have been too big for any scholar, however gifted. As it was, Hertz was compelled to reduce the scope of his project from sin treated globally to sin in non-Western societies, with special reference to Malayo-Polynesian peoples.[79] In the evident belief that a change would be as good as a rest, he turned to writing up a project of a different sort which he had conceived the previous year while on a walking tour of the Alpes Grées in north-western Italy.[80] There, high in the mountains near the village of Campiglia, above the Val Soana, he had witnessed the celebration of the Catholic cult of St Besse, supposedly a Roman legionary soldier and convert to Christianity who had been martyred in the late Empire and whose shrine nestles against a large rock. Next year, between 20th July and 1st September, he returned to the area, staying mostly in Cogne, in French-speaking Aosta, apart from two days during the festival itself over the mountains in the Italian-speaking Val Soana.[81] In other words, he accompanied the pilgrimage that was a part of the rite, an example of participant observation, however brief, that preceded Malinowski's by a number of years. This short burst of fieldwork was a rarity among the *Année,* and it was the only such venture that led to any substantial writing.[82]

Hertz gathered his information for his study of St Besse not only through direct enquiry and observation but also by correspondence, especially with local intellectuals, learned clergy and the local chemist in the Val Soana, as well as from Val Soanesi domiciled in Paris. For the historical background, he turned chiefly to published sources. Alice Hertz says that the study 'fascinated' him, its high point being the gift of an illuminated portrait of the saint from a local woman.[83] Hertz continued this research with a study of the myth of Mount Olympus in Greece, with its association with Athena, Pegasus, etc. Judging from what his wife tells us, part of the fascination of this subject for him was precisely the place of rocks in such legends, and of any sort of mystical projection from them. This included simply jumping from the rock, and clearly also those accounts of Besse's martyrdom that have him being flung from the rock where his chapel now stands (see Chapter Seven), but Hertz was also apparently interested in the possibility of assimilating to this image the flight of Pegasus and the springing forth of Athena from the head of Zeus. In this connection, he was planning a trip to Greece in the company of his friend Pierre Roussel (later Director of the Athens School) for September 1914, but war intervened. The result of this subsequent work was a draft essay which Alice entitles 'Légendes et cultes des roches, des monts et des sources' and which Durkheim refers to as a general, comparative study of certain myths of antiquity to complement the monograph on St Besse.[84] Mauss normally gives it the title of 'Mythe d'Athèna';[85] the result of nearly two years' work, it was in a fit state to be published, despite the fact that Hertz had not had the opportunity to act on his colleagues' advice and make some final revisions. After the war, Mauss repeatedly announced his intention of issuing it, but never got round to it. What has happened to it since is unknown, but it was probably destroyed during the occupation of Paris in the second world war. Early the same year, 1913, Hertz was back working, refreshed, at his thesis, but was not able to make much more progress with it before war broke out.[86]

There are several indications that his colleagues did not fully appreciate this aspect of his work. Mauss's comments to the effect that these were mere pastimes, entertainment, recreations, that his colleagues had been somewhat critical of them and so forth,[87] are only one hint of this. Durkheim too is noticeably non-committal concerning this work in his obituary,[88] while a letter from Hertz to Hubert of 1913 makes references to the latter's 'serious reservations' concerning the St Besse study, which had been relayed to him by Mauss.[89] At the same time, Hubert had taken some interest in Hertz's thesis, and Hertz pays tribute to the positive effect Hubert's own writings had had on him. We have only hints, no specific statements, as to what the objections actually were. Although Hertz had apparently set out to study the rite purely in order to show that it was the *conscience collective,* not anything physical such as the rock associated with it, that was its basis, he had ended by demonstrating that a rite could generate conflict as well as bring people together as one before the sacred object. This in itself would have been seen as a problem for the new sociology, in which ritual marked the most intense, because most unifying, point in social life. Perhaps also the St Besse adventure was too close to classical folklore studies for the liking of some of the group. It is well known that Arnold van Gennep, who carried out many broadly similar studies, was not taken very seriously by them.[90] Maybe too, the idea of fieldwork was felt to be inappropriate for a group which always saw its main task as the interpretation of data, not its collection or mere description.[91] A connected objection might have been the adoption of a monographic rather than a comparative form of writing, this perhaps being what persuaded Hertz to attempt to widen the focus subsequently with reference to Greek materials. His activities in respect of this corner of Italy were not restricted to the academic: he contributed an open letter to a brochure issued by a committee for the defence of the French language in the Vallée d'Aoste in 1912.[92]

The coming of the war has prevented us from ever knowing whether these problems would have been resolved in course of time, or how this new direction would have fitted in with the rest of Hertz's own work or with that of the *Année* generally. There is reason to believe that Hertz himself was not at all intimidated by his colleagues misgivings. His paper on St Besse is certainly unique to the writings at least of the inner circle, and it may indicate that he would have fitted increasingly uneasily into the academic environment they were creating, though he was always personally loyal to his colleagues, many of whom were also his friends.

Hertz spent the last months of his life in the French army, stationed in the woods at Herméville, near Etain, as part of the defences around Verdun, not in itself a particularly dangerous posting at the time.[93] To begin with, he was a sergeant in a Territorial Infantry Regiment, with a half-section of about thirty men under his command.[94] In his letters home during this period, he continually reassures Alice and his mother that he is not in danger, that he is even relatively comfortable, living the life of the barracks rather than the campaign, and that it is those left at home, not those at the front, who are suffering most. Others are bearing the brunt of the fighting, and Hertz is still hoping that he may be able to remain in the reserves: 'Will we ever have to fire our weapons? Very doubtful.'[95] This confidence progressively diminishes. A letter written to his mother, just a month before his death,[96] finds him at the front, not yet in action, but saying that he would now feel ashamed to go home without having seen any.

While at Herméville, awaiting orders, he busied himself collecting stories and sayings from his troops, many of whom came from Mayenne. In a letter to his wife he commended, as with St Besse, the more authentic feeling of getting out of the library and doing some face-to-face enquiries, regretting only that he did not have the knowledge to take down the music as well.[97] Alice says that he was happy to be doing his duty for France in the war, and happy also to be able to disappear into the mass of French soldiery, to allow it, and the totalizing experience of war, to subdue his individualism. In her own words, 'instead of studying them in the abstract, he lived, and with what intensity, those formidable social experiences that wars are.'[98] The notes he collected were published in the *Mélanges* brought together by Mauss in 1928.[99]

Despite his note-taking, the inactivity agitated him, and in April 1915 he took the opportunity to volunteer for a more mobile unit.[100] This led to his promotion to sub-lieutenant in a different unit,[101] and soon to an action which none of those who were to take part in it had much confidence they would survive.[102] He was killed at about 3.30 on the afternoon of 13th April 1915, during an advance towards Marchéville on the plain of Wöewre, leading his section across open ground swept by German machine guns and pounded by their artillery. The enemy, alerted by movement in the French trenches, had had ample time to prepare to receive the attack. Altogether twenty-two officers and men, including Hertz, another sub-lieutenant and the lieutenant leading the attack, were killed. All three officers were found side by side by one of Hertz's subordinates, Sergeant Partridge, after nightfall, on the edge of the German trenches, and were buried in the cemetry of Haudiomont, Meuse (near Verdun).[103] Hertz was postumously awarded the Croix de Chevalier (Légion d'honneur) for his part in the action.[104]

The news took more than a week to reach Alice; it was conveyed to her initially by the wife of one of his comrades,[105] though in the coming weeks many were to write to her about what had happened. Almost immediately afterwards, in obvious reaction, she plunged herself back into her own educational work, which she pursued to excess, so that her health, delicate even before the war, suffered. She contracted consumption while on a visit to Verdun immediately after the armistice to erect a tomb for her husband. She died on 16th November 1927, while her husband's *Mélanges* were in press. Her ashes rest with her husband's body, in the cemetery at Haudiomont.[106]

There is no doubt that Hertz was keenly mourned by his friends and colleagues as well as by his family, as can be seen from the numerous letters of condolence sent to Alice immediately after his death. The feelings expressed are clearly more than just conventional expressions of regret. Perhaps Maurice Halbwachs sums up the significance of his death most aptly:

> We owe to him the health of our country and of our civilization; but with him has disappeared one of our main reasons for loving this country and for maintaining life as it was for us before this war.[107]

Hertz's volunteering for the dangerous action that cost him his life has been taken as evidence of a death wish by some, the inevitable fate of a rather sombre character interested mainly in the negative aspects of human life. Isambert, for example, sums him up like this:

> his personality was many-sided, even contradictory: his taste for the sombre coexisted with perfect married happiness; he hesitated ... between a sense of duty to teaching and a taste for studious leisure, to which must be added a strong militant streak; and finally, his interests ranged from economics to mythology and folklore.

This suggests a soul in torment, a view whose origin Isambert traces to Mauss, with his talk of Hertz's obsession with 'the dark side of humanity'.[108] Some basis for it can be found in correspondence of the time and earlier, as well as in what we know of Hertz's difficulties in deciding between the life of the study and activities where he could be useful. A letter from a fellow soldier, E. Vermeil, to Alice, sent two weeks after Hertz was killed, tells her how much he was '"dedicated" to his task', how 'he turned his duty as a soldier into a sort of religion.' Hertz himself had told him, 'our task is equivalent to being a veritable sacrament.'[109] Other correspondence is also interesting on Hertz's state of mind in these last days. In a letter to Alice of 26th March, he complains of having spent five months at the front only in a nominal sense: 'I continually have an appetite for more complete dedication ... I almost *envy* those who are more exposed' (original emphasis). He realizes that there is a conflict here with his duty to his family and to his work, but so many others have fallen - which, he now knew, meant his colleagues Antoine Bianconi[110] and very probably Maxime David too:

I am nostalgic for that burning region where sacrifice is consumed in
full. But be calm, this is just a state of vague impulse which reason
keeps repressed. And I do nothing – and until the arrival of new orders
shall do nothing – but follow my destiny and remain in my place.[111]

On 28th March, Hertz wrote a letter to a fellow officer named Chiffert,
who only received it two days after Hertz was killed. Chiffert later sent this
letter to Alice, together with one of his own.[112] Hertz had told him that he
had been suggested as sub-lieutenant, which pleased him greatly, though he
felt it was due more to his station in life than to his military capabilities.[113] In
the event he was not selected, because he was married and at 33 was considered too old. For the same reasons he had not been expected to volunteer,
but did so anyway after a few days' reflection and hesitation. He was then
sent briefly to the front, only to be sent back to Verdun again almost immediately, leaving him disappointed at not having seen action.

However, the background to his decision to volunteer for more active
service is actually more complicated. In October and November 1914 he was
in correspondence with two of his brothers-in-law, Léon Eyrolles and Léon
Gorodiche, asking them to intervene with the authorities to get him posted
to a more active role.[114] He explained that he was not looking for promotion
or greater responsibilities, just more active service. At this point, it was less
service at the front that he was thinking of as his becoming an interpreter or
liaison officer with a British unit, given his fluency in English and his knowledge and experience of the country. He made it clear that it was not simply
boredom that was weighing on his mind: 'There are cases and situations in
which one's duty is to do a little more than the average, which is exactly my
case.' He also seems to have thought he had acquired an unfair advantage
over his age-mates in more active units through an accident of career history.
As a youth, he had opted to do his initial period of military service a year
early, so as to be able to enter the ENS in 1901. This blip had now worked
through his career as a reservist, making him, at 33, younger than his comrades in the same unit, who were all at least 36 or 37, and in some cases in
their mid-forties. As a result, he considered it 'abnormal, even ridiculous,
humiliating,' to be sitting 'comfortably in a wood' with men senior to him,
instead of doing something more useful. These approaches came to nothing.
It was actually while his brothers-in-law were acting on his request that the
call for volunteers was made where Hertz was stationed, an opportunity he
eventually took, as a consequence finding himself in a unit in which the
average age was lower.[115]

It is difficult to argue from this that Hertz deliberately and recklessly
sacrificed himself. Such a view could only be sustained if a direct connection
could be established between his volunteering and the action which took his

life, which was known to be dangerous. Although there was only a ten-day gap between the two events, the particular action of the 13th April may not have been finalized or even planned when Hertz volunteered. Clearly, however, as the fighting wore on and casualties mounted, he took the view that duty demanded that he play a full part in the war, wherever it led him, a wish that the call for volunteers enabled him to turn into reality. There are other important considerations to be made. First and quite simply, Hertz was under military discipline, so that having volunteered for more active service in general, he was hardly in a position to refuse to take part in any particular action, however dangerous — that way lay only the disgrace of a court martial, and probably a firing squad, and we can be quite certain that Hertz never even considered it. Secondly, as we have seen, Hertz was only one of 22 officers and men who were killed in the same attack. Thirdly, it probably becomes a part of any war in which civilians take part en masse to believe that they are fighting not just for victory but for a better world. Hertz's letters to Alice from the front frequently make reference to this theme,[116] to which his ardent if intellectual socialism gave a more specific shape than can have been the case for many of his comrades. It is obvious too that he found in the war that sense of purpose which had not come easily to him as either a socialist or a sociologist. His keenness to play a full part had even led him to learn the army optical chart by heart in order to counter the possibility of his failing the medical test through his bad eyesight.[117]

However, other, later correspondence seems to indicate a markedly increased degree of readiness for self-sacrifice. A letter to Alice of the 3rd November 1914 explains his decision to volunteer for a more active role in terms of the various identities he could claim for himself - Jew, socialist and sociologist, significantly in that order. The decision represents

> the outcome of my whole life. My dear, as a Jew, I feel the time has come to give *a little more* than my due — because there are many who have given or are giving much less than they have received. There can never be enough Jewish devotion to this war, never too much Jewish blood spilt on French earth. [...]

> As a socialist, I have always claimed that the desire to *serve* the community can be a motive for action as powerful as the desire for profit or individual interest. Too many men, even at this time, hold themselves back, think only of themselves — it is necessary that at least some go *beyond* what is asked of them, ever ready to respond to the call for 'volunteers'.

> As a sociologist and rationalist, I have always maintained that the thought of the common good was enough to inspire and to uphold the giving of each individual, up to the complete sacrifice of self.... My

dear, you know well that I have done nothing up to now but receive, that to me has fallen the lot of an easy life, full of joy.... How could I remain deaf, in our present situation, to this appeal made to my good will — up to now, I have hardly suffered in the war....[118]

In contrast to Isambert and Mauss, Durkheim prefers to give us a picture of a balanced personality, versatile in taste and ability, alert but thoughtful, disciplined but energetic, incapable of a base or even mediocre thought.[119] Hertz's one-time colleague Hubert Bourgin — though politically opposed to the Durkheimian endeavour by the time he was writing, after the war[120] — offers a similarly sympathetic picture. He describes Hertz as someone who was not just a library-bound scholar but who reached out to life with an enquiring mind, a considerate nature and a courteous manner, serious and amusing in turn. He has also left us the sole physical description of Hertz:

> Tall, well built, clean-shaven, with a high forehead, blond hair, clear, soft, attentive, penetrating eyes, he resembled a 'fellow' of England or America, one of those young university savants who undertake scholarly researches, teacher-training, sports and social enquiry all at the same time.[121]

Finally, however, Bourgin too turns Hertz's inner conflicts into a death wish, suggesting that, in going off to war, he abandoned not only his work and his family, but hope itself, taking with him a premonition that he would not return. And he refers very directly to Hertz's Jewishness, confirming Hertz's own words on the topic to Alice with a gloss of his own:

> Jew by origin, and French by all the thoughts of his intellect and all the aspirations of his moral nature, he thought that the blood of men of his race and conscience would have been usefully spilt if it freed their children from any reproach, in the eyes of a suspicious France, of egoism, interest, particularism or indifference.[122]

Whether one views Hertz's death as inevitable or avoidable, as the outcome of a desire or simply a readiness for self-sacrifice, the war was clearly the culmination of a life that, while certainly not unhappy, was marked by conflict of purpose and a certain struggle in finding inner fulfillment. Hertz clearly had a concern for the social, political and economic conditions of his country, which was then at a critical moment of its history in its attempts to turn itself finally, after over a century of turmoil, into a stable democracy. The Dreyfus affair symbolized the political challenge it continually faced from the forces of reaction, while deteriorating working-class economic conditions were constantly threatening to undermine its social stability. Hertz's personal dilemma was the part he himself should be playing to help remedy the situation, a dilemma he felt all the more keenly as a scion of a bourgeois commercial family which enjoyed relatively comfortable circumstances, yet which on neither side was of French origin. He was early drawn into sympathy with socialism and trade unionism, but he came to prefer the role of intellectual to that of activist, that of a provider and disseminator of ideas to that of a politician. This explains the attraction of both Fabianism and Durkheimianism. The former discussed actual problems and sought remedies. The latter provided the theoretical background of what the life of men in society could and should be. Possibly it was this that initially led Hertz to Durkheimian sociology, and that it was only subsequently, at the insistence or at least the instance of Durkheim, that he undertook specifically academic studies.

Yet it is precisely where Durkheimianism branched out into ethnological materials and their academic study that one perceives a degree of tension arising in Hertz's attitude. Although he found the discovery of exotic facts exciting and intellectually rewarding, writing them up could be tedious, and the result often seemed devoid of purpose. Teaching was one solution, but his experience of it at Douai was marred by the indifference of many of his students, most of whom were privileged, like himself. Yet to obtain a worthwhile job in a university meant having to continue with academic work for a while longer. And underlying everything was the need he felt for a well-defined and disciplined role or task, a *métier,* of which wealth had deprived him and from which the pressure of his academic colleagues had somewhat diverted him.

The dilemma had still not been solved when war broke out in 1914. Death wish or not, the experience seems to have provided Hertz with an arena in which to satisfy his sense of duty, as well as a satisfying example, in the shape of the mass army, of the Durkheimian social in which to live to the full his liking for crowds. It also gave him what he missed in the way of discipline and purpose. Finally and perhaps most significantly of all, it offered him, as one born in France but of non-French parents, the opportunity to serve France to the limit of his ability, to prove that his Jewish and part-German background — which in a sense united in himself the two elements to which French nationalism had been most hostile in the preceding decades — did not undermine the commitment of people like himself to the country he was born into. The anthropological scholarship for which Hertz is most keenly regretted today may actually have meant least of all to him by April 1915. Indeed, there are signs that if he survived the war, he was preparing to abandon or at least reduce the time he spent on pure research in favour of giving greater attention to problems of education. This would have corresponded more closely to Alice's interests, and it may have been inspired in part by a concern to play a full part in his son's education and upbringing.[123] Whether this intention would have survived with him or was born simply of the heightened emotions of war cannot now confidently be answered.

Hertz's memory was kept alive initially by Mauss, in fulfillment of a promise made to Alice shortly after his death.[124] In 1922 Mauss published that part of the introduction to Hertz's thesis which had been written up, and in 1928 he reissued, in *Mélanges* (reprinted 1970), Hertz's three major separate articles (those on St Besse, death, and right and left) plus the material he collected from his soldiers and a long review of a book on a Russian Orthodox sect (the original published version of the latter, Hertz 1913c, is shorter). Mauss considered the work on sin important enough to lecture on himself regularly in the 1930s, largely though not entirely using Hertz's notes. It is a measure of the collective spirit of the original *Année* that Mauss undertook to work so hard to advance the reputation of his late colleagues at the expense of his own researches. One of his students was Louis Dumont, who taught in Oxford from 1951 to 1955. According to his own account,[125] one of the outcomes of his sojourn there was his reminding Evans-Pritchard of the value of Hertz's work. Evans-Pritchard himself subsequently lectured on Hertz as part of his general enquiry into the intellectual origins of anthropology, and it was under his auspices that Rodney and Claudia Needham translated the articles on death and the right hand in 1960 as part of a series of translations of *Année* classics.[126] Finally, in 1992 the Association pour la Recherche en Anthropologie Sociale in Paris launched an annual lecture in Hertz's name, the first being delivered by Carmelo Lisón-Tolosana in 1993, the second by Maurice Bloch in 1994.[127]

Hertz's academic career can be seen to fall into two broad phases, though there is a degree of overlap. First, there is the group of works on specific topics treated generally and comparatively, on death, on the right and left hands, and on sin. In practice, this covers the years from shortly after Hertz's departure from the ENS in 1904 up to about 1913, though the thesis on sin still had not been completed on the outbreak of war. In 1912 began the research on St Besse, which Hertz developed further into another general and comparative study, this time on the sacredness of geographical phenomena,[128] especially of rocks and of the theme of jumping, falling, being thrown or launching oneself from them. As we have seen, this phase seems to have implied a shift away from Durkheimian orthodoxy for his colleagues, in that it pointed towards the monograph rather than the comparative study as the type of composition, and towards topics which had more to do with traditional folklore than with either sociology or ethnology. But if the shift appeared as a regression to Durkheim, Mauss and Hubert in particular, it could also be argued to be forward looking. His three colleagues were by this time fully prepared to use ethnographic monographs as evidence for their general arguments, which were really based on the close and detailed comparison of such data. Hertz, it could be argued, was simply beginning to create his own monographs, as the group's post-war successors were increasingly to do. And in the general tenor of his arguments and his explanations of social phenomena, Hertz remained largely faithful to Durkheimian sociology, though there was some revision of it.

In the last thirty years, since the articles on death and right and left were translated, they have regularly served as an inspiration in anthropological analysis and as a source of debate. This is especially so of the latter, which deserves its place among the key texts dealing with dichotomous thought as the foundation of structural analysis. The article on death, similarly, belongs with the seminal works on ritual. The other major works, on St Besse and on sin, are also at long last beginning to be noticed, the former having been translated in the 1980s (Hertz 1983), the latter in the 1990s (Hertz 1994). The content of these articles and the use made of them subsequently are the subjects of the remainder of this book, but first we must say something about how they fit together with each other and with the work of the *Année* generally. To do this, we need to examine in a little more detail just what the Durkheimains were aiming to achieve with their new science of society, especially in respect of their sociology of religion.

CHAPTER TWO

The Durkheimian Background to Hertz's Work

THE GENERAL BACKGROUND[1]

The science of sociology that Durkheim wished to develop was concerned, perhaps above all, to distance itself from explanations of the social which referred to any aspect of individual psychology. This part of the critique against his rivals was particularly evident in his sociology of religion and bore especially on the so-called 'intellectualist' school of Herbert Spencer, Edward Tylor, James Frazer, etc. This approach tended to ground beliefs in man's perceptions of the world around him and his reflections about them, and it was at the root of the view that magic was merely false science, the result of reasoning from false premises. But it also promoted the argument that religion, like magic (from which it was distinguished), was primarily a belief in ghosts and spirits. This itself was supposed to have arisen as a reasoned but false response to the fear aroused by the phenomenon of death: the individual survived as a soul, even though his or her body decayed. For Spencer, the ghosts of ancestors were at the root of all religion, the earliest form of which was ancestor worship. Tylor generalized this to a belief in spiritual beings of all kinds, though he continued to distinguish souls from other sorts of spirits. Because of the plethora of spirits and souls which must have rapidly come into existence, the origins of religion were necessarily polytheistic.

Evolutionism was equally a mark of the intellectualist account. There was first of all a concern with the origins of religion, often developed as part of an atheist polemic against revealed religions, especially Christianity. The intention was to show, with reference to ethnographic materials, that religion, far from being divine revelation, could be explained with reference to human needs and capacities alone, that it was, in fact, a wholly human phenomenon. But this evolutionism tended to take on a life of its own. Tylor not only distinguished spirits from souls as such, he did so in an evolutionary sense. And Frazer set the already standard triple distinction between magic,

21

religion and science into a set evolutionary sequence, which led him to deny the priority Tylor had given to animism in favour of totemism (see below). Such views were an advance over earlier accounts of religion which saw the worship of fetishes as prior to either magic or revealed religion. Also, for all the identification of 'stages' of religious evolution, which were set in a sequence which was related to progress and was therefore hierarchical, the essential unity of the human species was unequivocally recognized. According to this view, it was only a matter of time before 'primitive' peoples would develop as 'civilized' man already had, given the undoubted ability to think rationally that all peoples, at whatever stage of 'progress', enjoyed.

Yet the intellectualist model did not long go unchallenged. There were two main reactions to it from within anthropology. In Vienna, Wilhelm Schmidt adopted some earlier ideas of Max Müller's to argue that all religions originally centred on a single god, any polytheistic notions representing simply the decay of this fundamental idea. This, however, was still an intellectualist position in that it derived religion, a social phenomenon, from the reflections of the individual. In this case, these reflections were generally supposed to have taken the form of an explanation for the universe in terms of its creation by a superior being.

The other reaction, more lasting and radical, came from specifically sociological approaches, which are mostly associated today with Durkheim and his colleagues. Certainly the *Année* scholars, in their collective work, developed the tendency to its highest pitch, but they were not without their precursors. As Nisbet points out (1975: 159–61), Comte and de Tocqueville had already insisted on the ubiquity of religion as a social force, and the latter had pointed to the essentially social nature of knowledge and belief. Durkheim's own teacher, Fustel de Coulanges, had stressed the religious nature of social forms, thus making a connection between society and religion that Durkheim was to accept, though he could never quite make up his mind whether it was religion or society itself that was at the root of the social (cf. Pickering 1984: 274). He also rejected his teacher's adherence to the earlier intellectualist choice of ancestor worship as the first form of religion, preferring to follow those who were already replacing this with totemism, such as Wundt, McLennan, Frazer and Robertson Smith. Here, he took most from the latter, especially as regards the rooting of totemism in a clan structure (the totem being the clan divinized), the distinction between pure and impure (which, modified, appeared as sacred-profane in Durkheim), the idea of sacrifice as communion with the sacred, and the general priority given to ritual over belief as the mechanism holding society together.

There were other influences too, drawn from philosophy: indeed, as Evans-Pritchard has consistently argued (e.g. 1960: 17; 1965: 49), Durkheimian sociology has roots in the thought of the Enlightenment. Although in some respects a neo-Kantian, Durkheim opposed Kant's doctrine of the innateness of ideas just as much as the Lockean derivation of ideas from experience which can be traced in the intellectualists. The first was specious, the second too individualist, and the social dimension was absent in both. It was Durkheim's life's work to establish that dimension firmly in intellectual discourse about the human condition, a task in which he has in general succeeded, though not without drawing much criticism to himself along the way. For all their radicalism, however, his writings are rooted in his time and its arguments, and he addresses himself specifically to his adversaries in the first instance. Thus he retained the conventional distinction between magic and religion, which has now largely disappeared from anthropological discourse or been modified into something which, whatever its surface similarities, at leasts omits the word 'magic'. Durkheim also retained an evolutionary perspective as part of the very act of confronting the intellectualists, though modifying it considerably (see Chapter Eight), as well as turning to it as a dubious procedure to explain away negative cases. But fresh arguments were also adopted, such as the idea of an inanimate force to replace spirits as the prime mover behind religious experience, and of totemism to replace ancestor cults as the earliest form of religion. Also, while the distinction between religion and magic was retained, that between religion and science was elided, on the basis that the latter too exists in a social environment. Even in these cases, however, the general context in which he and his colleagues wrote was one of opposition to the arguments of the intellectualists and other scholarly rivals.

For Durkheim, arguments from the individual to society are especially misplaced. Wonder and fear are not a sufficient basis for creating a religious tradition. Religion gives men confidence, it does not owe its existence to a lack of it. The direction of cause and effect has to be reversed. It is society that imposes its beliefs on the individuals composing it, since in whatever way they might have originated, beliefs exist only within a specific tradition and are transmitted with it down the generations. Moreover, their generality and obligatory nature give them an objective quality which conflicts with the theory of their genesis in individual minds. But above all they have a moral force, in that they promote the social solidarity that benefits society and its members. Moreover, they impose, or are backed up by, sanctions that are designed to bring about a sufficient measure of conformity to that end.

The human mind is by no means removed from Durkheimian sociology, but when it appears it is collectivized, quite literally: we have collective representations and the *conscience collective*. There are passages of Durkheim that one can characterize as a simple social psychology,[2] and he certainly takes the view that society depends on its individual members for its existence as much as they depend on it (cf. Pickering 1984: 255). On the other hand, society is sometimes attributed with so much causal force as to be seen to influence bodily functioning itself. This is true of Hertz's essay on the right and left hands, where social control is seen as having greatly magnified a propensity grounded in a slight physical asymmetry, and also of Mauss's essay on bodily movements ([1936] 1950, Part 6; this contains a reference to Hertz, *ibid.*: 375 and n. 1). The most striking claim is thus the affirmation of the autonomy of the social as something more than the sum of its parts, as the source of all the beliefs and even actions of the individual, and above all of the obligations he or she must fulfil. And it is society that creates and gives man the categories with which and through which he thinks: gods are conceived, not perceived.

How does this moral force that is society make itself felt in its members? The short answer is ritual, which has to be taken in a broad sense which for Hertz included auricular confession, for Mauss prayer (cf. Evans-Pritchard 1960: 16–17 n. 1; Pickering 1984, Part IV). Indeed, the Durkheimians, although fully accepting the importance of belief, tended to stress ritual rather more as an explanatory device, the reverse of what the intellectualists had done. In particular, rites do not arise out of beliefs in spiritual beings but may themselves give rise to them or at least promote them. Ritual occasions are where society stresses its values, inspires its members with collective feelings of social solidarity and generally represents itself to itself. Rites were thus not to do with efficacy, *pace* Frazer, but with developing a sense of communal well-being and of the strength of man in society, a strength greater than when he is alone. Religion, through ritual, shows the individual something superior to himself. In Durkheim's own words (1915: 414), 'beliefs express this life in representations; rites organize it and regulate its working'.[3]

This was, of course, an intensely objective and positivist view, one that took no account of the fact that for the people actually present at a rite, its intended purpose is often not at all certain to be fulfilled, or that indigenously much ritual is seen explicitly as creating the world, society, the cosmos, and so on. The consciousness of a compelling force that is society is often absent in the minds of its members, and where exactly to locate society in the overall model the *Année* put forward has often been seen as one of the most intractable parts of their approach. This was freely admitted (e.g. Durkheim 1915: 209), indeed seen as an essential part of that model: it is because the actual source of conformity is not seen as society that men are led to create gods. Where the idea of society is present in the minds of the individuals who compose it, people have something concrete to resist and rebel against, and social solidarity is that much harder to achieve.

Durkheim's hostility to Marxism is well known, and we are not being offered an argument whereby ideology and ritual are instruments of power exercised by one class against another, an argument that tends to endow the first class with strong meaning-making powers and the second with few or with none at all. To put Durkheimian sociology into Marxist language for a moment, if religion is the opiate of the masses, then it is the opiate of the other classes too, because all of them are subject to a common if variant tradition. And if religion and ritual are not exploitative, nor are they subversive: ritual overcomes all fissive tendencies in society. The problem is that tradition may not always be seen in the same way by different social groups or even be the same one, as Hertz was to establish in his study of St Besse (see pp. 163-72). Perhaps more significant here is the fact that an implicit recourse to intellectualist arguments based on individual psychology suddenly makes its reappearance in this context: men create gods not because of fear or wonder, but essentially because they do not realize that they form the society that is forcing its conformity upon them.

Of course, if social solidarity is proposed as the purpose of ritual, one is at the same time virtually admitting that some individuals still have sufficient minds of their own to threaten this solidarity and, more generally, that there are aspects of individual existence that disturb the collectivity. This, broadly speaking, is where Hertz's own contribution comes in, especially in the earlier phase of his career. We have seen that there were personal reasons for his wishing to concentrate on this particular aspect, arising out of his concern for what he perceived to be the instability of contemporary France and his belief, evidently taken from Durkheim himself, that sociology might help provide solutions (see previous chapter). But his choice of topics can also be justified intellectually. Where Durkheim and Mauss were mostly concerned with how social solidarity was created and maintained, Hertz took upon himself the task of studying the responses of society to breaches in that solidarity, whether these are seen as inevitable or as the wilful act of an individual. While Durkheim's and Mauss's themes included how relationships are established and maintained through gift-giving, how societies classify, mechanical and organic solidarities, joking relationships, the concept of the person etc., Hertz concentrated, in Mauss's words, on 'the dark side of humanity'.

We can see this more clearly by taking his major works one by one. His barely begun work on sin examined society's response to more deliberate transgressions of its injunctions by its members, which did not stop at considering just social sanctions but covered also how the sense of sin arose in the sinner's breast and made him repent — how, in other words, the force exerted by society on the individual is moral as well as merely punitive, how it convinces the individual rather than merely forcing him to believe. The essay on death set out to show how death ritual was designed to repair the breach in the social fabric caused by the sudden loss of one of its members. Death itself is often, of course, taken to be a wilful act by someone unknown in societies which lack any conception of natural death. In so far as it is then regarded as a threat to society as well as to an individual, it can be subsumed under the general category of sin. The paper on right and left drew attention to the ways in which such negativity might be symbolized, the value 'left' being ultimately just the emblem for a whole class of symbols regularly opposed to those subsumed under the more positive value 'right' (cf. Isambert 1982: 243 n. 87). The monograph on St Besse, finally, drew attention to the fact that a specific rite, far from being the high point of sociality, may actually produce conflict between classes and even whole communities. At this point, Hertz overreached himself in the view of some of his colleagues, though not of posterity. Although his demonstration was not explicitly an attack on their common work and the assumptions that underpinned it, it could be taken implicitly as undermining the Durkheimian notion of ritual as an integrating mechanism, especially for those of his colleagues, like Hubert and Mauss, who were going more in an ethnological direction. It is not at all clear that this was actually Hertz's intention, and he may have been surprised at his colleagues' misgivings. As we shall see later (p. 165), it is in fact possible to provide an answer to the challenge from within the Durkheimian tradition itself.

Hertz's work is also of interest in that within it can be found not only the specifically Durkheimian doctrine, but also the seeds of most if not all the major approaches to ritual that have been developed subsequently. In this respect, it is Hertz's work on sin that remains closest to Durkheim's specific interests in its concentration on the relations between society, ritual and the individual, and on the effectiveness of ritual in enforcing social harmony generally. One basic concern here was simply to account for ritual as an aspect of the human condition, and Hertz played a part in this too. The similarity of the paper on death to van Gennep's more general work on ritual in its concern with structure and process has often been noted (see pp. 87–8, 104–5). In this regard, the paper on St Besse discussed not only the conflicts and contested identities that the same ritual can give rise to and more generally the fact that a ritual can actually have more than one group interested in it, but also the linkage between rite and myth (which is what the various legends surrounding it really are). The relevance here of the paper on right and left, being largely about an aspect of symbolism, is perhaps not so immediately apparent. However, it can be related to the many studies on the ways symbols convey meaning in ritual, an approach perhaps best exemplified by Victor Turner (e.g. 1966, 1974b), though certainly not confined to him. Here, of course, the influence of Hertz has been largely indirect, second to that of structuralism in general. More recently, however, many who have sought to pursue this approach have specifically counted Hertz among their intellectual forbears, though not without taking into account the revision of his work by Louis Dumont, whose followers and fellow travellers they mostly are (see pp. 85-6).

Two concepts in particular are of importance in assessing the Durkheiman approach to religion and its relation to society at large and the individuals that compose it, namely the sacred, and *mana*. We will briefly consider each in turn.

SACRED-PROFANE

The notion of the sacred is associated especially with Durkheim, for whom it was a key concept, although he originally found it in the work of Fustel de Coulanges and Robertson Smith. Pickering goes so far as to remark that 'Durkheim gives a prior place to the sacred even over religion itself' (1984: 115; also 151-3). Its importance was that it enabled Durkheim to define religion in terms of something which in a scientific sense could be said to exist as an idea, and not in terms of gods and spirits, whose existence Durkheim consistently and forcefully denied. One could not explain a phenomenon scientifically by means of something which did not exist (*ibid.*: 165, 187-8).

But also significant is the dichotomy that the sacred forms with the profane, which is dealt with at length in *The Elementary Forms of the Religious Life* of 1912 (translated 1915). The essence of this dichotomy is the absolute and unmediated opposition between that which must be protected and isolated (the sacred) and that from which it must be protected and isolated (the profane). In this view, the two poles account for the whole of existence, but they are mutually exclusive and should never approach one another or come into contact. This distinction is the most fundamental in human social life and transcends all others, even that between good and bad. Indeed, the latter is distinct, being located entirely within the sacred: the religiously inauspicious and impure are seen very much as part of the sacred, not the profane. Satan is an impure, not a profane being; a corpse, blood, etc. are sacred things, though impure. Durkheim is also at pains to stress that sacredness is not a matter of some quality deemed to be inherent in the object but concerns its endowment with sacredness by society. Again, this includes the impure and inauspicious too: it is society, not the act of death, that makes a soul sacred, a corpse polluting. Following on from this, he says that religion consists in beliefs concerning the sacred and its relation to the profane, while rites stipulate the behaviour appropriate in respect of the sacred.

On the whole, there has been much less difficulty in understanding Durkheim's view of the sacred as such than his view of the profane (see Pickering 1984: 133ff.). For many, for example Lukes (1973: 24ff.), the latter is really no more than the ordinary, everyday existence of the individual. But since Durkheim banished the individual and his psychology from the realm of the sociological, this has the effect of making the sacred coordinate with the social as a whole. The profane therefore becomes not the negative or evil but the religiously neutral, equally at risk from the good and the bad sacred. This itself is to exhaust the symbolic and the ritual, and therefore the social in Durkheim's terms, making the profane a sociologically empty category, one which can only refer to the individual, the everyday, as sociologically neutral and neutered. For Pickering (*ibid.*: 136–7), this impoverishes the notion of the profane unacceptably, depriving it of much of its force and reducing it to the level of a mere residuum which can hardly be seen as contributing to the formation of a dichotomy. And to quote Augé:

> if one retains the categories of profane and sacred, one cannot find social activities that are strictly speaking outside the sacred, nor sacred activities that have no social applications or implications. It is, in short, the notion of profane activity that eludes analysis. (1979: 31)

However, for Durkheim the profane also has the ability to threaten the sacred, which it is the purpose of interdictions and taboos to protect. We can again return to Hertz at this point and to his interest in the negative aspects of social life. Much of Hertz's work can be understood as being concerned with the circumstances under which the profane was led to threaten the sacred, what happened when it did so, and how the damage was repaired. In this respect, sin, death and the left hand were all aspects of the profane which threatened the sacred and therefore the very fabric of society. This entailed a modification of the original dichotomy (see p. 62).

The dichotomy has anyway often come under criticism. Stanner argues that it is unsatisfactory because Durkheim allows no mediating category between its two poles (1967: 229, after van Gennep). He suggests that a third category is required in order to account for the many items which, he says, aboriginal Australians use in ritual which do not threaten the sacred. Even then, he thinks that yet more categories will have to be developed in order to account for everything. Both he and Evans-Pritchard (1965: 64–5) point out Durkheim's complete disregard of context, for sacred items are not necessarily sacred all the time. Stones, for example, may be picked up for use during a ritual and abandoned unceremoniously afterwards. Evans-Pritchard argues that in any ritual context, sacred and profane form a unity, not a clearly demarcated dichotomy, and like Stanner, if for a different reason, he ends by dismissing the dichotomous approach as useless in either fieldwork or analysis (see also Goody 1961). A number of ethnographers have denied that this essentially Christian dichotomy occurs at all among the people they have studied (e.g. Schulte Nordholt 1980: 247; Barnes 1974: 141), though Hicks goes out of his way to confirm its relevance in understanding Tetum dual symbolic classification (1976: 20-1).[4]

A balanced view nonetheless seems possible. Das (1977b: 115ff.), for instance, would retain the concept of the sacred in cases where it stands for the axiomatic in social life, for the values which society regards as unevadable. This implicitly generalizes it and removes it from any association with the divine exclusively, reinforcing the view that by it, Durkheim really meant society itself. Ritual in particular was the means whereby society reminded individuals of its values, especially those whose 'profane' activities might threaten it. It was van Gennep's contribution to realize that the threat also (or instead) comes from the unavoidable liminalities which arise out of the individual's life cycle and which necessitate a change of status that temporarily, at least, threatens the social order by muddling the classificatory principles on which it is based. The purpose of ritual is to effect this change in such a way as to preserve social order and continuity in the longer term. There are also problems with the further dichotomy into good and bad sacred. As Pickering points out (1984: 128-9; also Lukes 1973: 27), this produces a situation in which some sacred beings and substances threaten rather than uphold the social, thus logically detracting from Durkheim's account. This leads him to argue that society may create a belief in malevolent forces as well as in the power of ritual action to overcome them. Pickering compares this with Tylor's and Müller's theories of origins, which Durkheim was normally so keen to eschew, but it also comes close to being a theory of the manipulation of ideology for political ends, of the sort more normally associated with Marxism. It seems to have been the former that Durkheim was most keen to counter.

As Lukes makes clear (1973: 435-6), the sort of dualism exemplified by Durkheim's dichotomy between sacred and profane was part of the intellectual inventory of the period, being drawn ultimately from Kant, through Charles Renouvier, Octave Hamelin and other neo-Kantian philosophers.[5] While accepting it, Durkheim regarded Kant's explanations for it, in terms of its supposed innateness, as tautological, hence the search for something with which to replace the latter as the ultimate explanation for all dichotomies. This something else was society. But it is not a case of society itself being divided into sacred and profane. Society *is* the sacred, the religious, for Durkheim, i.e. it itself represents one pole of the dichotomy, the other, the profane element, being the individual and his private interests. In effect, society was Durkheim's own essentialist explanation, which Ladd (1957: 99) compares with Rousseau's General Will, Kant's Rational Will and Hegel's *Weltgeist.*

In a retrospective on his own career written some time during World War I, Hubert tells us how the sacred came to play a role in the Durkheimian sociology of religion:

> The problems we had to solve were the following: the nature of religious phenomena, the conditions of religious phenomena, the nature and conditions of myth. These problems did not present themselves in an abstract manner: the particular way in which they were posed gave rise to our works on myth and magic. [...] In the analysis of religious facts, the problem that demanded immediate attention was how to analyse the representations that preside over the development of these facts and regulate their logic. We isolated the concept of the sacred as a category of the mental operations involved in religious phenomena. (1979: 206, quoted in Isambert 1983: 156)

Elsewhere (1904), he calls religion 'the administration of the sacred' and the sacred the 'mother idea' of religion. He also defines ritual as the means whereby one gains access to the sacred, whereby one enters and leaves it. It is through such access that the individual is impressed with social values.

MANA

One of the most significant examples of a sacred object for Durkheim is the totem (e.g. 1898a; 1915). However, each totem object is sacred only for the clan that owns it, whose members characteristically may not kill or eat it, nor marry others having it. For other clans it is accessible both as food and in marriage, and is therefore profane. Thus each clan is sacred for only a part of society, though each part has one, i.e. each part orients itself towards something sacred to it. For Durkheim, totemism, especially when it occurred with a moiety organization of just two groups, was the earliest form of religion, associated above all with Australia. It was made necessary by the lack of any other focal point in mobile, dispersed societies, such as locality or kinship. Only later, as social evolution progressed beyond this stage, did a single great god come to symbolize the unity of the whole tribe against the particularity of the clans.

This interpretation of totemism has long been considered faulty on both ethnographic and theoretical grounds (see the review in Lukes 1973: 454–5, 477–8; also 513, 521, 525–7; Lévi-Strauss 1962). Nonetheless, it was for Durkheim an essential alternative to the intellectualist reliance on spirits and ancestor cults to explain the origins of religion. For Durkheim, the 'totemic principle' was the earliest form, in evolutionary terms, of a belief

accounting indigenously for what as a sociologist he identified as the com-
pulsive force of society over its members. All other forms of religion, including ancestor worship, are a development of this. Totemism did not take the
form of a belief in spirits: it was not the worship of animals or plants or of
any spirits that might be supposed to dwell within them, nor did it have a
material or utilitarian basis, as advocated by those who felt only 'useful'
plants and animals were the objects of worship. What actualized the belief
into action, what divinized the totem as the clan god, was its ability to represent the power of the collectivity. A corollary of this is that when the collectivity was worshipping the totem, or indeed any other sacred thing, it was
really worshipping itself, though it did not realize it: society symbolizes itself
through the notion of divinity.[6] This power was likened to, even perceived
as, a force which Durkheim called *mana,* made evident to the individual
through symbols, of which the totem was the earliest form.

The Durkheimians took over the notion of *mana* from Malayo-
Polynesian languages and put it to use as a concept of general significance in
their sociology. Since Keesing's revisionist studies (especially 1984) arguing
that *mana* is used variously as either a stative verb or as a noun denoting the
condition of 'efficacy, success, potency', it has become less feasible to represent it as any sort of force or power or invisible energy able to project itself
and act directly on something or someone else. *Mana* actually describes
something that works and even, metaphorically, whatever makes it work, but
not a force entering or leaving it in order to do so. The only exceptions,
Keesing says, are found in eastern Polynesia, where *mana* is frequently attributed to chiefs in a substantivized way. Keesing attributes this substantive
view to the influence of European nineteenth-century physics over early
ethnographers (cf. Needham 1976, on headhunting). Nonetheless, this was
what was emphasised by the Durkheimians, following Codrington (e.g.
Hubert and Mauss 1904: Ch. IV, part iii), and that is what is significant here.[7]

Mana was grasped by the Durkheimians as a non-intellectualist
replacement for the reliance on reasoning from dreams, personal experiences, the association of ideas, etc., found in psychological and intellectualist
interpretations of magic. Its value for them was freely admitted (e.g. by
Durkheim 1915: 363–4) to be that such an idea could not arise from anything
in the physical environment and therefore had to be social. Following
Codrington, it was seen as being both abstract and concrete, something
whose variability defies analysis, so that one must be content to describe it.
In view of their debates with the intellectualists, Hubert and Mauss are
careful to distinguish *mana* from any idea of *a* spirit, though it is still spiritual
in nature, and spirits, like people, may have and use it; it is an impersonal
force, not any species of animistic being. Moreover, it is both material, and

transferable to other things or people. Above all, its importance lies in the fact that it marks out what is of 'magical, religious and even social value.' Chiefs have *mana,* and the 'importance and inviolability' of the taboos that surround them depend on it.

In short, *mana* marks out the sacred, an equation the authors make explicit in identifying *mana* with the Malay concept of *kramet* 'sacred', from Arabic *haram.* Their keenness on the idea as a potentially universal and not specifically Malayo-Polynesian notion is seen not only here but also in other cases in which the relevant word is linguistically unrelated to *mana* (e.g. Iroquois *orenda,* Mexican *naual*), blithely ignoring the obvious possibility that such words, found at a remove of thousands of miles, might mean something radically different. There is the usual resort to evolution to explain away negative instances – in India, *mana* has turned into the notion of *brahman,* in Greece it has become a proto-scientific concept. The absence of it in many ethnographic accounts is attributed to the fact that people do not always realize or cannot always express the notions that form their thought and direct their actions. In any case, its connection with the sacred places it beyond all discussion or enquiry for those in the society. It is analogous to a category and thus 'makes possible magical ideas as categories make possible human ideas' (1950 [1926]: 111).

The connection between *mana* and the sacred was important for the Durkheimians, but they were not entirely consistent on the question of the identity between the two (cf. Isambert 1982: 228–9). This is partly because they retained the intellectualist distinction between magic and religion, though Durkheim himself left its definition and treatment largely to Hubert and Mauss. In their view, magic, though forming a continuum with religion, consists essentially of those rites which are directed at, or by, the individual rather than the community, tending at the end of the continuum towards the illicit, the malevolent. Magic was distinguished from religion by having no church or community, being instead a nucleus of ritual practitioners recognizing the participation of the laity only as clients and/or as victims. While both the community and the supernatural would punish the breach of a religious interdiction, only the latter is involved in breaching a magical taboo. Magical injunctions thus lack reference to the sacred and therefore to the morality imposed by the society: 'there is no sin in magic' (Durkheim 1915: 301). Thus it is circumstance, not evolution, as for Frazer, that separates magic from religion. In a sense, magic was defined residually, as extra-social and extra-moral, in order to break the connection between it and deities made by the intellectualists. For Douglas, this created a problem for anthropology for a long time after (one which her own *Purity and Danger,* 1966, set out to solve). Of course, the Durkheimians would still have accepted that magic *as a belief* is part of a social tradition: it was in its purpose and character *within* that tradition that it differed from religion.

Hubert and Mauss certainly saw *mana* as the essence of magic, calling it its 'mother idea' (1950: 130), just as the sacred was the essence of religion (cf. the quote from Hubert on the sacred, previous section; also, Durkheim 1915: 201). However, they did not see *mana* as magical *rather than* religious. Magic, a ritual technique made efficacious through *mana,* could be used to protect the sacred as well as to threaten it. Magic nonetheless leaned towards the profane, in so far as this could threaten the sacred. It is in accordance with this emphasis that the authors picked out particularly the dead and women as manifestations of magic par excellence, both having primarily negative connotations vis-à-vis their opposites, the living and men. In other words, their association with magic comes from their relatively inauspicious position in society, which endows them with their particular qualities (the latter are not inherent in them). The association with the dead is especially significant, given the disputes with the intellectualists. The magic is not in the soul but in the soul's *mana,* which the magician takes over and subsequently controls. It is a notion that society controls, by making *mana* a category suggesting variously efficacy, influence and protection of the sacred. Souls and spirits are its vehicles, not its owners.

Magic is thus both distinct from and a part of ritual, which itself is designed to reinforce social solidarity through contact with the sacred. It is such ritual as the latter, representing ultimate, transcendent values, that can be called religious, but magic shares with religion the intimate connection with belief, which it both reinforces and draws on for support. It is in this way that both *mana* and sacredness are attributed to things and people by the collective sentiments of society, not by the assumptions or reasoning of individuals based on their personal experiences.

At the same time, *mana* appeared to Mauss and Hubert to be more general than the sacred, precisely because of this association with magic as a technique available to both sacred and profane. This evidently involved some contradiction with Durkheim. Mauss explained the situation in a review of his own career, dating from around 1930 (see Mauss 1983: 149):

> ... at the foundation of both magic and religion we [i.e. Mauss and Hubert] discovered a vast common notion which we called *mana,* borrowing the term from the Melanesian-Polynesian language. The idea of *mana* is perhaps more general than that of the sacred. Later, Durkheim tried to deduce it sociologically from the notion of the sacred. We were never sure that he was correct and I still continue to speak of the magico-religious basis. In any case, like the notion of the sacred, magic presents itself as a category ....

Elsewhere in this period, in 1933, Mauss referred to the sacred as being 'an extremely restricted notion of religion' (1969 II: 147). In other words, he eventually rejected his uncle's reduction of *mana* and magic to the sacred and religion (cf. Durkheim 1915: 201-2). This was perhaps an element in his later breach with other propositions of his uncle's, especially the unity of sacred and society (assuming that the existence of *mana* was taken as showing that the sacred did not exhaust the social). This may also have reflected the circumstance that Durkheim was more concerned with the epistemological bases of the new sociology, something which his followers could be more sanguine about. For Durkheim, it was essential to begin with establishing the conjunction of the social and the religious, and he left it to Hubert, Mauss and Hertz to fill the gaps, to put some flesh on the skeleton.

Isambert (1982: 215-45) sheds more light on these issues. Durkheim was faced with the problem of avoiding a circular argument which explained the sacred by the religious and the religious by the sacred. The problem was realized at the outset (1899), but the solutions appeared in full only in *Elementary Forms of the Religious Life* (1915). In order to escape from this dilemma and arrive at a proper explanation, he chose to develop the idea of the sacred on grounds independent of its association with religion, with the help of Hubert's and Mauss's work as well as his own. One step was the development of the idea of the interdict, via that of taboo (cf. Durkheim 1898a), as something isolating the sacred from the profane. Another was the declaration that a sense of sacredness did not depend on the idea of God (1899: 15) but was whatever society chose to regard as sacred. This had the effect of freeing religion from the idea of divinity and extending it to any collective concern with the sacred, however defined, including law, and morality in general (see also previous section).

Mauss and Hubert's contribution (1899, 1904; also Hubert 1905) had been to stress the further widening of the sacred to include what is impure as well as what is pure, an idea that they, like Durkheim, took over from Robertson Smith and which Hertz also adopted in his paper on right and left (see pp. 59-65). This led to the idea that the sacred has a double nature, both desirable and threatening. Thus sacredness was relativized: things are no longer absolutely sacred or non-sacred but more sacred or less sacred. Moreover, sacrifice is the one means whereby the profane can attain contact with the sacred safely, through the intermediary of a victim. Despite the literal meaning of the word, sacrifice is all about communion with the sacred, not about foregoing something. In this way, the profane itself becomes temporarily sacred, hence the need to 'purify' oneself at the end of a rite, which is actually rather a means of being able to return to a suitably profane condition in safety. This overcame the problem of how the sacred and the profane can approach one another while remaining strictly separate: in doing so, the profane itself takes on sacredness.

Sacredness thus came to be isolated from religion partly by means of this ritual occasion, marked by a particular space and time, in which the sacrifice took on something of the nature of a crime. Another means was the incorporation of *mana* into the model, as the force which both protected the sacred and gave it its power. This in its turn had the merit of giving the sacred something by means of which it could be distinguished from the profane, which otherwise might seem to be defined simply by their opposition to one another. For Durkheim, who took this notion over into his theory of religion, this was enough. For Hubert and Mauss, however, *mana* was not exhausted by its association with the sacred; and since *mana* and the sacred were the bases respectively of magic and religion, this also meant that magic appeared as more extensive than religion. Yet all through this process, the sacred remained the basis of religion. What changed was that it itself received an independent basis through taboo, sacrifice and *mana,* so that religion need no longer be seen as *its* basis: the circularity of reasoning had been broken. Moreover, the idea of *mana,* generalized into a force *sui generis,* now became the means whereby society made its prescriptions and values felt among its members, whereby the collectivity responded to its own coming together at ritual moments, whereby it was impressed with the reality of something superior to itself as a mere collection of individuals. This was necessary because the social could not become religious on its own. As a result, there was no longer any need to rely purely on vague notions of effervescence and on the mere obligation to believe, as earlier with the Durkheimians, nor on reflections on individual perception and experience, as with the intellectualists. Religion was the expression of the will of the group, operating through *mana.*

Isambert is no doubt right in seeing in this use of *mana* an ultimate resort to a mere 'communal mysticism' as an explanation (1982: 242). Added to the dubious ethnographic extension of the concept, and Keesing's demonstration that, even in most of Oceania, *mana* is not what it was originally thought to be, one sees clearly how much the device was made to fit the theory. Nor was it the only instance. Lévi-Strauss (1950: xxxvii–xl, xlvi–xlvii) argues that Mauss's use of the Maori notion of *hau* as a concept of general significance in his work on exchange — the idea of 'the spirit in the gift' — (1950 [1925]), was directly inspired by the Durkheimians' exploitation of *mana,* of which Mauss clearly regarded the *hau* as a version. As Casajus points out (1984: 67), Mauss was consciously using *mana* as a sociological category of general relevance here and realized that among the Maori, the indigenous word *mana* is 'reserved for men and spirits, and [is] applied less to things than in Melanesia' (Mauss 1950: 158 n. 4). *Hau,* conversely, was used of things. Like Durkheim, Mauss was faced with a problem of explanation, namely how to account for the triple obligation to give, receive and return objects that were objectively lifeless between subjects who were objectively autonomous. In other words, what made the gift the medium of a relation between substances? The answer was the *hau,* the *mana*-like spirit of the gift, which not only resides in the gift but in anything stolen.

Mauss relates (1950: 159 n. 1) how Hertz was also planning to use the concept in the work on sin: the *hau* is the *mana* which, in the form of taboos, forms the sanction against the theft of personal property (cf. p. 139). Mauss drew on Hertz's notes here, which had even been annotated for his attention, though there is no reason to think that he owed any aspect of his own interpretation directly to Hertz: the essentials were all in Elsdon Best's ethnography. Hertz's reliance on this concept in his published writings is not so prominent as it is with his colleagues, but here is evidence that it would have formed a more important part in his central work, had he lived to finish it.

CHAPTER THREE

Hertz As Reviewer and Pamphleteer

HERTZ AS REVIEWER

Book reviews are normally among the more instantly forgettable forms of academic writing, even more so than some of the books they discuss. For Durkheim and his colleagues, however, they were one of the most important ways in which their own still to be established ideas could be propagated and directly confronted with those of their rivals. They were also a principal means of working out the methodology of the new sociology in a manner that was more compressed and often more obviously polemical than was the case in the articles and books they wrote. Their journal, the *Année Sociologique*, was originally intended primarily as a vehicle for discussions of contemporary anthropological writings, as befitted a group of scholars whose raw material was almost exclusively the previously published work of others, and reviews remained important right through Durkheim's custodianship of the journal, even when articles also began to be included regularly.

Hertz played a full role in this activity. His reviews are to be found in three different periodicals, *Année Sociologique, Revue de l'Histoire des Religions* and *Notes Critiques — Sciences Sociales*. Those in the first two are purely academic in type, whereas those in the latter concern more the political and social problems of the day. Generally, Hertz's reviews faithfully follow the Durkheimian line, but they are useful for showing us his particular slant on the new sociology, and sometimes he has interesting points to make that are outside his usual range of concerns. They are therefore well worth discussing in their own right, especially since they provide us with a typical example of what was a key activity for the whole group. Hertz's academic reviews can be divided into four broad themes: the relation of sociology to other disciplines; the sociology of religion in general; sin and expiation; and other.

Thus in the first group, Hertz praises the attention given to social conditions by King, who argues that collective beliefs are taken for granted when conditions remain stable and that they only come to be seen as 'having a value in themselves' (Hertz 1905b: 196) when these conditions break down and nothing replaces them. Similarly, Hertz appreciates Simmel's view of conflict as a type of social relation, though criticizing him for abstracting it from its spatial, temporal and social contexts as a series of 'types' (Hertz 1905a). Hertz is particularly hard on attempts to argue for differences in the essential nature of religion and morality between societies or between societal types, whatever the differences in detail. He deplores the view of the English moral philosopher Hobhouse, who is more concerned with moral improvement through the ages than with 'the objective norms which regulate the conduct and relations of men' (Hertz 1910h: 277). Hertz also criticises Gomperz for basing his arguments almost exclusively on individual psychology and the logic of philosophical systems rather than on sociology. However, he does not reject philosophy outright:

> Although philosophical systems are powerless to account for moral reality, it does not follow that they have no interest for the sociologist. In fact, objective rules are not the whole of morality, which comprises the set of notions which are current in a society on the nature of the moral agent, its motives, and the sanctions on its conduct. (1906c: 272)

For Hertz, as for Durkheim, modern morality, individualism and rational ideals are as much the product of society as 'primitive' beliefs.

His review of Ehrenreich, who had argued that mythological traits had been diffused from north-east Asia into the Americas, shows a degree of agnosticism concerning diffusionism: 'The readers of the *Année* know that we do not attach any fundamental importance to these questions. In any case, great care and rigour are needed to avoid falling back into the errors of the former "theory of borrowings"' (Hertz 1907b: 329). A degree of disquiet is evident even here, however. The concept of independent origin (e.g. of flood myths; Hertz 1913h, on Gerland) seems to have been less problematic to accept, though generally the Durkheimians shied away from speculations about origins, even history being a social creation.[1] Much more firmly rejected were attempts to choose one of the higher religions or a type of higher religion as the source of all others, despite the fact that the Durkheimians tended to endow totemism with this status. The Egyptologist G. Foucart's tendency to see all 'primitive' peoples as religiously Egyptian is one example condemned by Hertz in a quite polemical and ironical review of 1912 (Hertz 1912a). This was part of a continuous battle involving also F.B. Jevons and ethnologists of all sorts, and Hertz finds himself defending Frazer and van Gennep as well as the Durkheimians on this occasion. Like Durkheim's great rivals Bergson and Tarde, Foucart had a chair at the Collège de France (from 1906), and he clearly lacked any sympathy for the new sociology. While Foucart accuses ethnologists of simply ignoring Egypt, Hertz mocks his condescension in allowing African religion, 'still alive and vigorous' (Foucart), some value in comparison with Australian religion, which was supposedly on the brink of extinction. This, and the label 'totemic school', were clear digs at the Durkheimians, whom Foucart, according to Hertz, was seeking to part from other ethnologists (Schmidt, Hartland etc.) in the interests of an entente with Egyptology that would ultimately freeze the latter out altogether. Hertz manages to make Foucart seem at once intellectually arrogant and a cultural imperialist for his insistence on the virtues of Egyptology versus sociology and of the ancient Egyptians versus the whole of non-European humanity.

Hertz was only slightly less dismissive of Jevons, whom he regarded as little more than a Christian apologist of the Bergsonian persuasion (Hertz 1909c, 1911a). This was despite the fact that Jevons was claiming to develop a science of religion. For Hertz, it was legitimate to use science to argue the case for theology, but not to treat theology itself as a science, especially when it was intended to press the virtues of Christianity on readers (cf. his work on sin, p. 127). The first and longer of these two reviews carries an interesting comparison with Frazer, an adversary of Jevons as well as of the Durkheimians. While Jevons aimed to argue that all peoples are at root monotheistic and claimed to see an incipient Christianity in all 'primitives', Frazer claimed that monotheistic religion was an evolutionary development out of an earlier stage of magic. For Jevons, magic, fetishism, polytheism and monotheism are not evolutionary stages but different routes to the discovery of God, only Christians so far having found the right one. Both writers, says Hertz, have an essentially Christian view of religion, though Frazer excludes much ritual activity from the term and sees it instead as magic. While supporting Jevons's anti-evolutionism against Frazer, Hertz agrees with the latter's rebuttal to Jevons regarding the universality of Christian principles, however embryonic. Like Hubert and Mauss, he follows Frazer in regarding magic as distinct from religion but regards it as often co-existing in the same society and as having the same ultimate source in a more basic 'magico-religious complex' (Hertz 1909c: 222).

Hertz's review of the third (and therefore twice-expanded) version of Frazer's own magnum opus, *The Golden Bough* (see Hertz 1912b) was more sympathetic, though still sarcastic in parts. For instance, he starts by comparing the mere accumulation of examples in each successive edition of Frazer's with the Durkheimian practice of focussing on 'a group of ethnographically limited and typical facts' or 'a specific institution' (*ibid.*: 385–6). But there are also changes of substance in this edition. Frazer now brings in Hegel in support of his existing theory that magic is 'the immediate product of the

empirical consciousness of the individual' (Hertz *ibid.*: 388), the mere association of ideas being sufficient to explain it. For Frazer, magic is a matter of
man thinking he is exercising physical control over the universe, like a falsely
premised science. Religion, conversely, is a matter of impersonal forces, represented by supernatural beings. In effect, says Hertz, Frazer confuses beliefs
in spirits and beliefs in forces, which the Durkheimians separate, and also
natural spirits and spirits of the dead, all of which he connects with magic,
while separating these from the supernatural spirits and their powers that
supposedly inform religion. But these distinctions are ultimately false: in particular, 'the point at which a force is applied does not alter its nature. Now, it
is on this arbitrary delimitation of *natural* and *supernatural* forces that
Frazer builds his entire theory of the relation between magic and religion'
(Hertz *ibid.*: 392). As we have seen (pp. 30–6), the Durkheimians tended to
reduce any spiritual being to the force acting within it. Moreover, they did
not restrict the idea of a force to religion but saw it as underlying all manifestations of the sacred, those involving magic too. Hertz also opposes both
Frazer's reduction of taboo to negative magic – taboo is actually 'the type par
excellence of a ritual interdiction' (*ibid.*: 391) – and his reduction of the
Durkheimian concept of *mana* to a mere mode of transmission, when what
is really involved is a force.

Similarly unsatisfactory to Hertz, despite its erudition, was the work of
the Viennese Jesuit-ethnologist Wilhelm Schmidt, who also sought to prove
an original monotheism for all peoples, a thesis developed here with respect
to the Indonesians and New Guineans. Hertz (1913e: 281–2) quite correctly
condemns Schmidt's resort to 'degeneracy' to explain negative cases, an argumentative device that in the case of the Durkheimians, including Hertz,
became an almost equally dubious recourse to evolutionary change.

Closer to the Durkheimians was the work of the Arabist Edmond
Doutté, who was even allowed to carry out some editorial duties for the group
(in *Année Sociologique* Volume XII). Following Hubert and Mauss, he claimed
to have found in the Maghribian concepts of *baraka* and the evil eye different
aspects of the local version of *mana*, though he hesitated to apply it to omens,
unlike Hertz in his review (1910e). Also arbitrary, for Hertz, is Doutté's concentration on impersonal forces and their typological isolation from the
various sorts of gods and spirits, which Doutté proposed relegating to a
second book he was planning. For Hertz, all these phenomena play an equal
role in both magic and religion because all are equally impregnated with
mana. Though spirits and souls must be distinguished from *mana*, they are
still actuated by it (cf. pp. 30–6). Other problems that Hertz identifies are
Doutté's reluctance to endow sacred forms with their properly 'imperious and
severe character' (Hertz 1910e: 197), and his occasional tendency to introduce

fear and desire as the foundations of rites, *mana* and gods, thus taking a couple of steps back towards the intellectualists. If, says Hertz (*ibid.*: 198), fears and desires 'did not already possess a sort of objectivity and transcendence, how could they come to dominate, even to overwhelm, the individual from whom they are supposed to emanate and to impose the belief on the whole group?' Such beliefs can only be collective.

Particularly interesting is Hertz's review (1910n) of Lucien Lévy-Bruhl's *Les fonctions mentales dans les sociétés inférieures* (1910). Lévy-Bruhl was on the fringes of the *Année* group but much appreciated by them. In some senses he took the logic of their views on religion to an extreme to which they themselves were reluctant to follow him, but he was significant to them as a rare example of a philosopher anxious to base his views of the human condition on ethnographic reports rather than his own cogitations or those of his philosophical colleagues and predecessors. He opposed himself especially to the English intellectualists, who saw all mentality as basically the same, though at different stages of development (cf. Durkheim's review of the book, 1913a: 35–6; also Mauss 1923: 26, on Hertz's work on sin). This latter view constituted an advance in that it accepted the fundamental unity of the human species, but at the price of encouraging a definite ethnocentrism. For Lévy-Bruhl, conversely, mentality varies with social conditions. Although he went further than the Durkheimians in identifying a distinct primitive mentality different from our own, his interpretation of that mentality used arguments very close to theirs. For instance, his idea of a mystical force or fluid in all significant objects and beings can be described as his own version of *mana*. For him, primitive thought was both more concrete, in that it viewed as real what we might regard as arbitrary or non-essential, and 'prelogical', in that it does not link cause and effect and can tolerate what we would regard as contradictions. These last two points were directed particularly against the intellectualists, as a challenge to the notion of reasoning from false premises that they largely relied on: for Lévy-Bruhl, primitive thought is on the contrary 'impermeable to experience' (quoted by Hertz, *ibid.*: 358). An example is his argument that primitive thought does not separate the phenomena of life, birth, death etc., because it disregards the physical aspects of these things. For Hertz, the merit of this argument is that it does not try to make primitive mentality understandable in terms of our own thought and logic — which would distort it completely — but in terms of its own.

Hertz goes a long way in accepting this account, remarking (*ibid.*: 362):

> the opposition between the 'prelogical' and the logical that M. Lévy-Bruhl has brought to the fore corresponds not to two extreme moments of a mental development, but to two irreducible manners of

thinking, the one collective, above all emotional and pragmatic, the other (relatively) individual and reflexive.

However, he regrets that the author has 'not insisted more on the negative aspect of primitive mentality, that which is expressed in the religious order by ritual interdictions' (*ibid.*). For Lévy-Bruhl, polarities such as natural and supernatural or sacred and profane are secondary to participation, an approach which tends to focus exclusively on the sacred. What is needed in addition is a 'law of mutual exclusion or polarity' (*ibid.*: 363), which will bring back into focus the difference between what possesses *mana* and what does not, whether temporarily (the sinner, for example) or permanently. Hertz's interest in negativity here is noteworthy, given its importance in his work generally (see pp. 25-6). It can be seen that he also stressed duality more than Lévy-Bruhl (his essay on the left and right hands had been published only the previous year).

Hertz reviewed a number of books on Indonesia, the area he was mainly interested in as regards his article on death of 1907 (1907a). A long review of *Het Animisme in den Indischen Archipel* (1906) by A. C. Kruyt (also spelled Kruijt) appeared in the *Revue de l'Histoire des Religions* (Hertz 1909d; the book was unknown to Hertz at the time he wrote his death article — see 1909d: 357 n. 2). The review should be compared with Mauss's less detailed notice of the same book in *Année Sociologique*, Volume 11 (1910), especially since running through both is a relentless determination to throw out souls in favour of *mana*. The author of the book in question had been a long-time missionary among the Torajas of Sulawesi, and one of his concerns was to contradict a work on the same topic by a colleague and compatriot, G. A. Wilken (see Wilken 1884, 1885). The latter was a strict follower of the intellectualists, especially Tylor, another of Kruyt's targets. Kruyt did not go far enough for the two Frenchmen, however.

Kruyt opposes the intellectualist view that souls are the chief mystical force, analogical to the human personality and arising out of the contemplation of death, dreams and nature, with the observation that in Indonesia there are usually two such entities. For one, identified with the human personality and enjoying a more or less continuous existence after death, he retained the standard intellectualist idea of a soul. To the other, an animating force in life which evaporates or finds a new home after death, he applied the Dutch word *zielestof*, literally 'soul substance'. In addition, he distinguished belief in the former as spiritism, reserving animism for the latter. Not surprisingly, both Hertz and Mauss seize on Kruyt's *zielestof* as a version of *mana* or an inanimate spiritual force pervading all things sacred or mystical. Hertz in particular appreciates Kruyt's view that headhunting and sacrifice have more to do with acquiring spiritual force than with propitiating ancestors or other beings.

Kruyt himself resorts to an evolutionary argument to explain the appearance of souls, one which draws partly on the intellectualist approach to religion, and also on the notion of an original primitive communism. At this early stage, mankind was nothing but a dense mass, where only *zielestof* was to be found. In course of time, individualism arrived, and with it the idea of an individual soul. This individualism itself grew out of the hierarchization of society, in which the chiefs were the individuals par excellence – Kruyt remarks how much more fuss is made of their souls after death than of those of commoners. With this tendency, much advanced by Islam and Christianity, arrive gods and other spirits, as well as the idea of survival after death – a need, says Kruyt, again versus the intellectualists, that is far from being primitive. Thus the recognition of the awfulness of death is a late development in the history of religious thought, one which led to the splitting off of the notion of soul from *zielestof* as a separate entity. This shift in ideas is therefore linked to a shift in social formation, though in another sense it is simply the intellectualist view delayed somewhat in history. This is not lost on Hertz and Mauss, both of whom criticize Kruyt's further claim that fear of the soul is behind death ritual, especially the participation of the bereaved in the condition of the deceased. Their reaction is to try to reduce any manifestation of soul in Kruyt's book to *zielestof*. Hertz does this by denying that death is the frontier between the two notions: it is inconceivable that the soul is not thought to be the living person too, or that *zielestof* is not thought to go on existing after a person's death. In other words, both entities exist in both the living and the dead, and after death it is the *zielestof* or other mystical forces, not the soul, that become a danger to the living, affecting simultaneously the soul and the body (cf. Hertz's article on death, Chapter Five). For Mauss, the *zielestof* has an aspect of individuality in both life and death, but since this individuality tends to evaporate after death, it is clearly ultimately reducible to the former. He especially regrets Kruyt's inability to address the question of the structural relation between the two. Hertz's answer (1909d: 360) is that 'they correspond, not to an objective division of things, but to different planes of consciousness.'

In respect of many societies, Kruyt has in fact been proved more correct than either of the two more famous parties in the early debates on the origin and nature of religion between which he was sandwiched (we shall meet him again in Chapter Four). Souls and soul substances, often in the plural, are to be found in many parts of the world, without there being any possibility of reducing one to the other (tribal India is one example; see Parkin 1988; 1992c: Ch. 10). Both are, of course, social facts in the Durkheimian sense, and Hertz and his colleagues had no need to reject the idea of souls simply because of its association with the intellectualist approach. Their own attitude here was very much bound up with their overall view of the relation between society and the individual. *Mana*, a force animating the sacred taken over from what was thought to be the Polynesian world view, was converted into a pseudo-indigenous analogue of the power of society over the individual and then generalized to all humanity. It must have been easier to conceive of something like *mana* entering people and things specifically at society's request than souls or spirits. Indeed, in the process *mana* was made to animate even souls, as if these had no capabilities of their own. Despite their advances in insisting on the social provenance of all social facts, one feels here that the Durkheimians simply succeeded in replacing one set of sweeping assertions with another.

Similar attempts to reduce souls to *mana* occur in some of Hertz's other reviews. In a notice of Warneck's book on the Batak (Hertz 1913d), the significance of death as the boundary between *zielestof* and soul is again challenged, the different names designating, according to Hertz, 'not radically separate entities, but different states of the same substance, corresponding to the stage of the funerary rite, the earthly destination of the deceased, and the number and power of his descendants' (*ibid.*: 275; also 1910k: 60; cf. the article on death, Hertz 1907a, and Chapter Five). One term, *sombaon*, meaning 'ancestor' according to Warneck, is glossed by Hertz as 'the Malay equivalent of the Arabic *kramat*' (*ibid.*), itself connected with Arabic *haram*, 'sacred', a piece of sleight of hand borrowed from Hubert and Mauss (see p. 32). Similar slides from obvious spirits into supposed mystical forces can be found in Hertz's review of two books on Arabia (1910c: 161, 162). Mauss averred on one occasion (1907b: 308) that Hertz had also found *mana* in Bantu Africa in his review of a book on fetishism by the missionary Nassau (Hertz 1906a), an adherent of the view that monotheism informs all the world's religions. For Hertz, this original god is really a legendary chief, perhaps a folk hero or origin figure. Nassau's view of a fetish as something having a soul is also found to be false. The myriad names for it indicate a lack of clarity in the native conception (that this might indicate instead a large number of souls does not seem to occur to Hertz), and what must really be at work is an 'inexhaustible reservoir of spiritual energy' (*ibid.*: 193). Thus for Hertz, the fetish is 'not only an object invested with a special power, it is this power itself' (*ibid.*: 193–4), which in this case inhabits cemeteries and magicians as well as ritual objects. Hertz objects to so much reliance being placed on this imported term and its unwarranted extension to all sorts of cults, rites and taboos — remarks which might apply to *mana* as much as to 'fetish'. Neither term, of course, any longer enjoys currency as a cross-cultural category, nor, even, do the properties once attributed to them (cf. Keesing 1984 on *mana*).

Another of Hertz's regular duties in reviewing books and articles was to keep a watch out for signs of totemism in suitable places, especially where the original authors were reluctant to see it or were simply oblivious to it. Totemism was important to the Durkheimians as their version of the original form of religion and as the original vehicle for *mana*, an alternative both to souls and spirits and to the one and only God. It was a stage in their own evolutionary model rather than an all-pervasive force, like *mana*. Its academic development owed more to Durkheim personally than was so in the case of *mana*, which seems to have been more Mauss's and Hubert's inspiration (see pp. 30-6).

A review of an article by Rivers (Hertz 1910b) sets the problem in the context of the debate with the intellectualists, for Rivers follows Tylor and Frazer in deriving totemism from the individual's animal protector or external soul, and from reincarnation beliefs. Hertz naturally rejects this, since such concepts are also found without totemism, and it is hard to see how any development from the supposed individualism to the collective clan can have come about. However, he agrees with Rivers in seeing the fragmentary facts in the latter's ethnography as evidence of evolutionary trends leading to the 'breakdown' of the original structure of beliefs and observances. In accepting this, Hertz also accepts arguments for the shift between matrilineal and patrilineal forms of social organization then still finding favour in some quarters in ethnology. Another evolutionary case, the extension of a tortoise taboo in Tikopia from a single clan to a whole tribe, followed subsequently by its restriction to the chiefs, is claimed by Hertz to signal a process 'from clan cult to caste cult' (*ibid.*: 104), a process he had previously identified, more generally, in the article on right and left (1973: 8). He ends by pointing out against Rivers and Frazer, justly enough, that belief in chance impregnation by animals does not necessarily deprive the father of all involvement in conception, though behind this remark seems to have lain a desire to preserve the continuity of descent that was seen to be an integral part of the totemic complex.

Hertz's discussion of the Tikopia material also hints at an association between the decay of totemism and the development of agriculture, a claim made more explicitly in another review (1913d: 274), where the Batak of Indonesia are described as 'a dense agricultural population arrived at a social state which it is difficult to see as compatible with totemism'. A similar evolutionary argument had been used in the paper on right and left to get round the negative case of the Zuñi (1973 [1909]: 18). A large part of the model set forward in that article is reproduced in another review dealing extensively with totemism (1913b) but which also shows how much dual organization figured in Hertz's thoughts on both topics. Elsewhere (1910i) he refuses, surely rightly, the status of totem to livestock and their body parts in a pastoral society in Uganda, despite Roscoe's use of the term, on the grounds that such animals rarely provide totems.

Two major reviews in *Revue de l'Histoire des Religions*, of Hartland's *Primitive Promiscuity* (Hertz 1910l) and Westermarck's *The Origin and Development of the Moral Ideas* (Hertz 1910m), concern more particularly the question of the interplay between kinship and religion. Hartland's book was concerned above all with the question of the origin of beliefs in supernatural births, meaning those which do not give a place to an earthly father in procreation but instead to spirits of various kinds, who enter the mother's body through food, water, the sun's rays, being in a sacred place, etc. Like the Durkheimians, Hartland seizes on the Australians as the archetype of primitive man and concludes that such beliefs were once common to all humanity. His thesis relies also on the then still common assumption that humanity started its existence under conditions of primitive promiscuity allied to matrilineal descent, both of which reduced the father's importance to little more than his being the mother's furtive lover. We can now see that, with this theory, several early ethnologists incorporated the origin myths of their subjects into their own academic discourse as fact. The argument suggested that the supernatural and miraculous births of later religions like Christianity were once the norm for all humanity, at a time when its ignorance of the mechanism of procreation through sexual intercourse led to this classic example of reasoning from false premises. Hartland nonetheless applies his ideas to societies with patrilineal descent too.

Hertz starts his critique by comparing Hartland's meticulous but tedious array of facts drawn from all over the world with the Durkheimian practice of studying social phenomena through one particularly highly developed form, itself in part a reaction to the scissors-and-paste methods of Frazer (cf. Hertz 1912b: 385–6, cited above). He then remarks justly that ignorance of physiological paternity does not necessarily deprive the father of all part in procreation (he may, for instance, 'open the way' for the child, even if he does not cause the actual pregnancy). This can be said even of the 'primitive' Australians, following Spencer and Gillen. In other words, Hartland is forced to choose between physical fact and arbitrary convention. A middle way is nonetheless possible, i.e. seeing in paternity a 'mystical relation, imaginary in our eyes, but endowed with authentic reality through collective belief' (Hertz 1910l: 226; there is a similar argument in the work on sin; see below, p. 127). Even in societies with matrilineal descent, there is frequently a myth and ritual concerning the periodic renewal of life through a sexual union of the heavenly father and the earthly mother. What is at work here is not a spirit but 'a powerful mystical efficacy' (*ibid.*: 227). In other words, the failure of the earthly father to contribute to procreation is taken up by a heavenly father. Further counter-evidence in Hertz's view is the existence of couvade in societies with matrilineal as well as patrilineal descent, and the fact that adultery, far from being lightly regarded in primitive societies as Hartland claims, often has deleterious mystical consequences, which may even concentrate on the search for the real father as the solution. Hertz links this last point to the identity of father and eldest son in the Hinduism of Manu, which resembles beliefs from such widely diverse areas as Brittany and Polynesia. He then compares this, very neatly, with the consubstance of Father and Son in the Holy Trinity, though not mentioning the third element in that Trinity, the Holy Ghost.

Hertz expresses wonder that Hartland, who knows the material so well, should chose to stress spirits at the expense of the mystical forces generated by, for example, sexual intercourse. Girls are kept in out of the sun after puberty not through fear of their being impregnated by it but because they are in a state of impurity that threatens it (here, the stress on a force is linked to the danger to the sacred coming from the impure). Similarly, taboos surrounding a newly married couple are not a survival from a supposed age of promiscuity but a mark of their marginal state until they have produced at least one child (this, rather than the wedding, cements a marriage in many societies and may even give the couple adult status).

For all his erudition, Hartland is thus a typical intellectualist, determined to seek the reason for collective ideas in a past of greater ignorance as to the true nature of the world rather than in present-day collective representations. Birth and reproduction are no less disturbing to social equilibrium than death (on which Hertz had already written, of course, 1907a). As a result, they release

> energies and powers which go beyond the organism and the individuals who are present. The contrast between the sexual act, common to man and to the animals, and the appearance of a new member of the social body provokes in the consciousness of men a painful sentiment which is expressed and allayed, to some extent, by magico-religious beliefs and practices. (1910l: 233)

We see here how ritual receives more emphasis than myth, as was usually the case with the Durkheimians. However, Hertz also remarks that it is hardly surprising if, at birth, the genitor is often transformed into a sacred figure who is the source of all humanity. In this way, whatever the ignorance that may lie at the root of these notions, in actual fact they become transformed into a collective 'truth' (*ibid.*). Hertz's review is much fuller than Durkheim's (1913b) of the same book, though of course both write along basically the same lines. Durkheim makes the additional point that with reincarnation by a spirit, the mother is often merely the vehicle for rebirth in a descent line other than her own, as with patrilineal descent. This argument, true in itself, easily links up with totemism.

Hertz's review of Westermarck (Hertz 1910m) starts with the same generous acknowledgement of his scholarship, as well as an appreciation of his ethnographic researches during his many vacations in Morocco. He thus united in his person the ethnographer who observes and describes with the sociologist who compares and explains. Much of the review in effect analyses the relationship between Westermarck and the intellectualists. On the one hand, Westermarck opposed Frazer's claim that in human sacrifice the victim incarnates a vegetable spirit in favour of a theory of substitution preventing disaster. On the other hand, he sees in attitudes at death ritual only 'senti- ments of fear and pity' and 'considerations of prudence and individual sym- pathy' (*ibid.*: 235). For Hertz, this is not enough:

> In reality, a man's death, especially if he is of high status, is, for the entire community he belongs to, a scar, an affront, a failure. The obser- vances imposed on the survivors do not merely express the distress and anxiety which take hold of the group, they constitute a sort of revenge for the death and a reparation, thus serving to reestablish peace. (*ibid.*)

Nonetheless, Hertz approves of Westermarck's general approach to the study of religion as 'a notable contribution to our science' (*ibid.*: 236). For the latter, religion is a matter of both the duties men owe the supernat- ural and the influence the gods have on men's actions 'as legislators and judges of human action' (*ibid.*: 235). Among the duties are 'prohibitions and interdictions [taboos] as well as positive obligations (offerings and sacrifices, prayer, glorification, duty towards faith and orthodoxy)' (*ibid.*: 235–6).

Westermarck rightly, in Hertz's view, draws moral ideas from mystical beliefs, and he also distinguishes religion from magic by making the latter a matter of impersonal forces working mechanically. Where he offends is in reducing religion ultimately to fear of evil spirits and efforts to avoid them, as with the intellectualists. Thus he too is claiming in essence that it is scarcely possible to talk of religion in the earliest stages of human history. One conse- quence of this is that he does not attribute the social importance to totemism that Robertson-Smith and the Durkheimians had, seeing in it just a magical operation ensuring animal and plant fertility. Communal meals, blood brotherhood and sacrifice were simply means of transferring or obtaining such powers, these notions being at the root of moral ideas. Thus men origi- nally secured and controlled such powers themselves, as host, suppliant, owner, parent etc. They were not given them by the gods, who were simply the later inheritors of the powers men had access to.

Westermarck thus appears to follow a basically intellectualist line while substituting Durkheimian mystical forces for their souls, ghosts and spirits as the prime movers of human relations. This in itself meets with Hertz's approval, and he is not wholly opposed to Westermarck's evolutionary scheme, even agreeing that gods appear relatively late in the sequence. However, this is not to say that early humanity lacked 'an authentic religiosity' (*ibid.*: 238). Hertz asks how these supposedly personal powers could be thought to have any effect 'if it is not by reason of the sacred character, the holiness, with which the community invests them and which is of a properly religious order' (*ibid.*: 238).

Nonetheless, as Hertz no doubt appreciated, Westermarck met the Durkheimians halfway. His independence of mind accounts for his particular approach to totemism. As Goody has observed (1962: 15ff.), the Durkheimians reacted to that part of the intellectualist message that placed ancestor worship near the start of religious evolution by linking such worship to the family. They then declared that the intellectualist view had to be wrong because it was the clan, not the family, that came first in the evolution of social groups. This enabled them to give the priority to totemism, which they linked to the clan. Westermarck, as part of his campaign to discredit primitive promiscuity, demonstrated the universality of human marriage and thus restored the idea of the family as universal too (in *The History of Human Marriage*, 1891). But the family itself was not a focus for developed religious activity. The cost of his restoration of it was therefore to move the development of religion forward in evolution, thus leaving primitive man with a fear of mystical forces, but no true religion.

Hertz reviewed a number of works on sin and expiation, the topic of his doctoral thesis (see 1910d, 1910f, 1910g, 1913f; also 1910j: 327). The longest review of this kind was of Windisch's work on early Christianity (Hertz 1910d), which Hertz considered truly sociological, in that it saw the Pauline message as part of a tradition, not the individual inspiration of a religious thinker (cf. Hertz's dismissal of Bennewitz, writing on sin in Israel, as the work of a mere theologian, 1910g). For Windisch, this tradition is to be sought in the change in Judaism from occasional penitence to total submission to Jewish law in order to remove sin, followed by final penitence allowing entry into the realm of God. Christ's crucifixion and resurrection abolished law, sin and evil at a stroke and made believers an elect through their baptism, which thus attained a concentrated significance absent from Jewish ritual bathing. Conversely, the idea of total absorption in the divine, through conversion, was retained: the Christian 'participates in the essence of Christ' (1910d: 170) and is himself sacred. However, the rigidity of the early doctrine in allowing no degree of sin to the convert proved to be unsustainable and over-exclusive,

and sin came to be accepted as inevitable, even within the Christian community, tolerable so long as it were expiated. Thus 'the ordinary Christian is no
longer a saint but a profane being of good will who inclines towards holiness
without claiming it' (*ibid.*: 171). Accordingly, baptism was no longer seen as
entry into a state of perfection – which was now postponed, as in Judaism,
until after death – but merely as entry into the faith, into the community of
believers.

Another review examined Schrank's book on expiation in Babylon
(Hertz 1910f), which concentrated more on the low status of the class of
priests concerned with it than on the nature of the rites of expiation themselves, which is what would have interested Hertz. Nonetheless, their whole
purpose was clearly to remove evil and restore the people and things affected
by sin to their normal state. One guesses that amongst their number would
have been healers and shamans not necessarily concerned with the problem
of the evil of the victim as such. Hertz agrees with the author in seeing in the
conjunction of concepts such as sin, impurity, sickness and possession their
confusion, but not as regards this being an evolutionary development: 'the
confusion is not here the effect of syncretism, it is original, primitive, essential' (*ibid.*: 211). Such a view aided, of course, the introduction of a single
force, *mana*, as the agent in place of the myriad ghosts, spirits and souls that
the intellectualists, not without reason, saw as inhabiting the world of so-
called 'primitives'. Hertz also mentions (1910j: 327) the diminution of a
person's sacredness through sin or loss of honour among the Bedouin,
restored through a 'whitening' ritual (in the second case, at least – in his
own work on sin, he was to draw a clear distinction between the two; see
below, p. 131).

Hertz's review of the book by Grass on two Russian Orthodox sects
was edited, probably by Durkheim, for the *Année Sociologique* (1913c), but
Mauss published the full-length version, that discussed here, in *Mélanges*
(1928). The two sects studied by Grass, the Chlusts and the Skopts, were het-
erodox and non-conformist in the extreme and proved hostile to enquiry.
Hertz accepts Grass's account as a whole, but as usual has interesting points
of his own to add. Orthodox belief, scandalized by the multitudes of christs
and mothers of God in the Chlust pantheon, analogous in a way to saints,
attributes to the Chlusts a belief in their reincarnation generation after generation in the community of believers. Hertz manages to read into Grass a
denial of this in favour of 'an impersonal [i.e. *mana*-like] force' (Hertz 1928:
193). The Chlusts also condemn the flesh as irremediably profane, only the
soul being 'capable of divinity' (*ibid.*: 196), i.e. sacred (cf. Lukes 1973:
432–3, on Durkheim). Hertz resolves Grass's 'paradox' concerning the co-
presence of asceticism and enthusiasm in the same sect with recourse to the

Durkheimian idea of 'effervescence'. The rules of asceticism, imposed like all other social rules, are lifted at particular moments in order to 'exalt all one's being in making it commune with the divine and thus give it a sense of unlimited power' (*ibid.*: 197). Children born of the sexual license that occurs at Chlust rituals are attributed to the Holy Ghost, and it is angels, not humans, who actually dance on such occasions. Such is the moral fervour of the sect and its sense of superiority over the Orthodox faithful that it struck Hertz as the perfect example of the doctrine of society being more than the association of its members, precisely because of its unifying moral force. The other sect, the Skopts, were in one sense yet more extreme in preaching and apparently practicing castration, though this modified the rest of their ritual life in making it less fervent — not because of the castration itself, says Hertz, but because the rite of castration replaces dancing as the most important. More definitive, and irreversible, in its nature, it removes the contingency of Chlust attempts to achieve union with the divine. For Hertz, nonetheless, effervescence links these Russian sectarians with totemic Australians as manifestations of the religious experience. But there are still differences, exemplified by the two sects. For the more fervent Chlusts, Christ is indistinguishable from the Holy Spirit, and represents an impersonal force. For the more centralized Skopts, Christ returns as a holy being, the Holy Spirit being merely one of his manifestations.

HERTZ'S POLITICAL WRITINGS

In the present climate, in which academics are expected to keep their private political attitudes separate from their professional teaching and writing, we are apt to forget just how politically committed the *Année Sociologique* scholars were. As an incipient 'science', the new sociology was to be of use to society and not merely a talking shop for an academic elite. It was a vital part of the scientific socialism which the *Année* were just as much concerned to promote as new approaches to the study of society as such. It led them to give almost as much attention to writings on contemporary economic, social and political issues as to those on ethnology, psychology and philosophy. Hertz's published contribution here consists of a couple of reviews in the *Année Sociologique*'s sister journal, *Notes Critiques — Sciences Sociales* (1902, 1903), and the pamphlet *Socialisme et dépopulation* (1910a), published in the series Cahiers de Socialiste, which he helped found.[2]

In this section, we look primarily at Hertz's pamphlet on depopulation, which has a distinctly polemical tone absent from even the most tendentious passages of his other writings. It was written for a more general and politically motivated readership than his other published work, and his treat-ment of the problem reflects this. It was a subject that had already been taken up briefly by Durkheim, in an early article concerning the link between the birth rate and suicide (1888; cf. Lukes 1973: 194–5), but Hertz does not refer to that here.

In his pamphlet, Hertz, as a socialist, starts by dismissing other political parties' approaches to the problem: the right, who blame the retreat from religion, especially the separation of Church and State and the lack of reli-gious education in schools; and the radicals, who think money and the exhor-tation to produce more babies will be enough to solve the problem. Socialists have two options: a neo-Malthusian approval of the decline in the availability of labour, with its consequent pressures on the owners in terms of pay and conditions; or seeing depopulation as an evil which must and can be solved. Hertz clearly prefers the second option and spends the rest of his time dis-cussing it. The method throughout is comparative, but the assumption is also that France represents the most civilized of the civilized, and that its depopu-lation threatens this excellence. Thus 'the only method in social anthropol-ogy', to paraphrase Evans-Pritchard, is wedded to a prejudice that would be intolerable in today's anthropology.

However, the target is not so much immigration (though Hertz excludes it as a solution) but the middle classes. Hertz's attack on them is equally polemical, and this prevents him from advancing as far with the problem as he might. He identifies a basic unwillingness to have children as the chief reason for France's depopulation. Immigration and emigration make only a negligible difference to the population rate, and there is no great dif-ference in the timing or incidence of marriage as compared with other coun-tries. This unwillingness is blamed firmly on the middle classes, both because of their own small families, and because they are responsible for working class conditions. The result is a worsening deficit, which is changing from being relative (compared to other countries) to being absolute.

One of the consequences of France's depopulation is the adverse mili-tary balance compared with Germany. Therefore the socialist campaign for peace benefits France. Moreover, 'the powerful diffusion of French culture is indispensable for the socialist civilization of tomorrow' (1910a: 10). Depopulation thus threatens both socialism and 'all civilized humanity' (*ibid.*). The problem is that, even within France itself, a high rate of fertility goes along with 'primitivism'. The Pyrenees, the Massif-Central, Brittany and Flanders are not only areas of high fertility but also areas where modern values have been slow to penetrate. England too has its 'primitives' in the Irish (Hertz cites Sidney Webb's fears that they will one day become predom-inant), Germany in the Poles. France, however, is compelled to import people from Italy and Poland to keep its economy going. Thus it is the most backward populations that are increasing in numbers, i.e. those most under clerical influence, most superstitious, most resistant to ideas of freedom. They are also, from the point of view of the socialist struggle, material for scabbing. Even if they could be assimilated and thereby become civilized, they too would lose their fertility. If the civilizing process that started with the Renaissance is not to come to an end, France must act: but as before in history, in doing so she will be showing the way to the rest of civilized humanity.

Immigration should be discouraged for another reason: it limits the power of the working classes by providing competition for their labour. This power will only become effective if working-class numbers are increased: limiting the numbers of children is no way to improve their conditions. Single-child families are unnatural and undesirable, since single children tend to lack initiative or else are too self-centred and prone to *arrivisme*.[3] Moreover, depopulation leads to a decline in economic activity through the restriction of markets and the non-availability of labour, and thus to general impoverishment. Neo-Malthusianism is thus rejected, especially since France is not short of natural resources. Finally, depopulation brings about an increasingly aged population, whose political conservatism dilutes the radical political activity desired by the socialists.

Thus Hertz concludes that it is an unwillingness to have children that is at the root of the problem and not any basic infertility. In other words, it is a social and hence artificial problem capable of being redressed, not a natural one that cannot be. Partly this is the result of changing attitudes, especially the new seriousness towards the very act of creating a new life. But still, the working classes have more children than the bourgeoisie. Despite the latter's greater ability to support large families, they prefer to make money (there is a lot of imagery in these passages about social and human capital). It costs the working classes more, proportionate to their income, to have more children in terms of feeding and clothing them. Moreover, a lower proportion of worker's children survive until marriageable age. Thus bourgeoisification of the working classes will only depress their fertility, since they will adopt the same deleterious attitudes.

Hertz then turns to remedies. The obvious and much-tried ones of rewarding the fertile and penalizing those without children are rejected as having no long-term effects. The basic tactic must be to abolish poverty, but this will take time, and in the meantime other reforms should be introduced. Hertz proposes a new ministry of public health, to counter the twin scourges of tuberculosis and alcoholism. Also, many more children would survive if their pregnant mothers did not have to work so hard – this alone would increase the population by another 80,000 or 10% a year. This deficit is partly due to the fact that a greater proportion of women in the population work in France than elsewhere. Mothers should be given maternity leave for the last three months of pregnancy and until the child is weaned, they should be paid maternity benefits, and local nursing facilities should be increased. Maternity should be treated as a social task, not a sickness, as in Germany.

Tax reductions should be granted to large families to offset the increase in the consumption taxes they have to pay. The bourgeoisie should be taxed to support lower-class families in having children. Subventions of FF 500 a year should go to families with more than three children (though this is surely rewarding the fertile — see above). Hertz compares this with subventions going to industry and commerce but, he says, children are the nation's most important future resource.

In conclusion, Hertz denies that this is all just socialist rhetoric — it is merely an accident that socialist measures happen to be the right ones. But public spiritedness depends on community spirit and is therefore opposed to bourgeois individualism. Fertility is a national task, to which all must contribute, according to their means: the bourgeoisie must adapt or die, i.e. give way to *social* democracy. It is not merely a matter of social justice or progress but of France's survival. But only the working class can achieve what is necessary, by sheer force of numbers. If all fails, at least socialists will have done their duty.

Though Hertz noticeably eschews obvious and easy answers, such a polemical piece of work is not difficult to criticize. There are many insufficiencies in Hertz's arguments, even in his own terms. A major contradiction is that the working classes are seen as potentially more fertile in arguments directed against the middle classes but, like all Frenchmen, as less fertile in arguments against immigration. Some of the comparisons made can only be superficial. Those involving France on the one hand and the USA and Australia on the other hardly compare like with like but instead take a relatively stable country in terms of demography and level of economic activity and set it alongside areas still experiencing rapid change in both respects. Even in Europe, comparisons with England and Germany — both highly industrialized and urbanized compared with France — were hardly completely apt. Indeed, there is no consideration of the inheritance pattern in France's rural areas, which still acts to divide landholdings and make them uneconomic, making France a land of peasants and small towns rather than large-scale agriculture and major industrial centres. It is also frequently seen as a factor of demographic significance in France.

The problem not faced, in Hertz's own terms, is that of preserving and increasing the fertility of the working classes while improving their standards of living. Experience since tends to show that the two do not really go together. It seems to be the increasing quality of life that makes the having of children, especially in large numbers, just one of many competing interests, even for those at the height of their fertility. The very effort involved in amassing sufficient wealth to support a large family in comfort is in itself a disincentive to having one, and even to marriage itself. The more non-work activities and entertainments become available, the less incentive there is to go without them by having a large family to look after. There has also been an increase in what is demanded of a partner for life, which extends the search for the most suitable one, and with it, the age at which child-bearing can begin — which in itself is made more feasible by increased medical care and life-expectancy. Conversely, of course, the very expectation that a marriage will last until the death of one or other partner rather than be dissolved halfway through has also taken a tumble. The necessity to educate children properly is a further disincentive. A technological and financially sophisticated society has no need of large families as additional labour and support in old age. Modern prestige depends on other achievements, and it has become almost axiomatic in many bourgeois circles that having great numbers of children is socially irresponsible in a generally over-populated world. Of course, not all these factors would have been relevant to Hertz, but he does not even begin to assess them; and his treatment of middle-class values, which he reasonably enough identifies as the root cause of declining population in France and elsewhere in European societies, is restricted to polemical diatribes. The fact that eastern Europe, which has only recently emerged from several decades of authoritarian socialism, have equally been involved in this decline suggests that his remedies, and their association with a particular political programme, have not been borne out either.

The pamphlet attracted considerable attention in left-wing papers at the time of its issue, but only one notice, Legendre's (1910), seems to have been at all critical. Even he restricts himself to pointing out that some socialists might be offended by the appeal to patriotism, which the *haute bourgeoisie* so noticeably lack, only to add immediately that Hertz is of a younger generation than Jaurès etc., a generation which is more prepared to face practical realities, one of which is certainly that the working classes are patriotic. Such appeals are decidedly startling when viewed from the other end of the twentieth century, especially when coming from a leftward-leaning sociologist. This applies equally to colonialism, which Hertz accepted without much question, despite his interest in the ideas and values of non-European peoples. His anti-imperialism was rather of the kind which supported the rights of minorities and small nations, such as French language rights in the Aosta valley and the Boers in their struggle against the British.[4] This too was far from being untypical of the time: contemporary discourse on colonialism tended to focus either on the balance of power in Europe or on domestic politics, not on the rights of 'natives' in the colonies. A letter to his Fabian friend, Frederick Lawson Dodd, shows this clearly. In it, Hertz complains that the socialists in France have no

> policy on the whole colonial problem, *one of the most fundamental aspects of our whole civilization.* In our French socialism ... you hear mainly a few negative and stupid phrases about the colonies being run only in the interests of a few greedy capitalists. [Yet:] The right of a higher civilization is superior to all the vested interests.[5]

Yet even here, there might be a Durkheimian dimension. In a earlier letter to Dodd, Hertz describes his pamphlet on depopulation as dealing with the 'problem of the perpetuation of a society under civilized conditions [which] socialists especially must take very much to heart'.[6] Patriotism was something Hertz advocated bringing into the service of France, for the sake of both its unity and its continuity. Patriotism was not alien to Durkheim either, though he advocated developing it so as to be of use to international relations (see Lukes 1973: 41–2, 87–8, 118, 350, 542ff.). Indeed, it might be regarded as a species of 'effervescence', of that spontaneous coming together of individuals in a society which contributed so much to social renewal and creativity in his thought (e.g. 1951: 134).

For a fuller idea of Hertz's overall attitude to socialism and to the social problems of his day, we can turn to the surviving lectures he gave to such bodies as the Ecole Socialiste.[7] The most academic of these is his talk on 'Saint Simon et les Saint-Simoniens', delivered at the Ecole on the 13th September 1910 (see Hertz 1910p). This applauded Saint-Simon's appreciation of social science as 'a methodological enquiry into the human past allowing remedies for the evils from which society suffers to be uncovered'.[8] Saint-Simon had also realized that society was more than just a collection of individuals:

> Saint-Simon had already recognized a truth which inspires the sociologists of today, namely that society is an organic reality superimposed on the individual, which must have its own goal. Men come together to create together, not to guarantee rights to one another.

Society also had to be 'hierarchical', i.e. have leadership, and be religious: there is 'no healthy society without a cult, which recalls men periodically to their common goal, to the grand interests of the community of which they are members.' From his early nineteenth-century perspective, Saint-Simon saw industrial society as the way forward, for it would promote both social well-being and stability. This required merit, not wealth or position, to be the basis of power and influence, which in its turn necessitated inequality.

Thus society would not cease to be hierarchical, it would be hierarchical in a different way: 'the social revolution would be carried out through a simple substitution of hierarchy.' Although the ordinary people would benefit, they would not be involved. Nor would they be free: liberty, the other main plank of the French Revolution, had no place in his scheme.

For Hertz, the chief faults in Saint-Simon's argument are that he did not see that privilege would obtain in industrial society too, and that capital and industry would tend to act in their own interests, not those of the community as a whole. This made the involvement of the masses, in the form of democratic control, necessary. But his ideas can still be an inspiration to socialists, in that he based them on 'a positive historical method', not on 'abstract metaphysical considerations', and saw periods of crisis as transitional from one form of society to another. This gave his ideas objectivity.[9]

Hertz appreciated the work of the British Fabians for similar reasons. In a second lecture given at the Ecole three and a half months later (13th January 1911; see Hertz 1911b), he began by praising their success in introducing some collectivist ideas into a society which until then had been a stronghold of individualism. Even the Liberal Party had adopted the minimal socialist programme, and although the Fabians as a group were officially allied with the Labour Party, five of their thirteen MPs actually took the Liberal whip. The influence of this reformist and non-revolutionary organisation was thus achieved tactically by a policy of what in the 1970s came to be called 'entryism', in that they concentrated on placing their members in strategic positions within rival or opposing organizations. But they were also able to take advantage of something Hertz had identified in the English character:

> This Fabian attitude is to be explained partly by the psychology of the English, who find very clear ideas, logical classification, repugnant, and who do not like to take cognizance of what they do.

Above all for Hertz, the Fabians saw themselves as scientific, basing themselves on 'social reality' — in other words, they always use 'the inductive method, by starting from the facts'. Although often criticized for intellectualism and lack of enthusiasm, their self-appointed task was to provide activists with concrete ideas, with exact concepts, with a research base, in short, with the intellectual underpinning of their propaganda.[10] Revisionist vis-à-vis Marxism, their arguments were directed towards the public consciousness of the average citizen, not workers specifically, nor the philanthropic conscience of the upper classes. This consideration affected political activities too. As Hertz argued in another paper (Hertz no date), experience showed that the idea of a political party dedicated to the working classes, i.e. to purely labour issues, was tactically wrong. Any such party had to be be prepared to tackle national issues on behalf of the whole country if in government.

CHAPTER FOUR

Right and Left

RIGHT AND LEFT IN HERTZ

The notion of binary opposition has come to be associated largely with Lévi-Strauss in anthropology, especially through his work on myth, in which contradictions are seen as being both identified and resolved through the manipulation of binary distinctions. But there is a separate tradition whose roots lie further back in the history of the discipline, though only developed fully much more recently, through the agency first of Rodney Needham, and later – and partly in explicit contradiction to Needham and to Hertz himself – by Louis Dumont and his followers. In essence, what started as a special case of the Durkheimian notion of sacred/profane developed first into a heuristic device for the understanding of a distinct and widespread form of classification (Needham), then into the essence of an interpretation of Indian society (Dumont), and finally into a general analytical tool in the comparison of societies (Daniel de Coppet, Cécile Barraud, André Iteanu, Serge Tcherkézoff, etc.). In this way, binary distinctions became linked not to myth, as with Lévi-Strauss, but variously to primary factors of experience (Needham), to problems of classification (Dumont), and to the analysis of ritual (de Coppet, *et al.*). In one respect, this reflects a shift away from narrow Durkheimianism, given that sacred/profane quite rapidly became unsatisfactory for many anthropologists – here, Hertz has lasted somewhat better than his master. But at the same time continuity is shown in respect, variously, of a continuing concern with classification, and with ritual as the chief arena in which the integration of society is demonstrated to its members. This chapter will concern itself primarily with the development of Hertz's insights in this paper up to and including that introduced by Needham.

Mauss tells us (1969 II: 156) that one of the first texts to impress Hertz with the problem of right and left was White's *Ancient History of the Maori* (1887–90), especially in showing the division of Maori gods into gods of the right and gods of the left, gods of war and gods of peace, gods of dreams and gods of magic, etc. Durkheim, as Hertz's doctoral supervisor, can be expected to have had some influence over him as regards the problem of right and left, but he himself was not entirely consistent, even the course of the same work. In some passages of *Elementary Forms of the Religious Life,* for instance, he concedes that the individual can distinguish right and left before he is socialized (Durkheim 1915: 145; Durkheim and Mauss 1963: 7). Elsewhere, however, when citing Hertz in the context of the social determination of spatial distinctions (which had already been argued by Durkheim and Mauss in 1903), he says: 'Thus the social organization has been the model for the spatial organization and a reproduction of it. It is thus even up to the distinction between right and left which, far from being inherent in the nature of man in general, is very probably the product of representations which are religious and *therefore social*' (1915: 12, my emphasis).

Hertz's first task in 'La prééminence de la main droite' (1909a) is to examine the possibility that the apparently physiological asymmetry between the right and left hands is in fact of social, not physical or organic origin. He starts by observing how all societies avert internal opposition by claiming to be grounded in 'the nature of things', an example being right-handedness. But right-handedness is not so axiomatic as is generally supposed. Not that there has been no scientific examination of the problem. The greater power of the right hand is known, he says, to be connected with the greater development of the left hemisphere of the brain, which controls speech and voluntary movement. The question is, *how* are the two connected? Biologists claim that the brain is the fundamental and controlling factor, i.e. that 'we are right-handed because we are left-brained'. But man is unique among primates in not being ambidextrous, suggesting that the reason for his handedness might lie outside the organism. Hertz therefore counters with the proposition that 'we are left-brained because we are right-handed' and that it is outside, cultural factors that have determined the preference for the right hand in both ritual and mundane tasks, this leading in its turn to the development of the left hemisphere being greater than that of the right.

This, left as it stands, would have been one of the more extreme examples of the Durkheimian sociological method and of the doctrine of the tyranny of society over the individual in the *Année Sociologique* tradition. In fact, Hertz retreats just enough to accept an underlying organic asymmetry, his real concern being how and why this asymmetry is exploited by society in its collective representations. This asymmetry is real but slight, and can be overcome physically with training (e.g. by a violinist) – it is society that gives it value. Hertz clearly prefers the evidence of those who point to variations in natural handedness and who stress the importance of socialization in promoting right-handedness as a norm: 'it is not because the left hand is weak and power-less that it is neglected: the contrary is true' (1973: 6). In other words, society takes this slight biological asymmetry and reinforces it through training, endowing the two hands with contrasted attributes, always opposed in any ritual or social context that refers to them. The right usually but not invariably has the more positive connotations, the left the more negative ones (see further below). As Mauss was to say of this text, years later, when discussing the use of the left and right hands by a Moslem (1950 [1936]: 375): 'In order to know why he makes this gesture and not another, neither the physiology nor the psychology of motor dissymmetry in man are sufficient; it is necessary to know the traditions that impose it.'

Like a true Durkheimian, Hertz dismisses naturalistic explanations for the asymmetry, i.e. those depending on a stimulus, such as attitudes to the sun. In this view the sun, as the source of light and warmth, shines on the right-hand side of the body when one faces east, the direction of the sunrise, in sun worship or other ritual, which makes the south auspicious. As Hertz points out, this cannot account for the values placed on right and left in all societies: e.g. for Hindus and Romans the south belongs to the dead and is therefore inauspicious. Moreover, the suggested association does not neces-sarily change among peoples in the southern hemisphere, despite the fact that the sun shines from the north there. In any case, this explanation can hardly account for the plethora of dichotomous and asymmetric associations that are encountered in many societies.

Another explanation rejected by Hertz is the 'military' one, i.e. that the right hand is the 'spear hand', positive, aggressive, the left hand the 'shield hand', yielding, defensive, the ultimate basis of this distinction being some sort of instinct. This, says Hertz, confuses cause and effect: a choice is involved even here, and it must have a social origin. He cites the Maori, who do not know the shield, yet 'among whom the distinction between right and left is particularly pronounced'. Such explanations do no more than highlight one particular example of the phenomenon that is to be accounted for, and it was Hertz's main intention to overcome this with reference to the new soci-ology of Durkheim.

But why does society elaborate the organic asymmetry so tremen-dously and endow it with such deep cultural relevance? Given such an insignificant degree of biological asymmetry, reason would lead one to expect that the hand that has been less favoured by nature would be trained up by society to parity with the more favoured. To answer this, Hertz invokes the human mind's 'innate capacity to differentiate', by which he means to dichotomize. This would have existed regardless of the organic basis of the asymmetry: 'If organic asymmetry had not existed, it would have had to be invented.' It would be over-generous to regard this as an explanation, however: the evidence for it — the 'innate capacity' — arises directly out of the phenomenon that is supposed to be explained. Rather, it is simply an acknowledgement of an aspect of that dualism dogmatically asserted to exist as the basis of all human thought by the Durkheimians (though Mauss later expressed some doubts — see p. 75) and of which Hertz gives a number of examples (his Sect. III). It is only by minimizing drastically the significance of the organic asymmetry between the two hands that he himself is able to avoid a naturalistic or intellectualist explanation for this dichotomizing. It may be true, as Schwartz says, that he 'anticipates Lévi-Strauss in recognizing the way natural polarities are appropriated by society for the representation of its own divisions' (1981: 32): indeed, his attribution of this propensity to all humanity invites a psycho-biological explanation in terms of the common structure of the human brain as much as a social one. Nonetheless, he remains closer to Durkheim in wanting to insist that the determinants that govern all human experience are ultimately social ones.[1]

The most famous expression of this dualism among the Durkheimians is, of course, the dichotomy between sacred and profane (see pp. 27-30). Hertz accepts both this and Durkheim's further division of the sacred into pure and impure, which, put together, can be represented thus: sacred (pure + impure)/profane; or, pure sacred > profane < impure sacred, in which the profane is threatened by both the pure sacred and the impure sacred (the arrows represent ritual danger). Hertz wants to relativize this, because he regards it as representing the perspective of the profane only. For the *pure* sacred, he argues, not only the profane but also the impure sacred is danger- ous and must be kept at arm's length. However, he regards the impure sacred and the profane as virtually identical. In this way dichotomy is restored, but refocussed: we does not end up with a triple distinction between pure sacred, impure sacred and profane. As Isambert remarks (1982: 243 n. 87), this makes the profane ambiguous, not the sacred, as with Robertson Smith, Durkheim, Hubert and Mauss. As Das says (1977a: 26 n.2), 'Hertz did not use the term "profane" in the sense of mundane. He used "profane" and "impure" as interchangeable categories'. His modification therefore takes the form: pure sacred/impure sacred + profane. He also indicates that he will return to the question elsewhere in order to justify this change properly (his note 14), but never did so.

Henceforward, Hertz applies the symbolic values of right and left etc. to the dichotomy between pure and impure, for despite continuing to use the words 'sacred' and 'profane' frequently, he seems to have regarded the former as 'more essential' (Granet 1973: 43). In doing so, however, he reverts to seeing them as emblems of or metaphors for sociocentric factors no longer

dependent on particular perspectives. On the whole, most of those who have
subsequently applied his ideas ethnographically have followed him in these
respects, and the actual notion of a distinction between pure and impure,
though apt to be modified into one between auspicious and inauspicious, or
positive and negative, has not come under fire like that between sacred and
profane. Nor are there the same conceptual uncertainties over the definition
of the less valued pole. Both of Hertz's poles are decidedly within the ritual-
cum-social: once he has disposed of the purely physical basis of the right-left
asymmetry in collective representations and modified sacred-profane, he recognizes nothing like the mundane as of significance. This amounts to the
view that society itself defines the threats to it coming from the individual,
which goes beyond Durkheim, who tended to see the individual as outside
society at such moments. However, Hertz follows Durkheim in regarding the
social as grounded in the religious (see his discussion of dual organization),
thus implying that every human activity, eating with the right hand as well as
right-left symbolism at a wedding or funeral, has a social or cultural basis. In
other words, the only distinction between normal and ritual activities is that
made by the society itself. This too has normally been perpetuated by those
who follow him, apart from occasional allusions to the right-handedness of
'everyday' (i.e. ritually or ideologically neutral) practices and situations (e.g.
Granet 1973; Matsunaga 1986), a debatable conception in itself. Hertz talks,
moreover, of 'a single category of things, a common nature, the same orientation towards one of the two poles of the mystical world' (*ibid.*: 14). This was
to come a bitter source of controversy in respect of the use Needham was to
make of Hertz's ideas decades later (see Chapter Four).

Hertz continues his article by giving a broader idea of the range of
values associated by society with right and left, the former being positive,
sacred, pure, good, auspicious, legitimate, homely, the latter negative or
ambiguous, profane, impure, evil, inauspicious, disorderly, hostile etc. (Hertz
himself does not use all these words). It is not, however, a matter of strength
and weakness, or of ability and inability; both poles have an equal but opposite effect. Right and left are associated respectively with life and death, as
well as being emblematic of a whole range of asymmetric oppositions, but
they are not their basis. He mentions especially the connection of right and
left with the cardinal points, though the associations of north and west with
left, and of south and east with right, are not so consistent worldwide as he
suggests. He is also over-confident in seeing movement to the right as being
essentially clockwise movement: it is anti-clockwise in parts of Indonesia, for
example Rindi and Kédang (Forth 1985: 105; Barnes 1974: 184), and in parts
of Greece (du Boulay 1982: 228). But in general Hertz realizes that what
counts as right may differ, citing as an instance the appearance of animals in

omens: it may be a good omen if the animal appears on the right of the person concerned, or alternatively if it appears on his left in such a way as to present its right side to him (cf. Leeuwen-Turnovcova 1990: 6ff.). In the penultimate section he gives some ethnographic examples of the use of the two hands in ritual activities and gestures. His closing remarks address the trend even then under way in his own society towards accepting left-handedness as natural and unproblematic. He clearly approves of this, looking forward to the full 'development of the [human] organism', and dismissing any thought that it would impair either aesthetic clarity or our ability to distinguish good from evil.

So many decades later, some might wonder whether he was not over-sanguine in these respects too. But then Hertz, like his colleagues, was no ivory-tower academic but a socialist-minded teacher anxious to prove the state of contemporary French society through education both academic and political. The problem of the asymmetry of right and left is therefore a special case, and for the modern age a rather irrational one, in so far as society has exaggerated it beyond its organic basis. Here, Hertz allows his own values to intrude in a way that seems out of place in modern anthropology. Yet in proposing equal treatment for the two hands he was fully in accord with key modern, progressive trends in the West. Thus he served as a fitting starting point for Louis Dumont, who clearly admires his work in general, when, many decades later, the latter set out to show the anthropological community at large how their devotion to notions of equality had blinded to them to its absence in the very 'non-modern' societies they were most likely to be dealing with (see sect. 4.3).

Handedness is a special case for another reason. For Hertz, right-left asymmetry is the cultural elaboration of a basic but not insurmountable organic asymmetry brought about by society in its urge to give everything a dualistic cast: 'organic asymmetry in man is at once a fact and an ideal' (1973: 6). The circumstance that right and left can be linked to the organism, and especially the human brain, does give the way they are valued a special character not replicated even in other obvious dualisms that are extraneous to it (day and night, for example, or even male and female). While Hertz concentrated on the explicit, ritual representations of right and left, many other manifestations of handedness are in effect automatic, unplanned and unpremeditated. But how much of this is due to the underlying organic asymmetry and how much to intense, persistent socialization? A mother may teach her child how to tie its shoelaces, but she does so in a particular way, which involves handedness; what is the basis of her choice, tradition, or instinct based on organic features? In truth, handedness is a problem of the same order as incest — a cardinal attribute of human populations, yet subject to varying degrees of representation and contradiction cross-culturally, existing wholly within neither nature nor society, but belonging partly to both and thus linking them.

THE REACTION TO HERTZ

Hertz's thesis was remarkable for its time, and even today its value is obvious. Unlike sacred-profane, to which it is clearly if implicitly an alternative for many anthropologists, it has not been dismissed as unworkable or irrelevant, and constant attempts have been made to exploit it and to extend and improve its use. Criticism has generally been muted and indirect, to such an extent that one feels that Hertz himself has taken on a rather sacred quality for many. Nonetheless, it is possible to criticize, though as usual in such cases only with the benefit of hindsight and subsequent research that were especially denied to Hertz because of his truncated career.

Many of these points surfaced in a paper on right and left in China read by Granet to the Institut Français de Sociologie on 9th June 1933 and in the subsequent comments of Mauss, who was in the audience (Granet 1973; Mauss 1969 II: 143-8). This was apparently the first time that Hertz's thesis had been subjected to a public discussion. As Mauss pointed out, the data from China and elsewhere, while they did not negate Hertz's thesis, showed it to be in need of modification. A general point for Mauss was that Granet had shifted from Hertz's metaphor of two opposed and unequal sides to a model 'of the division of all things into two symmetric hemispheres' (Mauss 1969 II: 143). There was also a need to introduce the idea of 'an imperative system of circumstances of rules with multiple considerations ... a structure of conditions and not just a system of simple and categorical rules' (*ibid.*: 144). By now, Mauss was also thinking that he and his colleagues had been too obsessed with ritual and action at the expense of mythology and thought, a circumstance which reflected their battles with the intellectualists (*ibid.*). This over-emphasis led directly to an over-concentration on the sacred, which Mauss was by now calling 'an extremely restricted notion of religion' (*ibid.*: 147; see also 1983: 149). Granet had sought to correct this by looking at the entire system of representations as an organic whole, at the same time introducing an overall symmetry into what was a comprehensive system of classification (*ibid.*: 146).

Central to Granet's paper was the point that Hertz had ignored even the possibility that for some societies the left may ordinarily be predominant and positive: he had dismissed the one exception that had come to his notice, the Zuñi, where left is associated with age and wisdom in at least one context, as a secondary development of a sort that might arise in agricultural societies.[2] For him, right was invariably auspicious. In fact, although the Chinese are 'normally' right-handed (i.e. in physical tasks and even in eating), their traditional values associate the left with the superordinate male or Yang principle, oppose it to the right, which is Yin and female, and altogether regard it as more honourable.

A little after Granet gave his paper, in 1938, Wieschhoff uncovered similar if untypical examples of left-hand predominance in northeast Africa (Wieschhoff 1973), and Vincent drew attention (1978) to the case of the Mofu of North Cameroon. Though again normally right-handed, for example, in eating, left:right::man:woman,[3] and men are dominant in society. The Mofu justify this by saying that the left hand is the shield hand (cf. Hertz); that the right hand is that used by women in their daily tasks, e.g. preparing food, so that unlike men, their right hand is stronger than their left; and that women, being weaker than men, are accorded the stronger hand in compensation. Men sleep to the real left of women, and therefore use their right hand in sex as in other impure tasks; they also occupy left-hand sitting positions in the home. Corpses are laid out on their left or right sides respectively for male or female, but both widows and widowers use the left hand in eating during mourning. Although generally left is auspicious, because of its association with maleness, an accused in divination must produce the opposite value if he is to be declared innocent.

Later still, Tcherkézoff pointed out the normal association of left with male among the Nyamwezi of Tanzania (1987: 35, 136 n. 16), though he also showed how the question of predominance varied with situation. Marcus (1984) has also denied the link between women and the left in Turkey, or indeed any link between gender and the organization of space, something which, she says, distinguishes Islamic societies from Christian ones. It is not that male-female differences are not expressed. Women are separated from men in the mosque, but they may sit either behind them, or upstairs, or to one side of them, which may be to the left or right. Moreover, in the Koran it was is Satan, not Eve, who caused the fall, so that the nexus between feminine, left and sinful sexuality is also absent. Instead, left and right are connected with boundaries. Whether man or woman, one steps into the mosque with one's right foot first, and leaves it with one's left first (cf. Bourdieu, on the changes in orientation produced by crossing the threshold; cited by Dumont 1979: 812). Boundaries themselves impinge on gender differences, in that, unlike men, woman cannot control pollution in the form of the loss of bodily fluids. Women unavoidably menstruate, whereas men can control loss of semen through celibacy. But this pollution is not related to sin:

> Such a view of women [i.e. the Turkish view] has nothing to do with
> distinctions between society and nature, with a left-right dichotomy,

with sacred or profane, or with morality. It results logically and unavoidably from the primacy of the inner-outer dichotomy, a definition of pollution based on the concepts of movement across a boundary, and on control. (Marcus 1984: 214)

She also suggests (*ibid.*: 211): 'It is possible that societies which are formally gender-segregated do not organize ground-space on a left-right principle.' Elsewhere, however, left and right are certainly frequently used as a marker of gender differences, if not in all possible contexts.

More generally, it is evident that there are no inherently good or evil qualities in particular ideas that are opposed cross-culturally. In many traditions, the negativity of death is balanced or replaced by the notion that it is but the transition to a better life to come. In Japan, Moeran associates death with the maintenance of youthful perfection and 'the prevention of ugliness', and he explicitly denies the usefulness of dualistic oppositions as a means of understanding either it or sex or violence (1986: 111). Similarly, although black widely has negative connotations, it is often positively valued (and white negatively valued) in east Africa (Rigby 1973 on the Gogo; Tcherkézoff 1985 on the Nyamwezi; both groups are in Tanzania). As Needham points out (1978: 35–6), the general association between witchcraft and black, darkness, etc. is not absolute: Catholic priests wear black, while Kaguru witches are associated with the colour white. Again, even numbers are often positive here, odd numbers frequently but not universally positive in eastern Indonesia (see Barnes 1985a: 101–2). Nor is the moon everywhere linked with the feminine, as among the Bunaq of Timor, for example (Friedberg 1980).

There is also reason to doubt that the refusal to discriminate against right-handedness is a purely Western and/or modern phenomenon. For the Foi of New Guinea, the 'strong' hand is 'the hand of habitual use, either right or left' (Weiner 1988: 246), something that, unlike Hertz, they are unlikely to see as part of a struggle against irrationality. An explicit distinction between symbolism and reality may sometimes be at work. Although the Nuer accord the left hand a negative symbolic value, they do not discriminate against left-handed people but simply say that for them, their left hand is their right (Evans-Pritchard 1973: 97). Firth remarks of Tikopia (1970: 194ff.) that although a left-handed person may be given a nickname, and although the house is divided laterally and symbolically (into areas associated with death and the sacred and areas associated with life and everyday activities), in general the right-left dichotomy is less important than front-back or high-low. Faron, conversely, takes right and left so seriously as the basic opposition that he feels compelled to make the point that its absence does not signal the non-existence of dichotomous thought (1973: 191). In his review of

Needham's handbook (Needham ed. 1973), de Josselin de Jong commented on Faron's reasoning (1976: 172): 'This seems a topsy-turvy argument; why not simply recognize that the right-left opposition is not a necessary ingredient of all dualisms?' Josselin de Jong points to a number of examples in this volume where it does not appear and to others where it is featured but does not have particular importance. Fiji and Indonesia provide yet others (see Firth 1970: 194ff.; Hocart 1954: 91; Fox 1989: 33).

One of the key examples of dichotomy for Hertz was dual organization, or the moiety system. This also linked in with totemism, routinely seen by the Durkheimians as the original form of religion. In dual organization, the totem is taboo, i.e. sacred, for its own moiety but not for the other, for which it is profane. The same remark can apply to the women of the respective moieties, and the general view goes right back to Durkheim's early article on incest (1898). For Hertz, one evolutionary development is that the opposition becomes hierarchized into a class or a caste-like structure, one sacred, the other profane and impure (cf. 1910b: 104). Another development is the breakdown of totemism in agricultural societies, of which the Zuñi are an example (they were also placed later in evolution than the Australians by Durkheim and Mauss, 1963 [1903]). The link is not made explicitly in this paper, but we can find it in two of Hertz's reviews (Hertz *ibid.*; 1913d: 274). In Hertz's mind, we glimpse the idea that the breakdown of totems among the agricultural Zuñi led to a reversal in symbolic values.

Historical speculation of a different sort, broadly connected with global changes in the nature of technology and politics, has recently been put forward by Leeuwen-Turnovcova (1990: 1, 14–15, 149–50). This is also linked to a discourse on dichotomy. In a world where all knowledge comes from the gods, male and female principles, though opposed, are more in balance, because they contribute equally to the creation and maintenance of the world. When mankind comes to develop technology and science, however, this balance collapses into a hierarchy, because men are involved in such prestigious developments more than women. The latter remain associated with nature, foreigners etc., but this now becomes more negative. In this view, the Pythagorean table of opposites appears as transitional: it shows a more concrete distinction between male and female, with devaluation of the latter, but maleness is still associated with limitedness, stasis, completion, femaleness with unlimitedness, movement, incompletion, associations some of which one might expect to be reversed today. The author explains the apparently aberrant Chinese example as a similar collapse from an earlier equilibrium into a hierarchy, but one in which left found itself associated with male (and with Yang). Modern politics has also produced a shift in values. Leeuwen-Turnovcova refers obliquely to the story that left and right in the political sense originated in the distribution of the sides in one of the chambers of deputies in the French Revolution (actually the Estates General of 1789; see Dumont 1991: 253; 1992: 264). After a period in which the traditional social order was expressed by seating which proceeded downwards from the king (though clergy were to the right of the nobility; see Dumont *ibid.*), the first two estates took the right side of the chamber, leaving the negatively valued left side to their social inferiors, the third estate, who rapidly became associated with radicalism. The upshot was that the right, originally standing for innovation and newness, became the side of political conservatism and stability, while the left, originally 'caring, reproductive', became the side of revolution and chaos.

The author's case is frequently overdrawn and very sweeping, collapsing an enormous number of contexts into two historical phases which are not clearly linked but which are nonetheless of supposedly universal import. However, she recognizes that analytical associations between the terms of a polarity are by no means predictable but rather arbitrary, at least when viewed from a more objective cross-cultural perspective. Similarly, she points out that women are linked to left in two radically different senses, denoting either fertility or danger and uncontrollability. Of course, in those societies in which taming women in order to control their fertility is the most persistent and pressing problem men face, one can quite readily find both values, the two being mediated by ritual.

Despite Hertz, the recourse to a naturalist explanation has also been remarkably persistent. Many authors, including Chelhod, Jenner, Bourdieu, Goody, Mimica and Leeuwen-Turnovcova, invoke such explanations in the context of dual symbolic classification. Chelhod (1973) gets around Hertz's objection that the values associated with the sun in the southern hemisphere do not change by putting forward the theory that these values were retained when mankind migrated there from north of the equator. Jenner (1976) apparently worked on dual symbolic classification among the Khmer in ignorance of Hertz's work, even though he cites two articles which themselves refer to it (by Cunningham 1973 and Kruyt 1973, both in Needham ed. 1973; Jenner refers to their original place of publication). His theory invokes the difference between the sexes as the initial stimulus for symbolic oppositions, the position also of Rosaldo and Atkinson (1975), and broadly of Meggitt (1964: 218), at least as far as the Mae Enga and similar groups of Papua New Guinea are concerned. The latter, however, also invokes the opposition between clans who both intermarry and fight, and hence are a source not only of wives but also both of debilitating female pollution and of physical danger to one another. 'That is, a chain of homologues can be traced from extra-clan military threat versus intra-clan military protection to feminine

pollution versus masculine purity' (*ibid.*). For Bourdieu, the basis of oppositions is rather 'movements or postures of the human body' (1977: 119). For
Goody, at least in part, it is the body itself (1977: 65). For Mimica, it is the
unequal power of the two hands (1988: 66-7), at least as far as the Iqwaye of
New Guinea are concerned. This point is also made by Hermann Baumann
(1955: 309-10), in explicit contradiction to Hertz's playing down of the
admitted biological dimension in favour of a sociological explanation.

At least some of these explanations are ethnographically specific, not
general. This is clearly the case with the Greeks studied by du Boulay (1974:
100ff.), among whom dual symbolic classification is not a matter of the particular properties and characteristics of right and left but of those of men and
women, two of which are certainly rightness and leftness. Leeuwen-
Turnovcova is more concerned with the association of right and left with the
two sexes in a general sense (1990: 145, 147 & n. 10, 148). Noting that both
men and women are normally right-handed, she goes on to focus her explanation on the fact that it is natural to cradle a child in one's left arm, where it
is next to one's heart and which also leaves the right hand free for feeding
and general care. This is said automatically to distinguish women from men,
given that the latter characteristically have little or nothing to do with the
upbringing of children until their initiation. This assumes that the latter circumstance is itself a matter of nature, not culture. It also does not explain
why the cradling left arm should be chosen to represent women rather than
the feeding and caring right. Victor Turner (1974b: 36-7) explicitly denies
the difference between the sexes being the basis of systems of dual symbolic
classification, principally because associations between terms frequently
differ with context: 'e.g., in one situation the distinction red/white may be
homologous with male/female, in another with female/male, and in yet
another with meat/flour without sexual connotation.'

Perhaps the biggest criticism that can be levelled against Hertz concerns his very stress on dichotomy. This has two sets of consequences, one
concerning the rigidity of the distinction, the other its incidence, both of
which were raised in the debate of 1933 involving Granet and Mauss.

For Hertz, the right-left dichotomy, like sacred-profane, was an
absolute one that could not be mediated and whose poles could never come
together. This is explicitly or implicitly rejected in many ethnographies. Thus
La Flesche (who seems to have written in ignorance of Hertz's work) tells us
that among the Osage the two main divisions of Sky and Earth — contrasted as
are right and left respectively — form an 'inseparable unity' essential for life
(1973: 32). Cunningham criticizes Hertz specifically if gently on this very
point as regards the Atoni house, which despite its symbolic divisions is also
in some contexts a unity (1973: 235). Granet remarks that Hertz's rigid

distinction is not found in China (1973: 44). Needham stresses the complementarity between the Mugwe or sacred leader of the Meru and the secular
authority of the elders (1973b: 117). Kruyt presents data from Sulawesi to
show that, within the same ritual, leftward movement or contact is used to
expel evil, while rightward movement or contact restores good — two
opposed but complementary stages linked in a van Gennep-like sequence
(1973: 85ff.). Beidelman has one clear example of mediation concerning
omens on a journey (1973: 134):

> If, on a journey, a person hears a turacu ... cry out on the right side, it is
> thought that something important will soon happen to his paternal kin;
> if on his left, to his maternal kin; if straight ahead, to his own house-
> hold (the social unit which unites both groups).

The Dogon are another group where duality exists within a framework
of complementarity (see Dieterlin 1968). On the one hand, the birth of twins
is valued as an 'ideal birth which is actually a favour' (*ibid.*: 151), since the
first humans were twins of opposite sex. The birth of single (i.e. non-twin)
right-handers is regrettably only normal, but the birth of left-handers, and of
albinos, is linked to the breach of an interdiction by the mother in the fourth
month of pregnancy, which had interfered with the birth of what were set to
be twins. Left-handers are the result of a fusion of two male twins, hence
they are powerful and skilful and can expect a numerous progeny, but they
are also inauspicious, because they will shorten their fathers' lives. Albinos
are the product of a fusion of twins of opposite sex, and because of their
ambivalence are preferred sacrificial victims. Both are therefore 'at once
sacred and, in a certain sense, impure' (*ibid.*: 152), being the product of a
wrongful denial of dichotomy. In other contexts, however, unity is preferred.
Both hands are used when accepting a gift or shaking hands, to signify acceptance with one's whole body. A one-legged person is the symbol par excellence of the universe, the ancestors etc., and among the Manding, ritual
officiants symbolize this unity by binding their legs together. The complementarity of a pair rather than their antagonism is stressed in the crossing of
hands, which mixes right and left, when rendering homage. According to
Dieterlin, a West African would complain of incompleteness if it were suggested to him that the right hand was dominant. Totality through complementarity is what is valued here. This complementarity clearly informs the
attitude to twins as ideal. Antagonism entered the world with the first human
to be born alone, without a twin, this being not merely a premature event
but also an act of deliberate ambition, of will, and, therefore, of rebellion
against God.

There have been more general suspicions voiced as to the legitimacy
of seeing dichotomous thought as universal. Dichotomy in Western thought

has been traced variously as far back as ancient Greece and as near as the Enlightenment. In Morris's view (1987: 289), much of the work of Lee and Whorf suggests that synthesis may be more characteristic of pre-modern thought, rather than Lévi-Strauss's dualism. Other challenges have been mounted against specific examples of the latter's dichotomies, such as the universality of the nature-culture divide, questioned especially by those working on definitions of gender (e.g. MacCormack and Strathern eds. 1980; Leacock 1981: 246–7; Strathern 1988).

Another illustration of the difficulties of a rigidly dichotomous approach is the Indian caste system as interpreted by Dumont (especially 1972). Here, there is a fundamental distinction between pure and impure, but these are just the two poles at either end of a continuum. Other points along this continuum vary in degree of purity or impurity, so that the two run into one another, and it is in general impossible to draw a definite boundary between them when this continuum is set alongside the whole caste system that is supposed to give it expression. This is especially so since in the middle levels above all, it is difficult to get informants to agree on the niceties of caste ranking – the answer very frequently depends on whom you ask. Thus there may be two ideal, abstract, opposed values, but the way they are applied, which is just as important anthropologically, leads to a rigid dichotomy rather than to a gradation. Moreover, even the extremes occupy the same ritual arena, interdependent and complementary: the Brahmans ensure the continuity of vital Vedic traditions, and the Untouchables ensure the continuity of the purity on which the Brahmans depend by removing pollution. Both act in principle for the whole of society (though rarely for each other in practice, the gulf in terms of pollution being too wide). Hobart advocates a continuum for Bali too: 'Applied to space in Bali, a formal analysis in terms of dualistic categories tends to be static and incomplete, as it ignores the problems of relative position and mobility' (1978: 5). Consequently, 'it may be helpful to view Balinese notions of space, not as a series of binary oppositions, but as continua between polar extremes, in which ritual movement parallels changes in social status' (*ibid.*: 22).

These examples are just one consequence of Hertz's over-dichotomous approach. What they also point to is the neglect of context, and of the particular phenomenon of reversal. Apart from passing concessions that the left hand 'has its domain' in certain situations, as do women in opposition to men, Hertz largely disregarded the contextualization of dualistic classifications. As we have seen (above), Granet seems to have felt that this was due in part to Hertz's over-concentration on ritual to the neglect of other collective representations. He pointed out that in China the left (here, 'honourable') is not always auspicious nor the right always inauspicious (1973: 44).[4]

There are a number of examples in the collection *Right & Left* (Needham ed. 1973) where the left is predominant in particular contexts (i.e. not normatively considered superior, as in China), especially where reversal is involved. Thus among the Temne, the left hand comes into its own in sleep and especially after death, for although it has been little used in life, it has been a silent witness to the individual's actions and is therefore listened to by God thereafter (Littlejohn 1973: 294). Among the Banyoro too, it is the normally hated left hand that holds the cowrie shells used in divination (Needham 1973c: 301). Elsewhere, Elkin mentions that the mythological hero among certain groups in Australia is a left-handed boomerang thrower (1961: 231 n. 1): 'The exceptional physiological endowment, left-handedness, is one of strength, not of weakness'.

Often, the same thing or person has different values according to context. Matsunaga (1986) gives an example from rural Japan in which use of the left hand, motion to the left, etc., are significant at both auspicious agricultural rites and at inauspicious funerals. His bewilderment at this violation of what he evidently sees as the normal inauspiciousness of the left leads him into a forced explanation of the agricultural rite in which – for naturalistic reasons, and because south and east are both auspicious directions – to face south (as the officiant does) is to have the east on one's left. A much more economical explanation, however, and one which Matsunaga almost reaches himself, is that use of the left hand is a reversal signalling a change from what Leach (1976: Ch. 7) and Bloch (1977) have called normal time into ritual time: the polarity of the rite in terms of auspiciousness or inauspiciousness is a separate matter entirely. Holy and Stuchlik (1983: 25–7) query Leach's argument (1976: 19, 27) that in Christian societies the white dress of the bride and the black dress of the widow are linked through the theme of marriage, the former indicating entry into the married state, the latter departure from it, and that they are linked more generally to other oppositions between the auspicious and the inauspicious. For Holy and Stuchlik, the fact that other mourners will also be dressed in black (and not only at the funerals of widows) suggests that what is really involved is status, not marriage (1983: 27). However, the two ceremonies can still be contrasted in terms of auspiciousness and inauspiciousness.

Moreover, particular values may have a clear ritual function in the sense of marking a boundary (Needham 1978: 35–6) or in effecting a change of status. Leeuwen-Turnovcova, for instance, reports (1990: 10) that in formerly German parts of eastern Bohemia, a bride on the morning of her wedding was first dressed right side to left and from bottom upwards, in order to be able to transfer her in the wedding itself into the male, 'patriarchal' sphere represented by her husband. In their critique of Dumont's *Homo*

Hierarchicus, Das and Uberoi (1971: 35) point out that in Hindu weddings and funerals there is not the complete contrast one might expect, despite the polarity between the purity of the bridal pair and the impurity of the corpse. Instead, there is simply the inversion of some values: the corpse's gown is put on upside down, yellow instead of white rice is sprinkled over it, and it is circumambulated anti-clockwise instead of clockwise and an odd number of times instead of an even number. The similarities are due to the fact that both events take place in a domain that the society defines as ritual as against everyday. The differences are due to the polarity in terms of purity between weddings and funerals, the latter being the most impure of ceremonies, the former the least impure.

What is needed, therefore, is a recognition that the symbolic use of particular values may signal entry into a ritual event as well as the degree of auspiciousness of that event or of a part of it. In the latter case especially, the reversal of values can signal a transition to another stage of the rite. Perhaps the chief problem with Hertz's model for later generations of anthropologists has been the belief that the left, and by extension other concepts that may have neutral value in the abstract, always mark the negative or inauspicious culturally. A famous example is Needham's difficulties in explaining the left hand of the Mugwe as sacred, since in rigorously following Hertz's view of the left as always inauspicious, he is led into the position of saying that symbolically, the Mugwe's left hand, which is that concerned with divination, is his right (Needham 1973b). This phrase could have been avoided by seeing use of the left as signifying simply a reversal. This sort of puzzle is not limited to the analysis of ritual but can involve classification too. J.A. Barnes, talking about Luther's metaphor for God's two kingdoms – one of the right hand, which is heaven, and one of the left hand, which is here on earth – points out that 'Luther does not equate God's left hand with damnation, as in Matthew 25, v. 31–46, but with secular life here on earth' (1971: 10). Wilson (1983b: 250–1) puzzles over the association of female saints with the right rather than the left in the distribution of their images in Parisian churches, saying that this runs counter to Hertz's theories. His tentative answer refers to the fact that the left side is normally occupied by the Virgin, from whom other female saints are kept apart. The real distinction in fact seems to be between the Virgin on the left and all saints, regardless of gender, on the right. One might nonetheless introduce a gender aspect in observing that the Virgin is the preeminent female intercessor with God, saints, at least in these churches, being predominantly male.

There are other problems with context. One relates simply to perspective: what is right for one person will be left for someone standing facing him (Mauss 1969 II: 144, 147). In India, the Kshatriyas may be considered female in relation to the superior Brahmans but male in relation to the inferior Vaishyas, although the Brahman is also said to have been the womb from which the Kshatriya was born. Similarly, the Sky is feminine in relation to the Sun, masculine in relation to the Earth (Beck 1973: 396, and Needham 1973a: xxvii, both citing Coomaraswamy). Sometimes one pole is subdivided, one half then taking a value associated with the other pole at the more inclusive level. A common example is the dichotomy between good and bad death, when death is itself one pole of a dichotomy with life. Among the Osage the two social moieties, Tsízhu and Hónga, are associated respectively with left, east, north and sky, and with right, west, south and earth (land and water); but Hónga itself is further divided for some purposes into land and water, associated respectively with east (cf. Tsízhu) and west. In another context, the final ceremony before the break-up of the camp, there is a ritual reversal in which Hónga is located to the north and Tzízhu to the south (La Flesche 1973: 33, 36-8). The Winnebago division between heaven and earth becomes threefold in some contexts, in which the earth divided further into earth and water (Lévi-Strauss 1956: 119-20). Friedberg (1980) provides further examples from the Bunaq, Schulte Nordholt (1980) from the Atoni, both of Indonesia.

In these cases, it might seem that a triadic form of symbolism would be more appropriate: logically, odd-number classifications are recalcitrant to a dichotomous reductionism in a way that even-number ones are not. But often a triadic system can be reduced to a dyadic one (or is so reduced in particular contexts). King (1980: 13–14), discussing Schärer's data on the Ngaju of Borneo (1963: 21), notes that the triadic distinction between white, red/gold and black, which is also one between the Upperworld, the Underworld and what Schärer called 'the evil aspect of the total godhead', is reduced to two on occasion, when the first two come together in opposition to the last. In King's words (*ibid.*: 14), 'a dual division is located within another dual division.' Similarly, the structure of what Lévi-Strauss calls generalized exchange is in one sense triadic (there are three groups to be identified, wife-givers, wife-takers and one's own), but in another sense (that of particular exchanges) dyadic. Ultimately it all depends on the ethnography, for what to us is logically possible is not necessarily a social fact. Fox (1989: 37 n. 2) even experienced disagreement among his informants in Thie, Roti, Indonesia as to whether their domain was symbolically dyadic or triadic.

Thus as Mauss pointed out in his comments on Granet's paper (Mauss 1969 II: 145; cf. Durkheim and Mauss 1963), classifications need not be dichotomous at all but can be based on other numbers instead. Mauss mentioned the necessity of including up and down, back and front, as well as right and left in respect of the Maori, and he also brings in the centre on one occasion, perhaps with the Zuñi in mind. Mauss still regards Hertz's thesis as valid, however, and regards his observation as supplementing, not contradicting it (*ibid.*: 147). Granet also made this point in suggesting that a fourfold classification of sociocentric groups as typified by the Kariera was more fundamental than the dichotomy represented by dual organization (1939: 166ff.). This suggestion has recently been revived and much developed by Allen (1982, 1986, 1989a, 1989b). It rests on the realization that dual organization takes into account only the vertical distinction between exogamous groups and neglects the horizontal division into generations.

A number of other early anthropological writers were nonetheless prepared to accept the fundamental duality of human thought, without necessarily mentioning Hertz. Unlike many of their contemporaries, they sought its basis not in natural phenomena but in the collective life of man in society. For many of them, unlike Granet, this basis was dual organization (e.g. Rassers 1959 [1922]: 3ff.; Hocart 1970 [1936]: Ch. XX; 1954: Ch. XI). This idea was influential in the work of Dutch anthropologists in particular, as was the idea that the symbolic order is based on the social order, drawn from Durkheim and Mauss's article 'Primitive Classification' (see 1963; originally 1903), which was very influential in Holland. For Hocart, 'the most persistent feature of the dual organization is not intermarriage, but mutual ministration [i.e. ritual services]. This feature is so persistent that it outlives dual organization' (1970: 284). Other basic dichotomies that he identifies are those between sky and earth — usually but not always the former is male and the latter female — and dual sovereignty: '[the] earliest form of dual kingship [consists of] a sky-sun king who regulates and an earth-king who executes' (*ibid.*: 286). However, he admits that in the absence of dual organization things tend to look less dichotomous, and, after asking 'whether this dichotomy is traditional or innate in man', opts for the former. 'Perhaps it is a law of nature, but that is not sufficient to explain the dual organization, for dichotomy need not produce a pair, except fleetingly as a first step. In the end it may produce any pattern, threefold, fourfold, fivefold or more' (*ibid.*: 289).

THE ADOPTION OF HERTZ'S WORK BY OTHERS

Later developments of the theme of right and left took place only fitfully for many decades after Hertz's article was published in 1909. As we have seen, it was the subject of a debate involving Granet and Mauss in 1933, the former being closely associated with the *Année* group though never strictly a member, in a meeting concerned with China. The following year, Mauss mentioned Hertz's text in a paper presented to the Société de Psychologie on the social variability of even basic bodily techniques such as walking or eating (see Mauss 1950: 365-86). The subject of right and left was also taken up by Wile in a book published the same year (1934), which was the inspiration for an article on right and left in Africa by Wieschoff of 1938; and in an article by Kruyt of 1941 concerning Sulawesi (see Needham ed. 1973 for both). The citing of Hertz's work by Kruyt indicates that his ideas had reached some quarters of Dutch anthropology by then. It remains a question, however, whether they were actually present as such at Leiden at this time.[5] P.E. de Josselin de Jong surmises (1976: 172) that 'the influence of Hertz on that tradition was only slight', and he does not mention him in his review of the *Année's* influence on inter-war Dutch anthropology (1972). Although like other Dutch anthropologists of the period, van Wouden had absorbed the work of Durkheim and especially Mauss from J.P.B. de Josselin de Jong's teaching, he makes no mention of Hertz in his famous monograph on eastern Indonesia (1935), despite his own extensive discussion of dualistic symbolism. In fact, despite the obvious richness of dual symbolic classification in many Indonesian societies, it is only recently that the Leiden school has really begun to interest itself in a tradition that can be specifically traced to Hertz, and then more in respect of its Dumontian revision of the 1980s (pp. 85–7).

Hertz's work was also kept alive by those sociologists of the 1930s who were attached to the Collège de Sociologie, especially Georges Bataille, Roger Caillois and Michel Leiris, its founders. They were in general much influenced by the *Année Sociologique* school, though far from being devoid of ideas of their own. Hertz is among those frequently mentioned in their work, though they did not all interpret him in the same way. For Bataille, for instance (especially 1988 [1938]), an intensified focus on the sacred is what distinguishes human from animal societies, for the direct inter-attraction of individuals in animal societies has to be mediated by something where humans are concerned, and this something is the sacred. However, this is a sacred, protected by taboo, which is based originally on disgust and horror. Such feelings are what first brought humans together, and they are manifested in ritual by such things as the aversion of one's gaze at the moment the sacrifice is carried out, the silence of communion and revulsion at the sight of a corpse. Thus we already have a deviation away from Durkheimian orthodoxy and back in the direction of intellectualism in that the feelings and perceptions of individuals are seen as lying at the root of social forms. But further, taboo objects in themselves have the ability to keep things at a distance. 'It is, in essence, not a case of objects consecrated by beliefs or fixed rituals — it is corpses, blood, especially menstrual blood, menstruating women themselves. [...] These objects, at any rate, are impure and untouchable, and they are sacred' (1988: 121). They are also left, inauspicious: 'On the whole, that which is left entails repulsion and that which is right entails attraction' (*ibid.*). But each object itself has its symbolically left and right aspects, for example a corpse: associated with the left *qua* corpse, it becomes progressively right as it decomposes, bones often being auspicious, a source of positive power. Ritual space is simply where such transformations take place, though such transformations remain the essence of the social. As for Hertz, so for Bataille, death is the supreme example because of the threat to social continuity that it represents. 'The death of an individual can be considered one of the most alarming expenditures for human beings united in a group. The corpse is treated, in fact, as a reality that could continue to spread' (*ibid.*: 123; cf. Chapter Five). Even more than with Hertz, however, do right and left become mere metaphors of auspicious and inauspicious, of pure and impure. The sacred as such is reduced to objects of horror being manipulated and transformed by ritual action into the socially efficacious — repulsion into attraction. For Bataille, it is less a source of attraction in its own right, which the members of the society seek to unify with, to gain access to, through ritual action.

In fact, in this view the sacred becomes transferred from the god or spirit *in* the rite to the object — person or thing — *of* the rite, in this case from the ancestors to the corpse. It is true that, like the corpse, initiands and virgins may be inauspicious, for it is their anomalousness or incompleteness that has made the rite necessary. Not only they are taboo or sacred, however. To use Bataille's terminology, there is certainly both attraction and repulsion, but it is the former that endures, overcoming the latter. Hegelian negativity and Freudian guilt complexes here interfere seriously with the Durkheimian view of society as a positive force that is frequently but not permanently threatened by the inauspicious. The sacred as society itself, making itself felt in ritual, almost entirely disappears.

In this sense, Caillois remained closer to the Durkheimians (see especially 1939). Leiris more occasionally referred to Hertz on right and left in writings that were as much literary as sociological, such as *Tauromachies* (1937; cf. Jamin and Lupu 1987: 52 n. 7) and his essay 'Le sacré dans la vie quotidienne', in which, in the words of Jamin (1981: 108 n. 3), he 'insists on distinguishing the right-hand pole (his parents' bedroom ...) and the left-hand pole (the WC ...) in his sacred geography' (i.e. of his childhood home).

It was in Oxford, however, that the decisive steps were taken to bring Hertz's work to the general attention of anthropologists and to establish his reputation firmly. Dumont claims (1979: 816 n. 14) that during the 1950s, while he was teaching in Oxford, he had reminded Evans-Pritchard of Hertz's work in the course of a lecture on Mauss (published in Dumont 1986: Ch. 7). Certainly Evans-Pritchard lectured on him regularly at this time, and it was under his auspices that Hertz's article on right and left was translated, along with that on death, by the Needhams in 1960. A further step was the publication of a 'handbook' entitled *Right & Left* assembled by Rodney Needham in 1973 (Needham ed. 1973) and headed by a slightly revised reprint of this translation.

Needham himself, from the late 1950s onwards, pioneered a trend towards much more elaborate and ambitious explorations of the theme of dual symbolic classification in articles on east Africa, the Indo-Burman borderlands and northern Indochina. He shifted the focus away from the Durkheimian reduction of classification to society and instead saw dichotomy as more basic, in the sense of being a global feature of human thought, a position which has certain affinities with that of Lévi-Strauss. Hertz had concentrated on a rather narrow selection of oppositions in his article and had regularly associated them with right and left, though he regarded this opposition as only one aspect of the more general Durkheimian dualism. Needham's studies went further in establishing a whole series of oppositions in particular societies, oppositions which need not be directly connected with right and left at all. Although this opposition would normally feature, it was 'not a determinant of the other oppositions' (1981: 45). Needham recognized that dual symbolic classification did not necessarily pervade the symbolic representations of any particular culture: classifications based on other numbers than two might also figure (1979a: 9ff., 12ff.). Nevertheless, he was especially keen to incorporate analyses of dualistic classifications into his studies of societies with prescriptive systems of affinal alliance, since he felt that 'the structural concordance between ... the social and symbolic order' was particularly impressive in such cases (1960a: 108). Indeed, 'social organization and symbolic forms in such societies are aspects of one conceptual order, only arbitrarily to be separated for our purposes of description and analysis' (*ibid.*: 108–9; see also 1960b: 105; 1959: 134).

Thus in the case of the Lamet of northern Laos (1960a), we are first shown how asymmetric dualism obtains in respect of the opposition between wife-givers and wife-takers, both in the kinship terminology and in respect of actual alliances, wife-givers being superior. The analysis then proceeds to show the same dualism in respect of the layout of the house, prestations between affinal alliance groups (of goods and services as well as women), the village layout (though this could only be speculative on the data available to Needham, which was basically Izikowitz's monograph of 1951), and the different sorts of spiritual being. The demonstration culminates in a double-column table in which 'the oppositions are listed seriatim as they have been elicited or inferred in the exposition of the relevant facts' (1960a: 115). It is not claimed that the analysis is exhaustive, nor is this necessary: 'in

making this analysis we are discerning a *mode of thought*; and further oppositions would not be of value in "completing" the classification, but in illus-
trating in other contexts how exactly this mode of thought has been
apprehended and in extending the social and natural range of its recorded
application' (*ibid.,* original emphasis). Indeed, so much are they reflections
of a common mode of thought that in making demonstrations of this kind it
hardly matters where one starts (cf. Needham 1973c: 330). Among the means
of identifying oppositions is reversal, e.g. aspects of movement between the
world of the living and the world of the dead, or between the realms of religion and secular authority (e.g. Needham *ibid.*: 306ff.).

Needham carried out similar analyses around the same time of similar
groups living in the Indo-Burmese borderlands, the Kom (1959), Aimol
(1960b) and Purum (1962a; also 1958), as well as the Wikmunkan of Australia
(1962b). The inspiration of Mauss's 'total social fact' is very evident.
However, it was already clear that this total method of analysis could not be
applied to all types of society. Needham suggested that

> in societies based on descent such symbolic representations may be
> expected to correlate with the type of descent system. Roughly, in cog-
> natic societies the relation of symbolic to social order may be indefinite
> or minimal; in lineal systems the relationship may be discernible in a
> limited range of particulars but not commonly in a comprehensive
> manner; and in lineal systems with prescriptive affinal alliance there is
> usually a correspondence of structure between the two orders such
> that one may speak of a single scheme of classification under which
> both are subsumed. (1973b [1960]: 111)

And further: 'In lineal descent systems without prescriptive regulation
of marriage a total structural analysis is generally far less feasible, and in cognatic societies it is even less possible' (1960a: 117–18). This was strikingly
shown subsequently by Howell, one of Needham's students, in her work
among the Chewong of West Malaysia, a group with cognatic descent and no
positive marriage rules: she was not able to identify many oppositions that
were ordinarily considered asymmetric (1985). Nonetheless, such oppositions can still be discerned in societies not regulated by prescriptive kinship
systems, as Needham himself endeavoured to show with respect to two
African ones (1973b, 1973c). This was presumably one factor making
Durkheim and Mauss's specific reduction of symbolic classifications to social
ones unsuitable as a model. Although Needham applauded Mauss's holism, he
declined to follow his and Durkheim's specific evolutionism, taking the view
that lack of concordance between the two sorts of classification could be
explained synchronically if both were referred to underlying principles of
order, like opposition (cf. Needham 1972: 154ff.).[6] Similarly, Needham

retained something of the inspiration of Lévi-Strauss without following it in every detail. Here, the configurations of the symbolic order led Needham to reject Lévi-Strauss's notion of exchange as a fundamental feature of the human mind in favour of opposition, of which exchange, like reciprocity, was merely one manifestation (e.g. 1960b: 105ff.). One can exchange wives, after all, but hardly symbols or values linked by dual classification. In the case of dual symbolic classification, this focus on abstract principles of order extends to analogy and homology as well as opposition, though homology was the most contingent of these. In this respect, Needham drew inspiration explicitly from Hertz's essay, which he saw as a disquisition on opposition and polarity as principles of order, while also modifying, to the point of denying it, Hertz's assumption that a homology necessarily existed between the terms in any system of dual symbolic classification (Needham 1972: 154–5, 210; 1979b: 296–7).

Meggitt (1964: 217–18) goes still further in specifically denying any correlation between the two sorts of classification on the basis of his own field researches with two different groups. One, the Mae Enga of Papua New Guinea, have a richly elaborated scheme of dual symbolic classification, despite their lack of a prescriptive alliance system, while the other, the Walbiri of Central Australia, have the latter but lack the former. In accounting for the Mae Enga case, however, he resorts to a naturalistic explanation – here, man versus woman as the basic opposition, from which the rest are derived – of the sort that Hertz dismissed as inadequate. Needham, conversely, has deep mental structures in mind. The marriage system is by no means the explanation, just one of many areas of social thought where a basic principle of opposition is applied.[7] Faron tends to move in the other direction, going out of his way to emphasise the strong preference for mother's brother's daughter's marriage and semi-permanent distinctions between wife-giving and wife-taking patrilineages among the Mapuche (1973: 190–1, 198ff.), not as the basis for dual symbolic classification, but as another characteristic example of this sort of coherence, even though the terminology is not prescriptive (see Needham 1967: 40).

Needham's analyses of dual symbolic classification have frequently been criticized, and from several points of view. Goody (1961; 1977: Ch. 4) and Beattie (1968) have both called into question their very status as actual collective representations supported by firm ethnographic evidence. This sort of criticism is often made of the study of symbolism in general. The assumption seems to be that symbolic associations always have to be made explicit – during ritual, for example – in order to count as social facts. This depends on the definition of ritual and on deciding where the boundary between the ritual and the non-ritual actually lies – if, indeed, there is one.

Even though it is more likely to be appreciated by the analyst than the man in the street, one inference to be drawn from Hertz's work is that we are making a ritual gesture every time we pick up a pen or a knife and fork (cf. Howell 1989: 244 on the difficulty of distinguishing the ritual and the every-day among the Chewong). This in turn suggests that many oppositions, if not actually unconscious, are at least felt rather than expressed, taken for granted and made almost automatically, albeit as the result of an early and basic con-ditioning (cf. Needham 1973a: xix–xx). There is a general recognition by those who support such work (e.g. King 1980: 6 n. 9) that oppositions may be either explicit or unconscious (though in the latter case they are admitted to be harder to verify), and may indeed be perceived only by the analyst. These realizations do not prevent their being analysed and might even be said to constitute a necessary preliminary to analysis. Verification is anyway never straightforward. Explanations for the symbolizations the people carry out may be produced, but only by referring to another part of the culture in question. Sooner or later the anthropologists is likely to be told simply that 'that's the way it is', at which point explanation, and with it explicitness, run out.

A less radical version of this criticism poses it rather in the form of whether the oppositions are themselves always seen as the anthropologist thinks. It has indeed become a standard criticism of binary opposition in structuralism that the links between the poles of an opposition are frequently made by the analyst, who is only assuming, without verifying the fact, that the link is indigenously recognized. According to Ellen (1986: 25), for instance: 'The Nualu do not say that MALE is "opposed" to FEMALE; or that MALE : FEMALE is analogous to SEA:MOUNTAIN. We formalize by seeing those symbolic relations in terms of conventions of perception which are not necessarily those of our informants.' There are, on the other hand, excep-tions, such as the Chinese division of all things into the categories Yin and Yang (see below). Goody also questions (*ibid.*) the assumption that such oppositions are basic features of the human mind and therefore universal. Needham has himself subsequently queried this assumption as regards partic-ular types of opposition, though he sees less of a problem with the faculty of opposing itself (see especially 1987). Terence Turner has objected in a more general way (1984: 339; also 337–8) to the tautology involved in accounting for binary opposition through 'fundamental structures of the human mind' when the only evidence offered for these structures is the very existence of the oppositions they are supposed to account for (see also Allen 1989b: 46; Tcherkézoff 1994). Conversely, it can be argued that if this faculty does exist at a deep level of consciousness, it is more likely to approach the universal than explicit social facts, which are more likely to vary cross-culturally. At the very least, it is obvious that its distribution is, if not universal (i.e. in the sense of existing absolutely everywhere), then at least global (i.e. appearing in all regions of the world).

Hallpike (1979) takes something of a middle way here. For him, tables of oppositions rely on many implicit assumptions concerning the culture being examined in their construction. Speaking of Needham's Banyoro analysis, he says: 'the classification ... is based on imagery and association, not on any taxonomic principles' (*ibid.*: 232). The tables of Needham and others are 'very much the product of literate thought ...; collective representations may have a dualistic structure which is beyond the capacity of the individual members of a culture to employ explicitly in their own reasoning' (*ibid.*: 233). It is only with the arrival of science and scholarship, i.e. reflective thought recorded by literate cultures, that the idea of a binary structure really comes to be exploited, something which for Hallpike concerns Yin and Yang as much as the scientific taxonomy based on perpetual subdivision. For him, binary opposition as a structure is less significant in other, non-literate or 'primitive' forms of thought, as his own experience among the Konso of Ethiopia and Tauade of Papua New Guinea has shown him. 'What *is* developmentally significant is the extent to which binary categories are systematized, either into an integrated explanatory framework such as that of the Chinese, or into exhaustive and hierarchically organized, goal-directed, classificatory procedures' (*ibid.*: 232, original emphasis). In other words, the dualistic structure may be implicit and taken for granted rather than normally expressed and reflected upon by the culture, the latter generally being a relatively late development in human thought. As Fox points out (1988b: 27), 'the cultural criteria used to order a system of dual symbolic classification are rarely explicitly given.'

Hallpike's explanation for binary classification is partly naturalistic, being based not only on the ability to distinguish, but also on the way the world is empirically ordered: 'the prevalence of dualistic classification is not principally a manifestation of a binary property of the human mind, imposing itself on a neutral range of phenomena, but rather an accommodation to a dualistic reality' (1979: 228). This is not to disregard a definite human propensity to reduce things to pairs, but this does not exhaust the human capacity either to perceive or to classify. His main concern, however, is to argue against duality itself being a basic feature of the human mind in the way that Needham has frequently suggested: 'The only fundamental binary structures of the mind ... are differentiation and comparison ...' (*ibid.*: 235).

For Needham, conversely, following Durkheim, it is not necessary for all individuals in the society to be apprehending their symbolic classifications all the time for them to exist. Despite its acknowledged jadedness, he brings in the analogy of the grammar of a language, which is followed by its speakers without reflection, let alone analysis on their part (1973a: xix–xx; also Beidelman 1973: 152–3). More recently (1987: 202ff.), he answers Hallpike's assertions concerning the mind's accomodation to empirical dualism in the classifications it makes:

> If there are natural pairs in our experience of the world, and if the mind is supposed to accommodate itself to them, it needs to be explained under what constraint or impulsion the mind tends to do so. [...] If, on the other hand, binary classification reflects features of the physical world, it needs to be explained why it reflects dyadic features rather than others. (*ibid.*: 205)

Needham's own claims rest ultimately on certain assumptions. 'The idea that it is an intrinsic property of the brain to order representations by pairs is an inference from the comparative study of ethnographic evidences' (*ibid.*: 202). Nonetheless, he accepts that binary structures do not exhaust human classification, even suggesting that technological and scientific progress has depended on transcending them (*ibid.*: 205). This has a certain resonance with Hallpike's overall concern to identify distinct modes of thought, though it is formulated quite differently.

Other objections have tended to revolve around criticisms of the use, by Needham and others, of two-column lists or tables to record the oppositions established in any particular society. These tables place each of the poles of each opposition in one of the two columns, e.g. right in one column and left in the other, an obvious enough form of representation. However, objections have been raised to them on two interrelated grounds, first, that they are insensitive to the various contexts in which oppositions find expression; and secondly, that they convey the false impression that the classification is a solidary structure, such that the terms in either of the two columns are fixed in their relation to one another, to the point that they necessarily imply each other and can represent each other. The sort of question then posed is, for example, is the left feminine or only associated with the feminine? (cf. Goody 1977: 66; Beattie 1968, 1976; Barnes 1985b: 15).

Although in his general statements (e.g. 1973a: xxv; 1973b: 117; 1980: 56–7; 1987: 150), Needham has been at pains to deny that there is any common property or homology between the terms of each column, in practice his analyses often seem to proceed as if the columns at least had the respective qualities of auspicious or inauspicious (cf. Makarius and Makarius 1973: 211–21). The difficulties that such a form of representation can entail can be seen from the examples of the Fulani of Sudan and the Purum of northeast India that he himself introduces (1973b: 121–2). In the Fulani case, the usual series north:south::junior:senior is reversed in the female context of where the beds of the various wives – who are ranked according to seniority – are placed in the homestead. The problem is that Needham's table can only show one order, otherwise confusion would result through some terms being in both columns. But this means that it cannot show that in this context the normal series female:male::junior:senior does not obtain, since the male category is absent and the female category itself split between junior and senior. In the Purum case, auguries at name-giving ceremonies for boys are auspicious if the right leg of the bird falls over the left after it has been sacrificed, while for girls the reverse is the case. Thus the transitivity of the sets right: left::male:female and right:left::auspicious:inauspicious does not obtain in contexts where left:right::auspicious:inauspicious. In both examples, one might speak of reversals, but what is really happening is that a person (a female) who would conventionally be placed in the inauspicious column is symbolized as important or auspicious through an attribute which is normally also considered inauspicious. Thus the Fulani senior wife sleeps to the north because north is a female-connected category, and a Purum girl receives a good augury when the bird's left leg is uppermost because left is a female-connected category. In neither case, moreover, are the contexts involved intrinsically negative or inauspicious. Thus these connections are context-specific and do not necessarily, or even probably, shape the whole symbolic system. Similar objections were raised to Needham's analyses of the Meru system (1973b; cf. Tcherkézoff 1987) and of the Nyoro system (Needham 1973c; cf. Beattie 1968, 1976).

Whether or not there is actually any conflict between Needham's programmatic statements and his actual practice, many commentators have chosen either to ignore the former or to regard them as unsatisfactory. The most radical challenges have come from the work of Louis Dumont and Serge Tcherkézoff in Paris (e.g. Dumont 1979, 1982, both reprinted 1986; Tcherkézoff 1987 [1983]; cf. Needham's reply, 1987: chs. 7 and 8; Tcherkézoff's response, 1994). Dumont chose Needham's approach as a perfect example of what seemed to him to be the neglect of hierarchy by his anthropological colleagues generally. For Dumont, Needham's tables were not simply devoid of contextualization, they presented oppositions as if they were basically symmetric, with an asymmetric overlay added on. This was quite different from Dumont's position, which was that any distinction necessarily entails a difference in value between its poles – and therefore hierarchy in Dumont's terms – a difference in value, moreover, that was intrinsic to any opposition or distinction, not merely an addition to it made after the event. And further, oppositions were not simply value-laden and hierarchical, they also entailed the encompassment of one pole by the other under most circumstances. Thus the opposition man-woman in the English language ceases to be an opposition when, as in certain circumstances, 'man' refers to all humanity, i.e. to men and women together. Dumont also prefers to talk of ideological level rather than context, the more global or inclusive level (man = human) being superordinate in relation to the level of distinction (man = not woman).[8] Tcherkézoff's contribution to the debate (1987) began with his critique of Needham's analysis of Meru symbolism (Needham 1973b), which he followed with his own account of the dyadic symbolism of the Nyamwezi, another east African people, using the notion of hierarchical opposition, which Tcherkézoff had developed largely in parallel with Dumont. Since then, Tcherkézoff has been one of a number of French scholars interested in applying hierarchical opposition in the analysis of ritual, following a suggestion originating with Daniel de Coppet (Serge Tcherkézoff, personal communication); others include especially Cécile Barraud and André Iteanu. However, some differences of interpretation have since emerged between Tcherkézoff and the rest (cf. Tcherkézoff 1994).

To deal with these developments in the detail they deserve would take us far beyond the bounds of this study, which is primarily concerned with Hertz's ideas and their more immediate impact.[9] Although there are clear intellectual links connecting Dumont *et al.* with Hertz, their modification of his model of asymmetric opposition is as radical in its implications for anthropological theory as in the form it takes. Suffice it to say here that their innovation has proved fruitful in the analysis of both classification and ritual, and that its applicability might well be extended. These developments also suggest that structuralism is neither dead, nor the monopoly of Lévi-Strauss. Needham's approach, by contrast, has always been closer to, though not identical with, that of Lévi-Strauss. His contribution has been to combine an amended version of the latter's thesis that global principles of order underlie variable cultural representations with Hertz's original model. Dumont and his followers, on the other hand, in opposing not only Needham but through him ultimately Hertz himself, are striking out into new waters. They may invoke the spirit of Hertz on occasion (e.g. Dumont 1972: 28), but the letter of their work has become significantly different.

CHAPTER FIVE

Death and the Analysis of Ritual

HERTZ'S THESIS

The anthropological and ethnographic literature on death is vast, and Hertz's name is not as singularly prominent in respect of it as it is with the theme of right and left. By no means all those writing on death find it necessary to mention his work, many mention it only as part of a routine survey of what has already been written on the subject, and only a few have examined his thoughts at all critically or sought to take them further. Nonetheless, he has importance as part of the Durkheimian shift from intellectualist to sociological approaches to the study of the topic. His essay, 'Contribution à une étude sur la representation collective de la mort' (1907a), has become one of its theoretical anchors, especially since its translation by the Needhams in 1960. The work is his longest, with a large number of detailed footnotes, and would have been longer still had not Durkheim and his colleagues pruned it considerably (Alice Hertz 1928: ix–x; see p. 4). Although it was referred to by Durkheim in his *Elementary Forms of the Religious Life* (1915: 402 n. 1), it is hard at first sight to disentangle what, if anything, Hertz brought to the topic that was not already implicit in the master's method and arguments. Nonetheless, although basically Durkheimian, it does have an originality of its own. Halbwachs regarded it as the most important of his works (1928: 201).

Hertz's basic theme is the phenomenon of second burial as final disposal of the corpse and the treatment of the corpse in the interim, as well as what this says about the state of the soul and of the survivors. In fact, these three aspects are seen as interrelated and as reflecting and impinging on one other, so that corpse, soul and survivors follow a common course. In this sense, the study can be regarded as structuralist. But Hertz's study also inaugurates the investigation of the dynamics of ritual that van Gennep was to make even more explicit, with reference to a much wider range of rites, two years later (van Gennep 1909). It is very much ritual as process that Hertz is concerned with, showing how society, damaged through the loss of one of its members, adjusts to its loss and makes itself whole again. The normal Durkheimian idea of a rite as the occasion on which society most strongly represents itself to it members, though present as a sub-text, is left implicit. The notion of sacrifice as the high point of any ritual, when the participants are closest to whatever counts as sacred, needed no special emphasis, thanks to Hubert and Mauss's earlier study (1899), even though sacrifice is a feature of death rites as of any other. It is in these respects that we find Hertz looking at the problem from a somewhat different angle.

Hertz begins with the remark that although death appears to be an emotional matter, only reason can examine the beliefs surrounding it and its biological foundations. It is the source of a social as much as a personal disturbance. The idea of the soul is used to express the end of life, but the body must still be treated properly, less for hygienic reasons than because, unlike the body of an animal, it retains something of the human status it had in life. Equally a moral obligation and therefore a social circumstance is the fact that the bereaved have duties to perform — grieving and other ritual actions — regardless of their personal feelings for the deceased. Hertz therefore proposes to examine death as a 'collective representation' (1960: 28) with special reference to the 'Dayak' of Borneo, which mainly means the Olo Ngaju of the southeast.

There are, of course, many differences of detail between societies concerning the treatment of death. In Western society death is regarded as instantaneous, as is the translation of the soul towards its maker; the only delay is to enable a funeral to be held. Other societies, by contrast, treat death more as a process, which may lead to a second burial some time after the first has taken place. In the West, this is but dimly manifested in later memorial services, which are held mostly for the prominent. Metcalf and Huntington point out (1991: 8) that although the phenomenon Hertz describes is actually quite rare, it does occur worldwide, a circumstance which tends to give it a true structural significance which is in no way the product of purely historical contingencies, such as evolution or diffusion.

Hertz identifies three phases of this process: the death itself ('in the usual sense of the word', 1960: 29), which occasions a temporary disposal of the corpse; the intermediate period; and the final laying to rest of the remains. The soul and the survivors undergo their own related processes in parallel, the three processes being intimately linked with one another. This is not invariable, but Hertz thought it convenient to assume so for purposes of exposition. When studying a social phenomenon, reasoned the Durkheimians, study it in its most highly developed form.

Among the Ngaju, the corpse is often kept at home temporarily, a practice which was diminishing at the time Hertz wrote because of Dutch colonial government prohibitions and what he calls 'inconvenience' (*ibid*.: 30). Here, Hertz seems to be trying to account for the relative weakness of this ritual practice among the Ngaju through the usual Durkheimian resort to historical change, though the evidence is circumstantial, if not weak. Certainly no clear reason is given why this 'inconvenience' should suddenly have arisen. But there are other options: the corpse may be placed in a separate and specifically built hut, in a tree or in a temporary grave, but always somewhere different from the final resting place. The delay before the final ceremony may be of months or years and depends secondarily on the requirement to provide an elaborate and therefore expensive rite, or to take a head, or primarily in Hertz's view, on the necessity for the corpse to rot entirely (this is important for Hertz's parallel approach). In the meantime the coffin is completely sealed except for the purpose of draining off the decaying liquids. This is done not for hygienic reasons or to avoid the smell of decay but to preserve both deceased and survivors from the evil threat coming from putrefaction. The latter is associated with a life-threatening thunderbolt, from which the corpse too must be protected. Hertz stresses particularly that it is mystical danger rather than fear of a soul which appears to be involved here. The pot used to drain off the liquids is itself clearly special: it may be broken and buried with the corpse at the final rite. Elsewhere, for example in the Andaman Islands, the threat from the corpse may lead to the settlement being deserted, together with the corpse and its possessions. In either case, corpse and living are set apart.

There is much concern with the changes to the corpse. In western Borneo, rice may be added to the liquids and eaten, while in other parts of Borneo a foul-tasting sort of rice is eaten which is symbolically assimilated to them. In Timor, they are smeared on the body. Such practices either have to do with the participation of the bereaved in the state of the corpse or else with preserving the substance, spiritual essences, etc., of the clan or other group. The corpse itself is open to evil influences, hence it is washed, its eyes and other orifices are closed, and spirits are deterred from approaching it or remaining with it in various ways, by noise, by keeping the corpse company, etc. Such matters must be handled properly, and they prevent immediate disposal of the corpse, which cannot take place until it is free of the pollution its death has caused.

As for the soul, this is a period in which it is not yet settled in its final resting place but wanders near the corpse and, more generally, in the earthly environment it knew in life. The Olo Ngaju in fact recognize two souls, or consider that the soul is split into two on death. One soul or part thereof consists of or relates to the personality, while the other is 'corporeal' (*ibid*.: 34) and lacks consciousness. Their survival depends not only on proper rites but also on the full decomposition of the corpse, which removes pollution from them as well as from the living. For this reason the soul proper, or personality, experiences a delay in its final entry into the world of the ancestors – i.e. it may visit there, but will not yet be able to find a permanent place of peace and therefore often returns to earth. Until this entry is assured, the deceased is not fully dead, and indeed he or she remains marginal, wholly in the world of neither the dead nor the living. This may be the reason, in some cases, for the corpse being temporarily placed in the desert or jungle, outside human habitation, and it certainly explains, more generally, the temporariness of its resting place during this equally marginal period and, where it is found, its need to be fed. Among the Ngaju, the corporeal soul accordingly remains with the corpse until the final rite or *tiwah*.

The soul is a potential danger to the living at this time, since death has given it the power to inflict them with disease if they neglect to care and provide for it as in life, with proper meals and so on. Its belongings must also be respected, avoided, perhaps destroyed, but they can no longer be used in a normal way. The closest relatives of the deceased are in a similar ritual danger to the corpse, and therefore they too are temporarily set apart from the rest of humanity. They are no longer a part of the community and may not eat nor behave generally as normal people. They therefore continue to be associated with the corpse in death as in life, but since the deceased has changed, so must they. At the same time, this is a part of the separation which must be effected between the deceased and those closest to him or her in life, something which is again a process rather than an event. The period of mourning may end with the final rite or may precede it if preparations for the final rite have to be prolonged – the argument from 'inconvenience' again. This creates the possibility that the mourners are liberated not at a single moment but in stages, as the danger coming from the corpse weakens. The severity of the restrictions affecting the survivors is said by Hertz to make it difficult for them to prepare the rituals that will release them. In most societies it is not the closest relatives who make these preparations. Others take on this role, and even feed of the survivors.

Hertz goes on to mention other forms of temporary disposal, from Australia, Papua New Guinea, sub-Saharan Africa, Polynesia and the Americas, all of which are structurally equivalent for him, whether they involve a temporary burial or temporary storage in the house, in a tree or on a special raised platform. He also brings in embalming and cremation, even though they appear at first sight to be radically different. Mummification, originally accidental, later became a means of disposing of the body with as little decay

as possible; like the bones left after decomposition, the mummy is permanent. Cremation, on the other hand, is rarely the final stage in the ritual
process, since the bones may be collected afterwards and then disposed of in
a second rite, though this often appears as continuous with the first.[1] In all
three cases, including embalming, the imperative is to deal in some way with
the dangers of the decomposition of the corpse and to convert it finally into
something permanent. In Borneo, one simply awaits its decomposition. In
India, one speeds up its disintegration through the action of fire. In ancient
Egypt, one avoids it by preserving the corpse as far as possible as in life.
Another tactic is endo-cannibalism, which preserves the powers of the
deceased's flesh so that they are not lost to the community. Yet another is the
Zorastrian exposure of the corpse in wild places (i.e. away from human
society again), where the flesh will be eaten by creatures of the wild, who in
this sense act as purifiers of its gross pollution.

The temporary and dangerous sojourn of the soul on earth corresponds to the time taken for the body to decay. Its destruction in this world
may be felt to necessitate its reconstruction in the next, which enables the
soul to be reborn, perhaps as an animal rather than a human being: for
example, in Madagascar fluids collected in jars are sprinkled with ox blood,
with just such a result in mind. The ancestors may help directly in this
process of re-creation: in north-west America they come from the next world
to take bits of flesh away with them for the purpose. Death is thus a transition to a new and often better life. Hertz specifically links this to the idea of
sacrifice as propagated by Hubert and Mauss (1899), which entails that sacrificial objects can only be transferred to the next world by being destroyed in
this. The theme of death as a sacrifice is, of course, well known in Hinduism
(cf. Das 1977b: 122–3), and it can also be discerned in the Christian interpretation of the death of Jesus. Hertz admits that the location of the soul in the
flesh is not invariable because it may be located in the bones instead, but he
maintains that the simultaneous destruction of the corpse and the appearance of the new body and soul in the next world are very general. Both are
gradual, however, and often the soul is unsettled, weak or otherwise imper-
fect while the decomposition of the corpse is still taking place.

The time between death and final disposal thus puts the mourners in a
special state, which may delay their ability to inherit, succeed or remarry.
The deceased retain something of the status they had in life until final disposal has been effected. This is why the death of a chief or king is often concealed until the flesh has decayed, despite the interregnum this causes. This
state, and the period of mourning which signals it, 'is merely the direct consequence in the living of the actual state of the deceased' (Hertz 1960: 51).
Mourners are assimilated to the corpse because, like it, 'their physical

integrity ... is impaired': as with sin, 'there is no clear distinction between misfortune and impurity' (*ibid.*). Hertz takes the opportunity to stress once again that mourning is a moral duty supported by sanctions, which may extend even to capital punishment; it is not simply an outcome of personal distress at the death. He also admits that the complex of ideas and practices he has just set out does not occur everywhere: in practice, mourning and the idea of the soul's temporary sojourn on earth may be found without a second burial. Nonetheless the process remains basically the same, in the sense that the soul is thought not to be fully at rest until the corpse has decayed, whereupon mourning ceases too. Thus the second rite is 'confirmatory in nature, rather than instrumental' (Metcalf in Huntington and Metcalf 1979: 80-1).

The final ceremony in Indonesia, including Borneo, is a community-wide affair carried out occasionally for several persons. According to Hertz, the expense in holding such rites is one reason for their frequent delay. The invitations are given widely and are never refused. But it is not this that ensures its collective character so much as the fact that it heals the breach in the community that is caused by any death. 'The final ceremony has three objects: to give burial to the remains of the deceased, to ensure the soul peace and access to the land of the dead, and finally to free the living from the obligations of mourning' (1960: 54). Whereas the earlier disposal had isolated the corpse, the soul and the mourners, the final rite marks a series of incorporations – of the soul with the ancestors, of the bones (i.e. the remains of the corpse) with those of the ancestors, and of the mourners back with the living. Indeed, this contrast between separation and incorporation is often physically expressed: first the corpse is isolated, then it is brought together with the remains of other deceased with whom it belongs. At the same time, in being incorporated with the ancestors, all aspects of the deceased, material and spiritual, are finally separated from, though not necessarily removed from all contact with, the living: 'henceforth the element of repulsion and disgust is no longer dominant, but rather a feeling of reverent confidence' (*ibid.*: 56-7). The remains are cleaned, in order to fit the corpse for its new position and signal that the polluting period of transition is over. Some of the remains, for example the head, may be retained by the family or descent group for protection or other benefits. Hertz is clearly determined to find this second rite everywhere. Thus the supposed tendency in parts of Borneo to collapse the two rites into one is attributed to 'spontaneous evolution or foreign influence' (*ibid.*: 58), the latter actually amounting to an admission that second rites are not universal after all, if, for example, Westerners or Moslems do not have them. Similarly, the second rite may be limited to destroying the temporary hut, the erection of a monument to the deceased or merely weeding the grave, none of which (except perhaps the first under certain circumstances) can be seen to have much to do with a secondary disposal of the corpse as such.

As vital as a second burial to the Ngaju is the introduction of the soul to 'the society of the dead' by specialist incantations and drumming, 'an arduous task' according to Hertz (1960: 58). The soul is reincarnated several times via animals and plants eaten by humans, so that death is not a unique event but is repeated for any individual. The priestly incantations also restore the living to normal life. This is accompanied by sacrifice, which for the Ngaju may be of a slave or a prisoner-of-war, whose soul is first ritually removed. His blood helps to reconcile the dead and the living and to purify the survivors, as does bathing. The parallelism between the rite incorporating the dead with the ancestors and the rite incorporating the mourners with the living is shown by the fact that both the bones and the mourners are washed — indeed, this is one and the same rite. In some cases, the dead may also be reincorporated with the living. One aspect of this is reincarnation. Another is the presence of some soul or part of the soul in the hearth of its home: perhaps the head or other body part is retained, this being the seat of the soul, in death as in life.

There are, of course, variations, but for Hertz they can all be seen as adhering to this basic structure. In totemic societies, such as those in Australia (which the Durkheimians placed at the start of attested human evolutionary development), individuals are merely the temporary repositories of ancestral souls, which otherwise have strict locations of their own connected with where the ancestral heroes originally left them and which are where the soul resides between incarnations. Here, the final union of the dead is with the totemic species, though the South American (e.g. Bororo) idea that the deceased actually becomes a totem is absent. This union is purely 'mystical', and there is no collective burial of bones. The connected rites take place at some remove after the death and are the analogue of secondary burial elsewhere. Sometimes, the radial bone or the cranium may be smashed to release the soul. This is not always connected with the second rite, however, as in a high-caste Hindu funeral (cf. Das 1977b: 124).

Other societies may collect all the bones of the deceased of the same family or clan together in one place, good examples being found in Madagascar (see, for example, Bloch 1982). 'The ossuary of the clan is not only the communal residence where the ancestors meet, but also a reservoir of souls from which descendants will issue' (Hertz 1960: 70). Hence it may be avoided at normal times, for fear a soul should enter one's own body. Hence also the fear of dying away from home, for the community as well as oneself, because a soul will be lost to the community, and presumably the cycle of reincarnations will also be broken. As with decaying flesh and the liquids of decay, the bones too may be ingested (South America), or at least worn (Andaman Islands), in order to preserve the soul of the deceased, especially to ward off evil spirits or to prevent interference by enemies with the remains themselves. Hertz also exploits reincarnation as a possible analogue of the secondary burial. Naming among Eskimos, as a part of initiation procedures, is connected with reincarnation and is their equivalent of the final ceremony. Hertz introduces a psychological motive here in claiming that in this way the bereaved avoid mourning. Reincarnation implies, of course, that the deceased achieves union not with the ancestors but with his or her family back here on earth. On Mabuaig Island death is seen as an initiation into the land of the dead, the deceased being killed there before being able to gain entry. This is perhaps the destruction associated with transition again. The re-creation of secondary rites also signals the re-creation of the nation in some North American tribes and of the very world among Hindus (e.g. Das 1977b: 125). Hertz ends this section by speculating on what happens where there is no secondary rite, the final disposal taking place immediately, without further ceremony. In such a case, there can be no identification of the mourners with the condition of the deceased, only the expression of sorrow (which is nonetheless obligatory), and there is no need of special measures to restore the bereaved to society. Instead, there may be a concern with the soul's salvation, as in Christianity.

In his lengthy conclusion, Hertz returns to the point that death is not a purely physical event, nor (*pace* Frazer and Tylor) just an occasion for horror. Reactions may differ according to the status of the deceased – a chief may be mourned to a high degree, a child not at all. Death also destroys the social person: 'his destruction is tantamount to a sacrilege' (Hertz 1960: 77), because it was society that had originally made him a social being. Thus death violates society's view of itself as permanent: 'it is stricken in the very principle of its life, in the faith it has in itself' (*ibid*.: 78). Hence the refusal to recognize 'natural' deaths and to attribute all deaths to the evil machinations of enemies or gods or ancestors is not as absurd as it is often felt to be. Relatives, spirits, even the deceased himself, perhaps through the violation of a taboo, may be responsible. Similarly, society cannot believe death to be irrevocable, especially if it believes in reincarnation, for it cannot lose one of its constituent souls. One version of this is the Christian promise of salvation, which takes place for all through the death and resurrection of Jesus Christ rather than through a specific individual or even collective rite: it is postponed until the Day of Judgement rather than periodically repeated. With his comment that the other world is simply 'the realm of the ideal' (*ibid*.: 79), since it exists only in the mind, to represent the soul's conquest over its earthly death, Hertz is clearly invoking the Durkheimian sacred. However, there is also an implicitly critical allusion to the intellectualist view of spirits and other eschatological elements as 'projections'. He attributes the full development of the idea of death as release from worldly concerns to the 'higher' civilizations, i.e. those where there is a clear religious environment separate from the domestic and political environments, though the germ of such ideas can also be found earlier in the course of religious evolution.

Hertz also spends some time putting death ritual into the general ritual context. As we have seen, death may constitute a sort of initiation into the world of the ancestors, or, through reincarnation, back into the human world. Conversely, initiation may involve the spiritual death and rebirth of the initiand, especially where a male child must leave the world of women and enter that of men. Elkin (1961: 231) associates Australian initiation with the rite introducing the dead to its spirit home, which makes the soul ready for reincarnation: in both cases, the same ritual process is involved.[2] Birth may be represented as death in reverse, involving the pollution of mother, child and father, and the necessity of giving birth away from the usual living quarters. 'The body of the new-born child is no less sacred than the corpse' (Hertz *ibid*.: 81). Hertz invokes the use of the veil by both bride and widow to set them apart from society. Marriage, like death, may certainly involve one's violent separation, especially if one is female, from one's nearest relatives. Marriage by capture is an especially dramatic demonstration of the violence of separation and reintegration elsewhere. As regards death, this may centre on the widow — bereaved but also suddenly unwed — her conjugal family wanting her to join the pyre and thus stay with her husband or to remarry into their family or clan, her natal family wanting her to return home. In his comparison with other rituals, Hertz puts the stress on the analogies between them as well as their structural resemblances: they all involve changes of status, accompanied by 'necessary but dangerous forces' (*ibid*.). This is distinct from the more modern point that different rites tend to implicate each other, for example the proper redistribution at death of the patrilineal bones and uterine flesh that had gone together to make up the person in life. The Durkheimians certainly tended to think of all life as ritualized, in the sense that everything has a socially derived meaning and purpose, but rituals themselves were occasional events, opportunities to make society's values felt. As Humphreys points out (1981: 6), it is only comparatively recently that anthropologists have begun to move away from seeing ritual as necessarily ephemeral and towards seeing it — in certain societies at any rate, including many in Southeast Asia — as continuous or at least of long duration. Often too, the neat divisions the anthropologist makes are felt less by the people themselves, as each 'ritual' runs into the next.

What of the West? For us, says Hertz, 'the successive stages of our social life are weakly marked and constantly allow the continuous thread of the individual life to be discerned' (1960: 81; cf. Mauss's much later essay on the person, 1938). Elsewhere, existence is divided up into discrete phases, each involving a different 'social class' (i.e. status). 'To the social conscious-ness, death is only a particular instance of a general phenomenon' (*ibid.*: 81). One of these phases is that between death and the final rite, which is neces-sary to enable society to adjust to its loss and to the new status it has to recog-nize. This, one might argue, is an explanation in terms of a generalized psychology rather than of sociology (cf. Evans-Pritchard 1960). Indeed, an appeal even to individual psychology is sometimes found, as where Hertz talks of the dead persisting in the mind as an image, which may generate further disturbance in the form of 'frequent hallucinations and dreams' (Hertz 1960: 150 n. 319). Of course, the content of dreams may also be culturally deter-mined. The idea of Purgatory is similarly transitional, though it applies only to some dead and is bound up with their need to rid themselves of sin before going to Heaven. Similarly, vendetta pacifies the soul of the murdered person, without which he cannot settle down in his final resting place. The problem is that society cannot accept disintegration and reintegration all at once. Also, the connection between the rite centered on the body and the belief concern-ing the soul comes from the fact that collective thought is primarily concrete and does not conceive of spiritual essences easily (cf. below). It also drama-tizes the situation for the society: when the flesh has rotted, the dead resem-ble all the other ancestors. This hypothesis is supported by the exclusion of some categories, for example children, from the second rite. Where children are not a part of society, their deaths produce no social consequences. They are easily reincarnated: the Ngaju, Papuans, etc., place dead children in trees, which is where men come from and must return to. The deaths of children merely represent false starts, and therefore they have not been separated from the world of the spirits. 'Naturally, the individual sorrow of the parents may be very keen; but the social reaction, the obligation to mourn, is lacking' (Hertz 1960: 152 n. 332). This explanation is at least as plausible as Pina-Cabral's alternative suggestion, that the practice represents a reversal of birth (1986: 114, following Schutte 1980: 262). There may, of course, be a general parallel between death and birth, or between death and initiation, even for routine deaths. In modern societies, it cannot be said that this distinction between adults and children really prevails: children have souls, are individu-als, just as much as adults, and therefore receive full funerals.

Others who are 'outside' society may also receive less or no attention at death. One example is Hindu ascetics, whose asceticism depends on their being socially dead — they undergo their own death ritual on becoming ascetics. Another is the very elderly in some Australian and Melanesian soci-eties, who have ceased to have a social role through their great age and are therefore already classified with the dead (cf. Rivers 1926: 40ff.). For the inauspicious dead, on the other hand, there is no end to the process of death, and their souls wander the earth for ever or go to a special place, never being reincarnated. Their bodies are disposed of, permanently, as soon as possible, and their bones are not put with those of the normal dead; mourning may be prohibited. This lack of ritual action, for Hertz, is a sign not of the weakness of emotion that such incidents generate, but on the contrary of its 'extreme intensity and suddenness' (1960: 85). Sometimes, as with the Aztecs, the inauspicious dead may form an elect, whose death is another occasion of joy. Ritual action is futile in the case of inauspicious deaths: 'reunion being impossible, delay is senseless' (*ibid*.: 86). Ordinary deaths, by contrast, are just 'a temporary exclusion of the individual from human society', and mourning is 'the necessary participation of the living in the mortuary state of their relative, [which] lasts as long as this state itself' (*ibid*.). Hertz's concern with the social aspects leads him to concentrate more on the living than on the body or the soul, as is shown in his final words (*ibid*.):

> In the final analysis, death as a social phenomenon consists in a dual and painful process of mental disintegration and synthesis. It is only when this process is completed that society, its peace recovered, can triumph over death.

THE SIGNIFICANCE OF HERTZ'S THESIS

As has already been pointed out (Ch. 2), the importance of the Durkheimians lies partly in their substitution of a sociological explanation of religion and ritual for the more psychological, intellectualist explanations that had prevailed until then. This is especially true of death ritual and beliefs, which, in their various ways, Spencer, Tylor, Lubbock etc. had placed at the root of all religion. This approach was essentially evolutionist. For Lubbock, eschatology arose out of dream experiences. For Tylor, primitive religion developed out of ancestor worship, which itself arose in the practice of making offerings to the corpse. Any eschatology depended on the all-important dichotomy between body and soul, and it was contemplation of the latter that led to beliefs in ghosts and spirits.[3]

The acceptance of these evolutionary theories was compromised because of the frequent co-occurrence of these supposed stages at the same time in the same society. For instance, the significance of dreams and of the body-soul dichotomy often exist together as a single complex of beliefs. There was also criticism because the connection between ancestor cults and the family that these theories presupposed conflicted with the postulated absence of the family from early society due to primitive promiscuity. This was the standard view until Westermarck (1891) rejected the argument concerning an original promiscuity in favour of a hypothesis of the universality of the institution of marriage. As a consequence, Robertson-Smith and Frazer preferred to stress totemism as the first stage of religion, thinking that this corresponded better with the notion of an initial stage of primitive promiscuity. Although certainly not an advocate of the latter, Durkheim retained the priority given to totemism, largely because it was, *inter alia*, an Australian phenomenon, like the clan system with which it could more readily be linked (the *Année* regularly saw the Australians as the most primitive of all societies). He placed ancestor worship firmly within later stages of civilization, such as China, Egypt, Greece and Rome, ignoring its presence in Africa, India and even Australia, as well as the fact that ancestor cults are regularly associated with descent groups. Moreover, ancestors and totems frequently interact in myth, so they cannot be restricted to separate stages of 'civilization'.

Thus even the Durkheimians had their evolutionary prejudices, and a modern anthropologist would find the debate futile. What really distinguishes the intellectualists from the Durkheimians was their different view of the interrelationship between belief and ritual, and of where the ultimate source of both was to be sought. Here death was primary, or at least archetypal, for both schools. For the intellectualists, eschatology was a product of man's contemplation of the horror of death, and the afterworld was an exact duplicate, an intellectual 'projection', of life in this world. Such beliefs led to the development of ritual actions of an essentially instrumental kind, in accordance with the view of magic as false science. The uncollectivized mind of man, together with his emotional and therefore individual reaction to the horror of death, was at the root of it all. The Durkheimians, however, stressed instead the collectivized society. Death creates a social disturbance, not just, or even primarily, an individual one, a disturbance which must be resolved through ritual action. Indeed, Durkheim even argued (1915: 399, 401) that the loss of one of its members through death actually brings a community together. The significance of the soul is not reduced, but its status as a special sort of spirit certainly is. What is significant about it is the force it contains, which is a property society endows it with (cf. pp. 30–6): 'a man feels that he has a soul, and consequently a force, because he is a social being' (Durkheim *ibid.*: 366); the soul is 'nothing other than the totemic principle incarnate in each individual' (*ibid.*: 248), i.e. '*mana* individualized' (*ibid.*: 264).

As regards the corpse, ritual action is less instrumental than confirmatory, its instrumentality residing in the opportunity it presents for society to demonstrate its own values to its members. This representation is no less a demonstration of belief, and eschatological ideas concerning the afterlife are presented both as reasons (to the people; they can only be rationalizations to the anthropologist) and as social ideals; they are not the result of abstract thought. Similarly, emotions are controlled, even generated, by the ritual; they do not in any way govern it, but even if formally represented are both stereotyped and obligatory. In this view, society regularly uses ritual to promote belief, whereas for the intellectualists, speculative beliefs based on individual observation led historically to collective ritual action, a view which makes the society little more than the sum of its parts. With the Durkheimians, it is society that is reified, not emotion, and the search for causal explanations receives far less emphasis than the demonstration of structural coherence.

This background explains Hertz's polemic against the supposition that horror of the corpse is the source of death ritual, and against the significance of the soul as the prototype of other spiritual beings. The soul is a very real part of the eschatology, but it is nonetheless a vague concept. Thierry is surely right in finding Hertz's whole treatment of the soul problematic (1979: 14). On the one hand, it is a necessary element in his argument, being an important part of what survives of the deceased in virtually all representations of death. On the other hand, there is a persistent tendency to see souls as vague entities when compared to mystical forces that have no sort of corporeal dimension, however evanescent. Evans-Pritchard (1960: 23) has pointed out the falsity of Hertz's denial to so-called 'primitive peoples' of the ability to conceptualize spiritual beings independently of something tangible (cf. Hertz 1960: 83). Hertz certainly tends to deemphasize the conceptualization of the soul among the Ngaju (e.g. *ibid.*: 34), denying at one point (118 n. 26) that horror of the corpse is related to fear of a soul rather than to mystical influence. What Hertz means is that it is through the body, and the ritual actions carried out upon it, that society impresses belief in the soul upon its members. This accords with the sociological explanation that society, not the individual's psychological needs, is the source of all belief, including belief in souls. However, spirits do enter the argument when Hertz wants to go further and offer an alternative to the intellectualist theory of horror of the corpse as the basis for beliefs concerning death. It is not horror, says Hertz, but pollution and other magico-religious forces released by death and personified as evil spirits which demand such careful treatment of the corpse. One purpose of the second rite is to signal the end of this pollution. Again, a personal reaction is replaced by a socially derived belief, though vague forces have to be introduced to provide the mechanism if the idea of a soul is not to be accorded undue importance in accounting for the ritual.

In reality, the soul may be more important than either the corpse or the mourners. Kligman says explicitly (1988: 151): 'The manipulation of the soul is to the understanding of death in Romania as that of the corpse is to an understanding of death in Borneo and Indonesia.' Cremation receives no favour here because it is thought to destroy the soul as well as the body. This is linked to belief in Purgatory as the initial destination of many after death (despite the offical status of the Orthodox Church, even under Ceauşescu, this part of northern Romania had been a Catholic part of the Austro-Hungarian Empire). The newly dead receive the prayers not only of the living but also of those have died previously, partly to help them on their journey to heaven, but also because the latter form a channel of communication between the living and the dead generally (*ibid*.: 158–60, 165). The corpse, by contrast, though washed and treated with respect (*ibid*.: 171), is clearly not the main focus of ritual action here compared to the laments with which the living communicate with the dead (*ibid*.: 154ff.). Similarly, among the Bassar of Togo, the soul becomes the very agent whereby the deceased's body is transferred to the other world (Pawlik 1990: 84).

Ultimately, it is a question of the significance of the soul rather than its absolute neglect by Hertz. Goody (1962: 26–7) makes the important point that for Hertz the fundamental problem was how society ensured its own continuity in the face of the impermanence of its members. This explains the universality of the body-soul dichotomy: if the former perishes, something must take its place and survive for this resolution to be possible. Ancestor cults and reincarnation both ensure that the deceased are not lost but remain a part of society. Reincarnation itself, of course, links death firmly to birth, while endocannibalism is also about preservation, despite, or through, destruction. Thus the body-soul dichotomy does not promote the hopes of the bereaved or even the development of an eschatology so much as make social survival possible. The true horror of death is the risk of social decay, not personal loss.

The Durkheimian view of ritual as simply the occasion for society to stress its own values has been questioned by those who prefer to see ritual as actually creating society rather than owing its existence to it (e.g. Bloch and Parry 1982: 6). There is an epistemological difference here, in that this creation is real for the society itself and is not a partly concealed mechanism, as ritual action largely was for the Durkheimians, at least as regards its social function. The earlier perspective remains fruitful for other modern anthropologists, such as Hockey (1990: 28, 35), who regards the very attenuated death ritual of the modern West as actually deepening the sense of loss of the bereaved. In this sense, death ritual corresponds with, even magnifies, the lack of meaning death now has in the West, so that the perspective of ritual as society imposing its own values on its members, even negatively, seems at first sight to be upheld. To believe this, however, one would also have to believe that it is the purpose of the rite to deepen this sense of loss. Hockey certainly does not suggest this, and indeed she obviously regards this circumstance as a by-product of the ritual, not as its goal. In the modern West, death ritual fails to satisfy either the survivors or society, partly because of fundamental changes in the relationship of the individual to society and partly because of scepticism about the value of any ritual in a rational world. As a result it has become perfunctory, which only reinforces this dissatisfaction. For Hockey, the crisis of the West is at least partly ritual.

Much of what Hertz says was anticipated by other Durkheimians. Hubert (1901: 192) mentioned the separation of the bereaved through, for example, veiling among Jews. Durkheim (1903: 363–4) set forth the view that fear associated with the dead proceeds from religious impurity to fear of the soul, not vice versa. This affects everything associated with the dead — relatives, house, possessions, but above all the widow — hence the separation that we call mourning. The fear of spirits is secondary, supporting the separation, but it is not its basis. Mauss, similarly, contended (1907a: 224) that the attitude to the dead entails more than a need to entertain the corpse through fear, it also involves 'adoration and propitiation'. These statements are all clearly anti-intellectualist in their tenor. The major early criticism from within this circle came from Lévy-Bruhl (1922: 194–5), who pointed out that *pace* Hertz, many societies keep contact with the dead rather than impose a definite separation. Separation is mainly a feature of the initial rites, though even the recent dead may well remain in contact with the living. The dead are fully a part of most societies. Nonetheless, he was prepared to use the elements of Hertz's model in his own writings on death (e.g. 1926 [1912]: 317, 319, 321). In fact, there is no necessary conflict. Hertz himself was keen to distinguish secondary rites from cults of the dead, which were presumably what Lévy-Bruhl had in mind,[4] and he also made reference to the reunion of living and dead through reincarnation.

Hertz himself realized that not all the ideas he presents in his essay would be found consistently everywhere, and he even suggests that they may be restricted to particular ethnographic areas or types of society. His, however, is the familiar Durkheimian technique of studying a topic in its most highly developed, one might say its most extreme form, and in concentrating on one particular ethnographic area, Borneo. This is what Mauss did with the gift and the Maori, what Durkheim did with religion and the Australians, what Hubert and Mauss did with sacrifice, Judaism and Hindu India, and what Hertz himself was to begin to do with sin and the Polynesians. In this sense, his essay on right and left was an exception, being much more wide-ranging, as is the theme itself compared with second burial. But the essay on death drew equally on a great deal of ethnographic material for comparative purposes, from all continents. In this way, Hertz was able to distinguish what Evans-Pritchard (1960: 12) has called 'the general from the particular and the social fact from its cultural form': that is to say, secondary disposals have a common function or structural position, despite the different ways in which they are represented in specific societies. Evans-Pritchard also maintains that the concentration on particular ethnographic areas enabled the Durkheimians to avoid the trap of wrenching ethnographic facts from all over the world and divorcing them from their context before using them to build their models of the chosen ethnographic theme. Conversely, Harrisson (1962) pours scorn on the idea that Hertz succeeded in this in the death essay.

This trap is particularly, perhaps, associated with Frazer nowadays, though he was not the only culprit. It also tended to be associated with psychological rather than with truly sociological explanations, such as Westermarck's view that incest taboos were the product of a common upbringing, or Tylor's and Frazer's account of death ritual as stemming ultimately from horror of the corpse. In addition, not only was the evidence fragmented, so, frequently, was the interpretation, in that particular facts were emphasized at the expense of others that were no less essential. Hertz's treatment of the soul, the body and the bereaved in tandem is an excellent example of an opposite tendency which sees the facts as interrelated and views the evidence as a whole. Indeed, as Evans-Pritchard also points out, this was the main task the Durkheimians set themselves; much less attention was given to origins or causal explanations. The difficulties of finding such explanations have, of course, become notorious in anthropology, to such an extent that one quite regularly encounters the opinion that the search for them belongs properly to other disciplines, such as philosophy or psychology. The Durkheimians may unwittingly have reflected this in their general distrust of causal explanations. Certainly, most of their attempts to introduce such explanations seem to refer ultimately to a function of psychological need or at least to social psychology, despite their parallel disinclination to recognize the validity of psychological phenomena as explanations for sociological facts. It is this disinclination that has been mostly influential, of course, but there have been discordant voices, for example Morin (1970: 37), who, while accepting Hertz's view of the social necessity of mourners participating in the state of the deceased, also talks about 'a permanent system of obsessions and anxieties', leading to what he calls a specific 'economy of death' in the form of spending on tombs etc.

The charge of resorting ultimately to some form of psychological reductionism applies to Hertz in this essay no less than to works by other members of the *Année*, as there has already been occasion to remark.

Otherwise, explanations are located solely in the specific ethnographic tradition being discussed, that tradition itself being seen as a totality. Of course, it is the ideas or 'sentiments' of such traditions that compel human action, ideas which have a moral compulsion and which constitute the society's values. This divorces phenomena such as ideas about death as a process from the biological fact of death, which is merely the occasion for their expression. This is especially pertinent in view of Hertz's association between representations of the afterlife and the ideal image a society has of itself, although this does not exhaust what the afterlife may consist of: many religious traditions have hells too.

The technique of studying ethnological phenomena in terms of their interrelationships and in respect of how they compose a whole was also how the Durkheimians chose to handle cross-cultural comparison. The search for common origins, whether evolutionary or diffusionist, was regarded just as dubiously as the search for causal explanations, unless these took society itself into account. In these senses, the new sociology was proto-structuralist, and the technique of comparing societies as wholes is still explicitly followed in Paris by many who see themselves as successors to the *Année*. Only when negative instances reared their ugly heads did Hertz invoke a sort of evolutionism, arguing that the situation once obtained but did so no longer. Durkheim and Mauss also resorted to this tactic and were even more positively evolutionist on occasion, as in their joint essay on primitive classification of 1903 or in Mauss's late essay on the person (1938).

As Bloch and Parry point out (1982: 6; also previous section), a more modern anthropologist would prefer to see society being re-created through death ritual rather than simply responding to the damage the death had caused it. This accords with their own stress on expressions of fertility in death rituals, something which Hertz practically ignores, despite his discussion of reincarnation. De Coppet makes a similar point (1981: 176), which Humphreys expands on by saying (1981: 9–10):

> It is an obvious ethnocentric mistake to assume that the behaviour
> evoked by death is to be seen solely as a reaction to the disruptions of
> social and emotional equilibrium caused by a particular decease. Death
> provides occasions and materials for a symbolic discourse on life....

Even of rural Romania under Ceauşescu, Kligman was able to say (1988: 151, after Ariès) that 'death and life are dialectically related', not dichotomized, as in modern thought. The same can be said of the Bassar of Togo (Pawlik 1990: 79–80). Mines remarks, of the approach advocated by Bloch and Parry: 'Theirs is a functionalism that does not simply rationalize funeral practices, but rather invites an exploration of the creative or reproductive processes triggered by death' (1989: 112). Her preference — in accordance with the approach of the Chicago school of McKim Marriott — is for a transactional analysis of death, which sees the deceased as a product of the 'transactions' and other sorts of relationship that he or she had been engaged in in life. Death ritual thus also provides an opportunity for relationships to be adjusted (*ibid.*: 118), a theme often explored elsewhere from different theoretical points of view (e.g. Huntington 1973: 83 on the Bara of Madagascar; see further below). One variation here is a concern with the problem of redistributing property after a person's death (e.g. Goody 1962, Weiner 1980, Moore 1981). Some of these examples might seem to signal anthropological obsessions with property and exchange at the expense of eschatology and death ritual *per se*. However, the idea that a person is the product of his relationships has also emerged strongly from the literature on New Guinea in recent years (for example, Strathern 1988, on Melanesia), an idea that certainly has implications for that person's fragmentation at death. Many of these works (Goody's explicitly, 1962: 37) seek to establish a unified view which brings together the belief and ritual that had been pulled in different directions to some extent by the polemics between the Durkheimians and the intellectualists.

The ending of pollution and the healing of a breach in the society is thus only one of the things achieved, or signalled, by this ritual process. Most particularly, of course, a change of status is involved. Hertz's comparisons of death ritual with weddings and initiations are designed to show how this is just one example of something very general. Moreover, such transitions are not instantaneous but processual, the main part of the process involving not only a social disturbance but ritual danger.

This is, of course, more or less the general thesis concerning the nature of ritual propounded by one of Hertz's contemporaries outside the *Année*, Arnold van Gennep, in *Les rites de passage* (1909; also translated in 1960). Indeed, the parallel was acknowledged, for van Gennep was one of the first commentators on Hertz's work on death. Van Gennep's own studies of ritual had showed him that death rituals stand out to some extent for the greater emphasis they tend to put on rites of transition, a main focus of Hertz's essay too. In fact, his own account even of death rites was more general, not being restricted to secondary disposals, and a number of important supplementary points are made, as well as criticisms. During the transition period, the corpse may be represented by something tangible, e.g. a doll, as among the Ostyak. Souls and bodies may be multiple, a point Hertz barely touched upon. It seems that van Gennep had less trouble than Hertz in accepting the idea of a soul as something intangible, since he says that both it and 'the contagion of death' must be guarded against (1960: 193). He also rejects Hertz's thesis that the flesh of the corpse is thought of, save exceptionally, as making up a new body for the deceased in the next world: the destruction of the corpse simply achieves the separation of the various bodies and souls. As we have seen, Hertz may have been strongly influenced by the work of his colleagues Hubert and Mauss on sacrifice here. Certainly van Gennep's view has a more modern ring, except that it is just as likely to be the separation of flesh and bone that figures in present-day interpretations. Van Gennep's other main criticism of Hertz is that he failed to recognize that mourning does not always end with the supposed acceptance of the deceased in the land of the dead (1960: 147 & n. 2). Against this, we have Hertz's statement (1960: 39–40) that the end of mourning does not always coincide with the second rite, which indeed is largely concerned with pressing the deceased's acceptance on the ancestors. Nonetheless, it is clearly what Hertz would like to have believed, and it is one of the places where we find him invoking the weak argument of inconvenience to explain the exceptions he is forced to acknowledge. In his general conclusion, van Gennep places Hertz among the many who had already pointed out general similiarities between rituals of various sorts, but he singles him out as the only one so far to see an overall structural resemblance focussing on the stage of transition between different statuses.

Chiva (especially 1986: 226–7) has argued that the parallels between these two figures consist basically of their abandonment of the search for causes in favour of formal analysis, their insistence on the social foundations of ritual action, and their recognition of the dynamic aspect in ritual – the 'rite of passage' idea – which before had simply been treated as static. He adds to this a stress on the necessary 'discontinuity' of both society and individual lives, which led van Gennep to the notion of ritual as 'passage' (ibid.: 227) but can also be found, very prominently, in Hertz's account of death ritual. Pace Chiva (1987: 16), this is not really so evident in Hertz's account of St Besse, which is less an account of a ritual than of the differentiation of tradition. If 'discontinuity' means anything here, it refers to the discontinuity of the versions of a particular tradition held by different groups in the same society (see below, Ch. 7). Nonetheless, he is surely right in seeing in this idea and in the consequent notions of 'sequential analysis' and 'transformation' early examples of 'a structuralist type of analysis allowing access to the unconscious categories at work in collective beliefs and practices' (ibid.: 17).

Other innovations wrought by Hertz in his death article are perhaps more specifically tied to his reliance on one ethnographic area, Borneo, in making his case. Bloch and Parry (1982: 3) mention the relative absence of the themes of fertility and sexuality in his work on death when compared with earlier studies by Frazer and Bachofen, the emphasis being instead on what they call 'the characteristic South-East Asian contrast between the

bones and the flesh'. Like the slightly earlier joint book by Huntington and
Metcalf (1979), that edited by Bloch and Parry seeks to merge the symbolic
approach of Frazer with the sociological approach of Hertz. However, the
editors feel (1982: 5-6) that Huntington and Metcalf had emphasised the
ritual treatment of the corpse and survivors and related beliefs about the soul
at the expense of Hertz's equal concentration on the way that society uses
ritual to control, even shape emotions in order to control the individuals that
compose it. Metcalf and Huntington have since defended their position
(1991: 3-4) on the grounds that for Durkheim, 'actions are prescribed, not
emotions', charging in their turn that Bloch and Parry's partly Marxist but
essentially functionalist argument is simply circular. Ritual shapes the emotions which, acting collectively, are supposed to have brought the society
together to begin with. Damon's introduction (1989) to a recent collection
on mortuary rituals in Melanesia neatly brings out the differences between
these two approaches, the one remaining explicitly close to Hertz, the other
seeking to supplement it in a direction which is many ways materialist:

> ... Bloch and Parry are more concerned with how mortuary rituals legit-
> imize the social order than with the rituals' form or grammar. And they
> think Hertz was more concerned with the sociology of emotion, with
> how the biological individual is kept in society, than with the struc-
> turalist reading that Huntington and Metcalf provide. Bloch and Parry
> deal with what gives rise to complex mortuary rites, not with the actual
> rites themselves. (Damon 1989: 16)

Against Bloch and Parry, one can argue that Hertz's text *is* structuralist
in the general sense of the term, at least as regards the parallelism in what
happens to the corpse, the soul and the survivors. Their further stress, also
highlighted by Damon (*ibid.*: 17), on the link between the degree of hierarchy in the society and the elaborateness of its death rituals, can also be found
in Hertz, but only in embryonic form. For Hertz, it is the importance of the
deceased in life rather than the nature of society as such that dictates the
elaborateness of the mortuary rite. Damon points out that Bloch and Parry
have sought to take this further, not simply by substituting the principle of
hierarchy for Hertz's 'great men', but in arguing that in controlling death
ritual, those with authority in the society are able to claim that it is they who
are responsible for the continuity, even the generation, of life. It is in incorporating reproduction and power into their model that Bloch and Parry can
be regarded as combining Marxism with Leach's brand of functionalism, as
Metcalf and Huntington are hinting.

Hertz's treatment of the contrast between the time-bound existence of
the individual and the permanence of the social order is explicitly invoked
by Bloch in his own contribution to the volume he edited with Parry (1982:

224; also Bloch and Parry 1982: 11), but the other contributors make only fleeting references to his work, if at all. The idea that society survives the disappearance of its members was not, of course, Hertz's invention. Something similar has been at the heart of legal theories of the corporation for centuries, and as such it has become part of the general sociological inventory of concepts. What Hertz did was to locate this phenomenon sociologically in the context of the ritual process with which it is most intimately associated, namely death ritual.

LATER DEVELOPMENTS

The general sociological direction of Hertz's work has proved less open to objection on ethnographic grounds than more particular matters such as the incidence of secondary burials or the duration of mourning. It is such matters as these that most of the renewed discussion of his essay has been concerned with. One of the earliest commentaries following its translation in 1960 was Harrisson's very patronizing article 'Borneo Death' (1962, especially pp. 29-41), which balanced the merits and demerits of Hertz's work and a diffusionist effort by Quaritch Wales (1959) against a long work by Waldemar Stöhr entitled 'Das Totenritual der Dajak' (1959). Stöhr comes off best in Harrisson's diatribes against all and sundry, though not totally unscathed. Hertz's work is declared to be 'juvenile' if also pioneering, and its recent reappearance in translation is called 'a surprise resurrection' (1962: 28-9). In Harrisson's view, Hertz had generalized too freely from a flawed interpretation of Ngaju ethnography, which was itself faulty at the time he wrote. *Pace* Hertz, burials in the forest are in fact rare and not temporary where they do occur but in reality the permanent disposal of the inauspicious dead or of strangers. Harrisson also denies that Bornean societies generally place dead children in trees or that they are indifferent to the fate of their souls. Much of Harrisson's contemptuousness here seems to stem from the view that Hertz denied feelings of loss to Ngaju parents in such cases, despite the latter's specific disclaimer (1960: 152 n. 332). The only source of Hertz's that refers unambiguously to the matter also mentions that shamans, who are very highly regarded, receive the same treatment. Whether this really invalidates Hertz's point is questionable, since however important shamans may be they, like children, are generally regarded as marginal and may be able to go straight to the land of the dead with little or no special ritual action. In any case, according to Hertz the return of children to trees is only exceptional, enabling them to be reincarnated much sooner (*ibid.*: 84).[5]

The question of inauspicious deaths has been taken up by de Coppet (1970: 760-1), who argues that among the 'Are'are, the Hertzian equation between death and sacrifice applies as much to murder as to other sorts of death. That is, murder is a different 'modality' of death which involves the taking of life by men rather than by ancestors, and although it is therefore an infringement of the latters' privileges, it is not inauspicious. The question of what counts as an auspicious or inauspicious death leads to a consideration of the cause of death, which is especially significant where the phenomenon of natural death is not recognized. Elkin points out how in Australia, it is the first ritual that concerns itself with this question (1961: 231), which is also true of some central Indian peoples (e.g. the Munda; Topno 1955: 718). The importance of the first rite over the second in a more general sense is also mentioned by Perrin, concerning his work among the Guajiro of Colombia and Venezuela (1979), though the remains are most dangerous in the second rite, which involves exhumation and reburial. This rather contradicts the idea we draw from Hertz that the danger decreases as the ritual process advances. In accordance with Hertz, the second rite here is a rite of forgetting, the dead eventually becoming anonymous ancestors, their remains being united with those of ancestors who have been dead for longer. *Pace* Hertz, however, their initiation as such takes place after the second rite, not before it. Here, death is not caused by infractions or human enemies but by supernatural beings.

Another study (Miles 1965) which appeared soon after Hertz's article was translated arose out of fieldwork among the Ngaju themselves, its ethnographic centrepiece. Miles focuses on Hertz's dismissal (1960: 31) of Wilkin's argument that the delay in the immediate disposal of the corpse is primarily due to the need to accumulate sufficient wealth to be able to carry out what is ideally a very elaborate rite. Hertz accepts this argument as a secondary variable but says that it is not sufficient as an explanation in itself: even if financially possible, a second rite could not be held until the bones were dry. Miles regards Hertz's interpretation of Ngaju death rites as basically sound (1965: 166), but he also found the *tiwah* or secondary rite to be 'a ceremony of conspicuous consumption' (*ibid*.: 168). From his case studies, he discovered much variation in practice regarding the incidence of secondary rites, which were sometimes held immediately after the funeral, sometimes delayed for a number of years, and sometimes never took place at all. In fact, the majority of ancestors in his sample had never received a second rite of disposal, due largely to lack of resources. There was also variation as to the complexity of the rites, their length, how many priests were used, and which sort of animal was sacrificed. Although the full rite involved disinterrment, even this was not invariably carried out, a flag simply being planted on the grave instead. Miles established two further points contradicting Hertz's thesis. One was that the cultural preference among the Ngaju was to hold the secondary rite as soon as possible after the death, without any delay. The other was that the responsibility for holding it rested not with the entire community but with the nearest relatives, starting with the surviving spouse and children. This does not in itself conflict with the idea of the ritual being a social obligation but simply narrows the responsibility for the actual holding of the rite. A further case study indicated that those nominally responsible often avoided holding a rite not so much because of poverty but to avoid an outlay of wealth they had already accumulated. For Miles, these cases weaken Hertz's idea of a 'collective consciousness' lasting any considerable length of time after a death. In these two cases, the gaps between the deaths and the time of writing were respectively 12 and 28 years, and still there was no prospect of any secondary rite being carried out.

Related arguments have been produced for another group in Borneo, the Berawan (Metcalf 1981). Metcalf starts with the observation that in many parts of the world rites are often compressed down from their ideal form for reasons of expense or convenience, and he points out that Hertz neglects this aspect in his study, except for supposed cases of later development or foreign influence. The alternative is to hold collective rites periodically for all who had died in the interim, as among the Ma'anyan of southern Borneo. The Berawan consider the full set of funeral rites to be ideal but usually only celebrate them for selected individuals, most having to make do with a reduced version. There has been a reduction in the number of secondary rites held in modern times, from an estimated rate of over one a year for all four Berawan communities to three in the ten-year period preceding the completion of Metcalf's field research in 1975. The reason for this is not expense, since the amount spent on funerals is generally large and always has been. The choice is to hold an immediate but expensive funeral and no secondary rite, or to hold a cheap funeral followed by an only slightly more expensive secondary rite later. Prestige may dictate choice of the former as readily as the latter. Nor do large-scale conversions to Christianity seem to have had any influence on the situation.

The key seems to lie in the character of the secondary rite, called *nulang* by Berawan, which is confirmatory rather than instrumental in nature — that is to say, the deceased reaches the land of the ancestors eventually, whether a *nulang* is held for him or not. Nor does he suffer particular disadvantages if one is not held for him, unlike the case with the Ngaju, where the comfort of the deceased in the afterworld depends on the expense of the secondary rite that is held for him (in the past, those accompanied by human sacrifice were the most favoured; see Miles 1965: 163). The main benefit of the *nulang* is that an occasional one brings together the living and the ancestors. There is no particular set of kin or affines who are invariably responsible for organizing and financing a *nulang*: if no one can be bothered, there is none. If one is held, however, it is necessarily a community-wide affair, less because of the rent in the social fabric caused by so many deaths as because labour and rice are required in abundance. There are economic grounds for the decline in the frequency of *nulang*, though they are not what one might expect. That is to say, the reason is not a shortage of resources but their suddenly greater availability. Given the ease of obtaining credit from Chinese merchants, many Berawan now have the wherewithal to hold an expensive funeral immediately after a death. A related circumstance is the availability of concrete, which though not cheap provides a quicker way of building mausoleums than the traditional wood, which had to be elaborately carved. In the past, this requirement itself imposed a delay of several months before the final rite could be held, and concrete is now being more widely used instead.

These changes have clearly been made possible by the impact of the modern economy on Berawan life, but they have still taken place within traditional Berawan eschatology. This suggests that while economics may influence the scale of a rite, its meaning and the symbolic devices that bring this about, however truncated, are not necessarily affected. For the Berawan, these aspects remain constant, whichever ritual process is chosen. Metcalf regards this as equally true of the Ngaju studied by Miles, who according to Metcalf (1981: 576-7) had mistakenly confused the *tiwah* with a second burial. Metcalf gives reasons for thinking that it is simply a celebratory rite, and Miles himself had admitted that secondary burial is not a necessary part of the overall process. In neither case, thinks Metcalf, do the economic arguments ultimately detract from Hertz's symbolic analysis, since the deceased reach the land of the dead regardless of which ritual is held for them. Essentially, he is arguing that economic arguments are irrelevant in these two cases because delays before final disposal are rejected in the one case and considered unnecessary in the other. Moreover, in the Berawan case the immediacy and abbreviation of the reduced rite go together ideologically: since the soul will not gain admittance to the land of the dead if the songs sung to accompany it there are sung too soon (presumably, that is, before the corpse has fully rotted), it is better to omit them altogether (Huntington and Metcalf 1979: 80). However, this denial tends to weaken Hertz's argument in other ways. At the very least, the necessity of a long period of social readjustment is not marked ritually. If the decay of the body acts on the soul and on the mourners at all, it would seem to do so without any ritual or other social action being necessary.

Metcalf concentrates more on the symbolic aspects of treatment of the corpse in other studies of Berawan eschatology (Huntington and Metcalf 1979: Ch. 3; Metcalf 1982). The Berawan regard death as unintended sacrifice, this being a way of communicating with the sacred through an object, the corpse, which has to be destroyed in this world before it can emerge in the next (1982: 95–6, 109). Although they store corpses in jars or coffins above ground rather than bury them, overall their eschatology corresponds very well to Hertz's account. One apparent difference is that the soul enters the land of the dead immediately upon death. Indeed, this entry actually constitutes death for the Berawan, and therefore it does not have to wait for the secondary rites to obtain entry. However, until it is finally settled in the land of the dead it wanders near the corpse and the mourners, being unable to re-enter the corpse because putrefaction has begun, but not yet entirely free of its earthly ties because that putrefaction is still in progress. Only after it is complete does the soul finally settle in the land of the dead. Metcalf also noted (1982: 84) that the Berawan are not indifferent to the sight and smell of the corpse, though this hardly detracts from Hertz's point that hygiene as we understand it is not at issue. *Pace* Hertz, the idea of pollution does not affect things, only persons, and this is a matter of closeness of relationship to the deceased, not contact with the corpse (cf. van Gennep, above). Indeed, the place of honour for the visitor is right in front of the coffin or jar. The surviving spouse and child are those most affected (1982: 149–50). The widow in particular may not bathe, wears filthy clothes, eats inferior food, and may not move from her cramped sitting position. This extreme discomfort has less to do with avoiding pollution than with avoiding the envy of the dead person: 'She must be made to suffer not because of the *corpse*, but because of the *vengeful soul* of the deceased' (Huntington and Metcalf 1979: 77, original emphasis). Thus it is not a sanction that is being applied so much as a prophylactic. Through her very discomfort the widow is being protected, not blamed: 'Only by sharing his [the deceased's] condition metaphorically can she avoid sharing it literally' (*ibid.*). This harks back to an original argument of Kruyt's (1906; not actually cited by Metcalf), which Mauss, in his review of the book, doubted because of its alleged utilitarianism (1910: 216).

Other Malayo-Polynesian examples cited by Huntington and Metcalf (1979: Ch. 3) tend to show that although the plan of death rituals may vary from the Hertzian model, sometimes quite considerably, there is still a concern with the proper fate of the soul or at least the assumption that it will eventually reach its final resting place. The variants are in any case usually consistent with other aspects of the particular culture. Thus the Mambai of Timor do not fear the corruption of the corpse because they see it as providing the black earth essential to all creation. Consequently, there is no secondary burial, just a final festival of the dead (cf. Traube 1980a, 1980b, 1986; see further below). A similar stress on fertility in death ritual is to be found among the Bassar of Togo (Pawlik 1990: 111). Among the Bara and Merina of Madagascar this means a lack of all but the most sketchy eschatology, though both groups carry out secondary burials. The problem posed for these two societies by the putrefaction of the corpse is not the wandering soul or evil mystical powers but the growing excess of order (represented *inter alia* by bone without flesh) over vitality and life. Death means less the disruption of society than the negation of vitality, and ritual action is concentrated on restoring that vitality for both the living and the dead. For the dead, transition to the world of the dead is no less a rebirth which must be accompanied by rituals stressing fertility. Perhaps the very sterility of the world of the dead ensures that no true eschatology is imaginable. The problem with Bloch's account of the Merina (1971) seems to be interpretative rather than factual, since despite his doubts concerning the relevance of Hertz's thesis, the ritual of *famadihana* is clearly a disinterment following decay of the corpse, which is itself followed by a permanent burial (*ibid.*: 145, 162). There are certainly some differences. Although the rite's main purpose is 'to make the dead happy', it is not thought to change the state of the soul, as Hertz's thesis suggests, nor is it linked with the end of mourning. Hertz's view that those who live together should be buried together is certainly validated here, since the Merina end up in large and elaborate tombs, one for each descent group (*ibid.*: 165–6, 169 n. 1). The rite also shows the living that the dead are irreversibly dead: 'While in the ceremonies considered by Hertz the dead are separated by being removed away from the living, in the case of the *famadihana* the living are separated from the dead by being removed from the dead' (*ibid.*: 169). The difference is hardly more than semantic on the evidence presented.

There is a wider degree of variation on the island of Roti, off Timor (Fox 1988a: 189ff.). As reported from elsewhere in this region there is no exhumation or second burial, and equally un-Hertzian are Rotinese statements that they like to keep in touch with the dead and do not regard the final rite as an absolute rite of separation.[6] Thus they neglect the corpse, once buried, but remember the spirit, the reverse of what Hertz's thesis predicts. However, aspects of their tradition point to a consciousness of secondary disposal that would bring them more within the orbit of that thesis. This comes partly from their mortuary chants, some of which allude to a past of secondary tree burial and special treatment of the bones. Another aspect, akin to a secondary rite, is to be found in the final mortuary ritual, which takes the form of a stone monument (*tutus*) being built around a large living tree. Trees form part of a range of botanic metaphors for life on Roti, and some ritual language pictures them as growing out of graves or buried bones (for which the stone is an obvious metaphor). In addition, the spirit of the dead is said to come back to the *tutus*. Fox does not mention the possibility of reincarnation, but all this symbolism is at least suggestive of the spirit being reunited with its bones and transformed back into life. True secondary burial is found on Roti, but mainly in the case of migrants to other parts of the island with which communication is not especially good and who had to be buried where they died but wished eventually to be interred in their home domain. However, Fox does not seem to think that this is merely a practical contingency, and it is not thought incompatible with other Rotinese mortuary rites. A more potent reason for the relative neglect of secondary burial here may be the circumstance that oratory and chants themselves have efficacy on Roti, and that non-verbal ritual action is accordingly uncommon.

DEATH AND DUAL SYMBOLIC CLASSIFICATION

A number of recent authors writing on death have taken inspiration from Hertz's article on right and left as well as or instead of that on death itself. One example is Hicks's work on the Tetum, of Timor. Here, we also return more explicitly to the theme of creation. This depends on the 'regulated' coming together of the sacred and the 'secular' (Hicks prefers this latter term to the more usual 'profane', 1976: 20-1), which normally have to be kept separate. Sickness involves witches, and death involves a corpse, both of which are 'anomalous' (following Mary Douglas) in being secular and sacred at the same time. Exorcism and death ritual are both designed to achieve this separation and to put everything back in its proper place, which as far as death ritual is concerned means the orderly transfer of the deceased to the next world (*ibid.*: 125). Although it is this aspect of Hertz's work, i.e. dual symbolic classification, that Hicks cites here rather than that on death, he makes use of the overall framework of the latter and he has some useful points of his own which bear upon it.

First, he points out that the Tetum are generally uncertain whether the soul has reached the land of the dead or when — hence the greater concern with the fate of the soul than with the state of the body or the mourners, and the greater amount of accompanying ritual. 'This uncertainty explains why each of the three stages for the soul is much longer than for the corpse and kin ...' (1976: 124). This suggests that although Hertz may be right regarding concern for the corpse, its complete actual decay need not always be important: either this is disregarded, or else it is assumed to have taken place, as must be the case if there is no exhumation and reburial as such. As Humphreys makes clear (1981: 5-6), bones are not the only possible metaphor for permanence, so that awareness of their physical presence is not always important. Not only can they be symbolized or replaced by other objects, but tombs or monuments may be found instead. That this is not only a matter of the West and its individuality, despite Humphreys' stress on this point (1981: 5-6), is shown by the example of the Merina of Madagascar, where tombs bring agnates together in death while removing the individuality they had in life (see Bloch 1971, 1982). However, Humphreys is right in pointing out that the dead do not always suffer this lack of differentiation (1981: 10). It is here particularly that the West stands out, allowing individuality to the dead as to the living, at least while the memory of the relatives is still alive, and even longer in the case of the famous. Apparent symbols of permanence may turn out to have a more instrumental purpose, as in parts of tribal India, where unmarked stones and megaliths are often thought to fix the soul in place. Examples include the Irula (Zvelebil 1988) and the Saora (Elwin 1955: 359).

The second point Hicks makes is that the Tetum lay the corpse out in the death house, which is usually situated on the edge of the village, between the village and the jungle, that is, between the secular and the sacred, and in any case 'at a place where they are symbolically united' (ibid.: 117). This accords with the 'anomalous' status of the corpse as something both sacred and secular at the same time. A similar point is made by du Boulay regarding Euboea, Greece, where the corpse links heaven and earth and is surrounded by sacred space (1982: 234; see further below).

A third point is the distinction between agnates and affines in respect of death ritual. The corpse is accompanied throughout by agnates, above all the closest kin, as mourners. They are the 'people of death', and so far there is nothing unusual in terms of Hertz's essay or of general ethnography. But it is the affines, both wife-givers and wife-takers, who conduct the ceremony generally. Nonetheless, they must keep away from the death house: they are the 'people who give life', and one guesses that too close an association with death might be dangerous or otherwise inappropriate for them (Hicks 1976: 115ff.). The association of wife-givers with origins, well-being and life itself is common in the anthropology of eastern Indonesia.

The use by Hicks of dual symbolic classification in respect of death ritual finds echoes elsewhere, sometimes in direct confrontation with the theme of death. Pina-Cabral declares: 'The life-death opposition is perhaps the single most important symbolic unit in the north-western peasant culture of Portugal' (1980: 1), a culture in which 'secondary disposal [of the bones] marks the complete separation of the deceased from the living' (ibid.: 5) in true Hertzian fashion. This separation is not always the purpose of the rite, as we have seen with the Rotinese in eastern Indonesia (previous section), who remain 'anxious to maintain contact with the departed spirit' (Fox 1988a: 189).

Other writers too have found Hertz's work on right and left, and on dual symbolic classification generally, just as fruitful in understanding death ritual as his work on secondary burial. This is often because the latter has to be modified. Among the Bara of Madagascar studied by Huntington (1973; Huntington and Metcalf 1979: Ch. 4), the key dichotomy generated by a person's death is not between body and soul – there is no true eschatology – but between flesh and bone. These are themselves metaphors for other oppositions, especially vitality and order, but also matrilateral and patrilateral relatives etc. The dichotomy between vitality and order is said to inform Bara concepts generally.[7] The individual is formed initially of the *ra* ('fertile blood') of the mother and the *rano-mamboatsy* (semen, literally 'water that arranges') of the father. Success in life depends on maintaining a balance between these values, as also between one's agnatic and affinal or uterine relationships. Death, like licentiousness but in a different way, upsets this order: 'dying, tombs, ancestors, father, social and moral order are all explicitly associated together by the Bara' (1973: 76).

There are three stages to the death ritual, which may be stretched out over many years: initial burial in a mountain tomb; the 'gathering'; and final reburial of the clean bones in a communal casket in the family tomb, also in the mountains. Of these rites, the gathering or *havoria*, a large but strictly optional display of wealth, is the most dangerous, because of the ever-present threat of witchcraft, and it corresponds with the most liminal and transitional phase of the whole ritual sequence. The process whereby the flesh decays and the corpse is progressively turned into pure bone is thought by Bara to signal an excess of order over vitality, which amounts to a denial of life. Thus each stage of the rite is characterized by a counterbalancing excess of vitality, taking the form (variously) of an abnormal degree of sexual licence, sexual imagery, drunkenness, dancing, cattle-riding, beef-eating (beef being an important life-giving substance), noise-making and general boisterousness. The purpose seems to be less to affirm life or restore it as to restore the balance that death has upset. Burial also uses sexual and birth images to introduce the deceased to the land of the dead, as Hertz would have predicted. This in itself requires the expression of vitality, just as the mother's fertility must be ordered by the father's semen in the case of a birth into this world. The reverse process is illustrated by the fact that the sacrifice which must be carried out to compensate for an act of incest must be of a bony cow; i.e. an illegitimate excess of vitality must be balanced by the offering of something symbolizing order.

Huntington draws up Needham-type lists to show these connected oppositions in Bara thought, but he argues that this thought regards some oppositions as complementary, others as antagonistic, in a progressive movement away from balance and towards the ultimate dichotomy between absolute order and absolute vitality (1973: 76–7). This transition is also one between life and death: the oppositions male-female, father-mother and semen-blood are necessary for life, whereas after death, death itself opposes birth, sterility fecundity, and tomb womb. The opposition bone-flesh partakes of both, being complementary in life, antagonistic in death. Here, Huntington introduces a level of dynamism into specifically Hertzian oppositions which was rarely seen up to this time in ritual analysis and which has only been matched subsequently by Dumont's followers (see pp. 85–6).[8] His representation is also, of course, firmly linked to the specific contexts of death ritual and the construction of the person, and is not generalized. But the ritual sequence can also be interpreted along the lines of Hertz's specific work on death: the initial burial is concerned with the treatment of the corpse; the gathering deals with the survivors and adjusts their relationships with one another (a common Africanist theme achieved here partly through witchcraft accusations); and the final burial is concerned with the bones and with their final interrment with those of the ancestors. As already mentioned, the Bara have little in the way of eschatology, and concern with the fate of the soul seems to be largely absent.

Traube also invokes both of Hertz's articles in her analysis of death ritual among the Mambai of East Timor (1980a; also 1980b, 1986). As she acknowledges, at one level her use of the right-left idea is simply that, as with Hertz's essay – and given that she is dealing with death ritual – she is focusing on the negative pole of life (1980a: 112 n. 3). However, other, more ethnographically specific dichotomies are also present. To begin with, there is the global division of Mambai ritual into the categories of 'white' ritual and 'black' ritual, which in broad terms are concerned respectively with agriculture and with death, and also with agnatic and affinal relations, although the two together form a balanced whole. This, rather as with the Bara, has an instrumental aspect, as expressed in the Mambai saying, 'when white is not enough, increase it with black; when black is not sufficient, augment it with white' (*ibid.*: 91).

Mambai thought concerning the origin of the person also entails dichotomy, being 'a variant on the widespread pattern wherein bone and flesh are created from paternal semen and maternal blood respectively' (*ibid.*: 98). Since maternal blood comes ultimately from affines, this also becomes a dichotomy between agnation and affinity in appropriate contexts, a dichotomy which further opposes permanence to the more temporary but also more highly ramifying nature of affinal alliance, in which blood appears as a key symbol. Bone is not used by Mambai as the countervailing symbol for permanence, and indeed neither secondary burial nor permanent tombs are used in funerary ritual. Nor does semen bring order, but instead fertility, since it is transformed directly into the mother's milk after intercourse (1980b: 310). Permanence is rather to be found in the metal swords, spears and breastplates that constitute the cult property of each agnatic group, having been transmitted agnatically to each generation from the founding ancestor. These objects are not exchanged in affinal alliance, though they may become dispersed through agnatic segmentation. Affinal exchange objects are less durable, consisting of livestock and of mats and baskets made of vegetable matter; mats are also used to wrap up corpses for burial. As with the Bara, order is static, enduring and stagnant and is opposed to life-giving, mobile vitality. 'Existence is based on a ritually secured balance of the two' (1980a: 100). Order is also represented by Father Heaven, who is the consort of but opposed to Mother Earth, whose repeatedly decaying body is the source of the soil through which all life is sustained.

Thus although death ritual refers to permanence, it does not use bone to express it. The overall ritual sequence consists of the burial, followed after an interval of indeterminate length by a final rite of separation that does not entail exhumation or secondary burial. This final rite is called *maeta*, one of the glosses of which is 'to dispatch the dead' (1986: 202, 203). It is held by a group of agnates for all their recently dead, but affines are also necessary because the dead themselves demand the continuity of affinal relationships. Moreover, since affines helped form the body in life they must help effect its separation into body and soul in death and ensure that the soul is properly embarked on its journey across the sea to the land of the dead. The spirits of the dead are associated with the horns of buffaloes given by wife-takers, which are placed on a bier called 'the ship of the dead' and finally thrown away into the bush when the spirits are thought to have reached the land of the dead. The latter event is accompanied by dancing and feasting off the flesh of the buffalo, which thus remains with the living as both symbol and provider of fertility. Despite being thrown away, the horns represent the permanence of the spirit and of agnation. The spirit escapes decay to live in the other world until it is reincarnated in a descendant of the same agnatic line, an event that is a subject for white ritual. To be reborn, however, it needs once again the fertility of flesh, derived from the affines. Life is thus the conjunction of flesh and spirit, while death is its separation not just as process but as existence. Moreover, although the central element in the white ritual cycle is a celebration of the blessings of life bestowed on the living by their ancestors, both the conjunction and the separation need the cooperation of affines (Traube 1980b: 299).

In Dumontian terms, therefore (see pp. 85–6), we might say that agnation and agnatic ancestry ultimately encompass affinity here. This can be contrasted with what Barraud (1990) has postulated for Tanebar-Evav, where one's wife-givers' ancestors are more important than one's own. There, wife-takers and wife-givers form a complementary whole, but as usual in such societies it is the latter who are normally superior, since they, in giving wives, give also life. Although marriage alliance is important, it is ultimately encompassed by the movement of the dead back to life:

> more than ensuring an arrangement of groups in the society, the marriage rules organize the relations of the living with the dead. The relationship to the dead thus encompasses intermarriage proper in extending it beyond the matter of marriage. Indeed, 'wife-givers' are more than wife-givers, they are ancestors, and marriage may be seen as an aspect of the relationship between the living and the dead. (Barraud 1990: 223)

In both cases, alliance is subsumed by ancestry during death ritual, but while in the former case ancestry is agnatic, in the latter it is ancestry through wife- (and therefore life-) givers.

Du Boulay's article on the Greek vampire also uses right and left in an analysis of what happens when death ritual goes wrong on the island of Euboea (1982). Death is conceived as the spilling of blood by Charos, the angel of death, the person dying when all the blood has run out of his or her body. After the body is washed, it is laid out and watched over in the period before the burial. The main concern, as elsewhere, is to see that the separation of body and soul that occurs on death is properly handled and that the soul reaches God without undue trouble. The problem is that this process does not take place all at once but only after the flesh has decayed (exhumation and secondary burial are practised in northern Greece). Ritual dangers lurk during the transitional period, one of which is the danger of creating a vampire. The ritual movements during the wake demand a particular lateral symbolism involving movement to the right (here, this means anti-clockwise movement). A spiral candle is set on the navel of the dead person to light his way to God which must be so constructed as to burn in a right-handed direction. The body is censed, and the singing of laments passed, round the body in the same direction (which is also the direction of the pattern in the dance). To reverse the direction is inauspicious. In this, it resembles reversal in any form of spouse exchange, even in subsequent generations: women, in leaving the natal home on marriage, take their natal blood with them, and this should not be returned before the elapse of three generations. As with correct motion around the corpse, the progression of women and blood through the community in this period is conceived of as right-handed.

But the proper direction would also be short-circuited by anything passing directly *over* the body. During the wake, the space above it is regarded as sacred, very probably, says du Boulay, because the body is felt to link heaven and earth, and perhaps also because this is the most direct route for the soul to go to heaven (though the soul also spends forty days on earth, being led round the sights of its life by an angel). To pass anything over the body would interrupt this connection and would certainly amount to an inauspicious reversal of direction. The soul and the blood would return, re-entering the body, reanimating it, and making it formidably dangerous: it would attack its own kin, suffocating them by trying to gain access to their blood through the nose. Vampires are thus much more to be feared than the merely sinful dead who cannot rot, and unlike them they return immediately and dramatically into the presence of the living. The only remedy is to destroy the vampire utterly by pouring boiling oil and vinegar into a hole in the grave accompanied by priestly incantations, whereafter nothing is left, not even the soul, so that no further ritual action is necessary, and none taken.

What is also striking here from a comparative point of view is the retention of a right-handed direction in the death ritual as in circumstances of life such as marriage and the dance: that is, there is no reversal on ritual occasions, even those associated with death. The local explanation is that left-handed (here clockwise) motion is 'the way of the devil'. Perhaps, in this Christian community, death, though a loss, is seen as an inevitable part of God's justice rather than an attack on the whole community by evil forces, as in many other societies. Certainly the concern seems to be with the proper flow of blood and other forces, in life as in death. Indeed, the important opposition would seem to be less that between life and death as that between good and evil – the great Christian battle. Danforth (1982: 48, 49, 68 n. 21) finds in the Greek 'soul with invisible human form' the local analogue of Hertz's 'spiritual duplicate' of the body, reformed, in the next world.

Barley (1981) offers a African example of a similar sort of analysis, though it might be called Lévi-Straussian rather than Hertzian. The essay of Hertz that he choses to cite is that on death, principally for its suggestion that the decay of the corpse can be seen as a transition from wet to dry, but also for the parallelism it identifies between what happens to the body, the soul and the mourners. There is also the parallel between death and initiation that Hertz mentioned, which the Dowayo make explicit. The value of wetness (especially 'still wetness', which is considered 'wetter' than 'moving wetness'), is associated with fertility and with women. Rain is another source of fertility, and the rain chiefs are in charge of male potency. Dryness and 'moving wetness' are associated with males, and initiation, in turning boys into men, is said to make them 'dry' as well being associated with the coming of rain ('moving wetness'). But secondary burials of the dead, at which the head of the deceased is removed (shortly after death), are also initiations, head-removal being explicitly assimilated to circumcision. Just as circumcised boys are able to approach the ancestors for the first time, so head-removal is necessary in order that they may join the ancestors when dead and may be reincarnated eventually. These are clearly examples of access to the sacred through ritual in the Durkheimian sense. There is also an association with the coming of rain. Women's heads are not removed, perhaps because they are associated with wetness already, and to remove them would risk flooding (this is certainly the case with the rain chiefs). There are severe restrictions on widows during the death ceremony, as Hertz predicted and as we saw with the Berewan (above). Equally Hertzian is the fact that a widow has to go through a rite which resembles the circumcision ceremony in all respects except for the actual mutilation. This reintegrates her into the community, which is thought to be simultaneous with her husband's acceptance by the ancestors. A further consequence of it, and of her not being allowed to have sexual intercourse during this period, is that she too becomes 'dry'.

Platenkamp (1992) locates the first and second funerary rites among the Tobelo of Halmahera in different 'levels of relationship' in a complicated study which owes much to the perspectives on ritual developed by de Coppet, Barraud, Tcherkézoff, etc. using hierarchical opposition (see pp. 125-6). While the first rite breaks the deceased's relations with kin and affines, the second starts by stressing the opposition, even antagonism, between 'houses' or agnatic groups. It ends with a communal meal signalling not merely their cooperation, but the incorporation of former affines into the house, as affinal links. In this way, relationships as well as substances circulate through the society in two different cycles of exchange linked as breakdown and renewal. If van Gennep's liminal and final ritual stages are seen as the first and second rite respectively, then it is also possible to suggest that the two rites and the cycles associated with them form two ideological levels. The former, being involved in the dissolution of relationships, is encompassed by the latter as reconstituting relationships of like kind. There must, however, be a transfer between the two cycles of exchange associated with the two levels so that this continuity can be maintained. Thus the second mortuary ritual not only achieves the incorporation of the deceased with the ancestors, as in the Hertzian view, but also renews the cycle which links death with life but which had been interrupted by the death originally dealt with in the first rite.

Despite their modifications of Hertz's original thesis, these accounts, like many other accounts of death ritual, all retain a recognition of the social dimension of death and of the collective concern for the proper treatment of the soul and the body, or at least a realization of the collective character of the event of death itself, an event which is at once private and public, individual and social. Death has always stimulated the anthropological imagination as well as providing the starting point for more than one general theory of society, a reflection of its actual significance in the ritual life of many cultures. It has often been used too as a peg on which to hang a general ethnography. Thus Douglass was led to to choose death as a 'heuristic device with which to approach the study of rural Basque society', given that 'no other life-crisis event serves to activate such a complexity of social relationships' (1969: 209, 218). Pawlik on the Bassar (1990: 80) and Goody's study of Lodagaa property and death ritual (1962) are similar examples. Modern anthropology has not dismissed Hertz's disquisition on death (Harrisson is virtually the only exception), though it has criticized and modified it where necessary. More importantly, it has sought to go beyond it in identifying images of fertility not merely as structural analogies, but as an intrinsic part of a continuing ritual process by means of which death is overcome symbolically if not instrumentally. In other words, Hertz's insights have been developed rather than discarded, and the ways in which particular ethnogaphers have been compelled to react to them has often reflected the relative weight their informants have given to the soul, the body or the mourners. For these reasons, a universal account in all the detail given by Hertz no longer seems possible, but the deeper sense of a transition for the deceased and for society remains, as generally does the brake on psychological speculations concerning the origins of beliefs and observances surrounding death.

CHAPTER SIX

Sin and Expiation

INTRODUCTION

Influential though they may have been in recent years, especially since their translation in 1960, Mauss tells us that Hertz's studies on death and on right and left were only supplements — 'prologue' and 'appendix' respectively — to the great work that really interested him (see Mauss 1925: 24; 1994: 51ff.). Had he lived, this would have been his doctoral thesis, supervised by Durkheim (Nandan 1977: li n. 20). In general, it was to have concerned the theme of impurity in all its forms, of which the impurity of death and the impurity of the left hand were only aspects (1994: 52). More generally still, Hertz was concerned with the 'dark side of humanity: crime and sin, punishment and pardon' (Mauss 1925: 24), the least studied and the most difficult to research. Compared with this, the studies on the cult of St Besse and the myth of Athena and the collections of folktales were no more than 'pastimes' (*ibid.*; see also pp. 10-11, 25-6).[1]

Although intended as supplements, there are obvious parallels between the two articles for which he is best known and this work on sin. First, the very identification of sin, and of the 'dark side of humanity' generally (Mauss 1925: 24), as something separate from the proper workings of the moral code in a society involved making yet another dichotomy of the sort for which right and left were the chosen emblems. Behind this is clearly the shadow of Durkheim's dichotomy between sacred and profane, which Hertz modified explicitly in his article on right and left (see p. 62) but which remains unmodified by him here. One profane object for Durkheim was the individual in relation to society, especially when he goes against society, his infraction of society's injunctions being sins. Really, sin is opposed to ritual action, whereby society, for the Durkheimian, stresses its values to its members. This was, of course, regarded as a more powerful social force than belief, which was what the intellectualists preferred to stress: hence the concern with the sources of moral power in societies and the stand against the alternative explanations of the intellectualists for their over-dependence on the workings of individual psychology. In a more general sense, one can say that much of Durkheim and Mauss's work concerned the nature and maintenance of social control; Hertz's magnum opus would have been concerned with the contrasting but related theme of what happens when the individual goes against society's injunctions. It was no doubt ulti-mately this that led Mauss to argue (1923), against Lévy-Bruhl's identification of a specifically primitive mentality, that Hertz had shown how the sense of sin hardly differed between our own society and Polynesian societies (Hertz's chosen ethnographic area for this study). Mauss was later (1994: 52) to use the term 'impurity' to link up Hertz's work on sin, death and the left hand, a term derivable in this context from Hertz's own modification of sacred-profane.

This leads naturally to the second parallel, namely Hertz's interest in how sin was overcome through expiation, how the breach in the moral code was mended. This clearly resembles his concern with how a society over-comes the loss of one of its members through death (Hertz seems to have col-lected information on the two topics simultaneously in the British Museum; see Mauss 1994: 54). One can also suggest that the state of unredeemed sin is another ritual transition of a marginal or liminal nature of the sort that Hertz identified for the corpse, soul and mourners after a death has taken place, which van Gennep analysed as a more general phenomenon in *Les Rites de Passage*. Finally, there is the usual evolutionism – the Polynesians are not as primitive as Durkheim's Australians, but they are still at a particular, and early, 'stage' of human development. And naturally, Hertz's view of modern civilization, with its emphasis on the tensions between faith and reason and the attempts of modern theologians to invoke the latter in support of the former, can only really be French.

At the time he was making these researches, Hertz seems to have been especially under Durkheim's influence (see Mauss 1994: 53). It is this text above all that is closest to one of Durkheim's main concerns, the importance of ritual in articulating the relationship between the individual and society, and the reasons for there being ritual at all. For confession and repentance, even though often effected in what seems to us to be a private sphere, are still rituals in that they bring individual and supreme authority together in a relationship of subordination. However, like any ritual the event is ultimately aimed at the former's oneness with the latter, who represents the sacred, and it requires the observance of certain procedures if it is to be effective.

Although little can be found in Durkheim on sin specifically, the latter did examine crime and punishment, especially in *The Division of Labour in Society* (1984 [1893], also 1901; see the review in Lukes 1973: 160–3,

257–62). He defined crime primarily as an offence against the collective consciousness, and it is the need to maintain this consciousness in the minds of members of society rather than the direct consequences of the crime as such that leads to the demand for punishment. Thus it satisfies the collectivity more than it reforms the offender. Indeed, punishment reinforces collective sentiments just as much as ritual does. It is, of course, frequently very ritualized and may itself constitute a ritual in all senses. Moreover, the nature of the punishment reflects the nature of the society rather than that of the crime. This is why punishments are becoming progressively less severe. The nature of the collective consciousness is changing: with the rise of individualism as the supreme value, the sense of a collectivity has waned. It itself is therefore less offended by crime, which is increasingly seen as an offence by one individual against another. This comparison would seem to take its starting point from the tyrannies and absolute monarchies of European history rather than the typical tribal society, where – feud excepted – capital punishment rarely seems to be imposed. There is also a problem with defining the severity of punishments: life imprisonment is not always seen as preferable to a death sentence, nor a death sentence to mutilation (cf. Talbot Rice 1987: 96–7, on Byzantium). Durkheim even came to see crime as useful in small doses, since it challenges state power and helps guarantee both existing freedoms and future improvements in morality. One is reminded here of the common populist argument whereby Englishmen owe their liberties to their willingness to break unjust laws. As we shall see, Hertz distinguished the criminal from the sinner because the sense of guilt is absent in the former but present in the latter, making him repent.

Mauss, who was witness to all Hertz's efforts (Mauss 1994: 52), realized full well the colossal nature of the task Hertz had undertaken. He relates (*ibid.*: 4) that although Hertz had assembled all the facts by 1912 and developed all the ideas, to begin with he recoiled at the task of bringing it all to order in a publishable text. He was also somewhat discouraged by the prospect of having to solve certain theoretical problems (left unidentified by Mauss), which would have diverted him from the joys of digging yet more interesting facts out of the ethnography. It was apparently at this point that he wrote up his studies of St Besse and the myth of Athena by way of relaxation. Mauss says that Hertz returned refreshed from these to his master work but did not make much more progress with the latter before the outbreak of war.

Nonetheless, a start was made with a nearly complete introduction (published by Mauss in *Revue de l'Histoire des Religions* in 1922), a draft of the conclusion, and many notes and sketches from Hertz's teaching on the subject at the Ecole Pratique des Hautes Etudes from 1908 to 1912, which Mauss used to teach a regular course on sin himself in the 1930s. These notes have apparently since disappeared, but Mauss gave their gist when reissuing the introduction. The latter's reports on his courses for the Collège de France are also valuable as a supplement and are available in the French edition of his collected works (Mauss 1969 III: 513-16). One of the courses themselves, from the year 1934-5, has recently been reconstructed by Jean Jamin and François Lupu from notes taken at the time by one Paul Lavaquery (1889-1960), a banker who interrupted his career briefly to study ethnology and related subjects but who never became a professional anthropologist (see Jamin and Lupu 1987: 44). Apart from this last item, which was published in the museological journal *Gradhiva* in 1987, all the other material, including Mauss's notes on his own courses, was reissued as a single book in 1988, with an introduction by Jean Jamin. The 1922 text has recently been translated by the present author, including Mauss's introductory and concluding comments (see Hertz 1994). Mauss had hoped to be able to reassemble the rest of the thesis from Hertz's notes, a hope he was still expressing as late as 1939 (see 1969 II: 163), but he never did so. Possibly these materials went the way of many of Mauss's other papers, when his office was sacked by the Nazis during the occupation. It must be remembered that while Mauss saw himself solely as an editor when reissuing Hertz's work on sin in the 1920s, by the 1930s he was developing the theme himself and using Hertz's original merely as one of the bases of his teaching. That he could even envisage doing this is another testimony of the extent to which the *Année* scholars regarded themselves as a team and to which Mauss regarded himself as the literary executor of his dead colleagues after World War I.

Using these sources, I shall offer an account of Hertz's ideas on the theme of sin and its expiation such as they can now be recovered, long after both he himself and his redactor have died. The introduction is all we have in his own words; its last section, which offers a provisional definition of expiation, was not written up, but the essence of what he proposed to say can be discerned from the notes he left. The remaining parts — three core chapters plus a conclusion were planned — are impossible to reconstruct, even with Lavaquery's notes (the latter are, of course, really notes of notes as far as their relation to anything Hertz wrote is concerned), though the broad lines of how Hertz would have developed his theme are reasonably clear. We start, however, with the published introduction (Hertz 1922; page references are to the 1994 translation).

THE PUBLISHED TEXT

In the first part of his introduction, Hertz introduces the concept of sin through the Christian tradition with which his readership — even the religious sceptics among them — are going to be most familiar. Sin and the redemption of Christ are central to Christianity since man is born in sin, hence the inevitability of death. Yet the sinner can ultimately be saved, a process which starts with baptism. Henceforward, man's life work must be the avoidance of sin, in order to avoid damaging this blessed state. If nonetheless a sin is committed, penitence can still redeem the sinner in the eyes of God. Penitence is thus like a second baptism, which renews 'the great cosmic drama' (1994: 57). Christians think of their 'nature, duty and destiny' (*ibid*.: 58) in terms of sin and expiation, ideas that lie so deep within the Christian consciousness that they seem certain and unavoidable. However, rationalist thinkers (Hertz gives Nietzsche as an example) regard them as a Christian invention, a priestly contrivance, and as not inevitable at all. Modern theologians have reacted against this, so that the battle between faith and reason is already joined. Perhaps, says Hertz, there is a middle way, one which will seek to understand such ideas in their own terms (especially their significance for social cohesion) but without succumbing to their embrace. This middle way is clearly that of the new sociology.

The second part of the introduction discusses the newer breed of rationalist and liberal theologian and the psychological and internalist explanations for the belief in sin that they have developed as a response to the sceptics. Perhaps Hertz is thinking mainly here of the Catholic view and is neglecting the way in which Protestantism long ago internalized sin in order to get rid of the phenomenon of confession, and with it, priestly intervention. Certainly it is noticeable how much Hertz's interpretation depends on free will as against predestination, since for the Catholic, sin is an avoidable act of the created. He admits that these ideas later came to be seen as less obvious and less acceptable because of the distortions introduced by the Church's worldly ambitions, but for Hertz this seems to be a matter of anti-clericalism or rationalist anti-religion, not of the Protestant reaction. At all events, these are not the only paths, nor is the attitude of modern liberal theologians an answer. While their modernizing tendencies are reasonable up to a point, their attempts to root religion in science are ultimately irrational, in that they are denying the force of history and of tradition. They are also being selective with tradition, retaining only those parts of it which still find acceptance at the present day.[2]

On the other hand, a truly 'critical theology' — he might have said 'critical sociology' — can make of sin and expiation 'a "moral reality" independent of any "juridicial fiction" or "priestly magic"' (1994: 63). Belief in sin and expiation is not irrational or superstitious, nor, despite Christian doctrine, is it just a matter of the individual conscience of the sinner — both sinner and God play a role set by the society. Hertz refers to the parable of the prodigal

son as an analogy of the sinner's redemption before God, which is only effective, he suggests, for those who already believe – i.e. it cannot be used as an
instrument of conversion. Yet this parable, with its happy ending of the
wayward son being joyfully accepted back into the arms of his father, is not
the only one conceivable: the Old Testament, like many other religious
systems, sees God rather as a punisher of transgressions, even through death,
whereas Christianity is all about the forgiveness of the repentant sinner, as
Christ himself forgave his murderers and betrayers. Thus the Christian belief
is contingent, not natural and obvious. Moreover, the sinner is not a free-
acting individual, despite what Catholic tradition might say – and despite also
the individualizing rationality of the modern republican democrat. Instead, he
is a social actor, with a social role to play: 'It is not the sinner who creates
sin; it is sin ... that makes the sinner what he is' (*ibid.*: 71).

Another essential element of sin consists in the feelings of fear and
guilt that the act engenders in the sinner. This can only come from an
ordered belief in the presence of an almighty god capable of both punishing
and forgiving. In its turn, this ordered belief can only stem from society
acting on its members, it cannot simply arise spontaneously in the conscience of the transgressor or be thought up by him unaided. The attempts of
the rationalizers to argue along these lines are ultimately false, since if the
sense of sin were left solely to the individual, the most hardened sinner
would be not only the most persistent but also the one who was the most
sheltered from the key consequences of sin, namely fear and guilt – and such
a paradox is hardly acceptable to any recognizable theology. In other words,
sin depends on its recognition by the sinner; without it, there is nothing to
enforce repentance, nothing to stop repetition, nothing to instil a sense of
fear and guilt. That recognition, in its turn, depends on the existence of a
sanction, of a punishing power, which may be identified as God but is in
reality society, society teaching the individual what to fear, what to feel guilty
about. Indeed, the sinner feels oppressed by his sin even if he is not directly
responsible for it (the sin of Adam, of one's parents), and he or she must
resolve it in expiation.

There is thus general agreement in all schools of Christianity, says
Hertz, that expiation is a matter of divine grace and power. But it is more
than merely an admission of sorrow and a pledge of future good behaviour,
more, despite modern theologians, than an internal conversion – it is a
matter of personal spiritual renewal which, since it amounts to an act of creation, also involves death and sacrifice. The crucifixion of Christ was not just
an example to man: 'the spilling of the blood of the perfect victim, devoid of
sin, was indispensible for the abolition of sin committed in the newness of
the world, and of all the sins of mankind.' (1994: 77). Penitence involves total

submission to God, which means the penitent sacrificing his self totally, and this renders punishment redundant. Penitence is also traditionally public, as with flagellation and even auricular confession. The latter takes place in the public arena of the church even though the contents are kept secret. This is another reason why the modern theologian cannot escape tradition by resorting to individual psychology: the Church is always present.

The third part is largely taken up with dismissing the interpretations of some of Hertz's contemporaries among ethnologists, especially those whose intellectualism has led them to introduce elements of personal psychology into what is properly a matter for sociology. At the same time, the plea for the merits of a truly comparative ethnology is developed as a middle way between rationality and modern theology. In place of a concern with the variations in feelings that sinners might undergo, there is an interest in 'the very ideas of sin and expiation, treating them as social institutions whose origin, meaning and function form a proper object of research' (1994: 81). This brings problems for ethnologists in freeing themselves from the feelings engendered by the concept of sin – either we ourselves are impregnated by it, or we regard it as absurd.

One fundamental task comparative ethnology should set itself is to decide whether or not ideas of sin and expiation are common to all humanity. The work of missionaries, in seeking parallels in indigenous cultures with which to explain sin and expiation, would seem to suggest not, given the troubles most of them have encountered in this respect. This is supported by Frazer's suggestion that primitive man is more interested in magical defences against malevolent powers than in recovering original purity through redemption. This in its turn would rule out a recourse to comparative ethnography, since if sin is not common to humanity and is only a matter for the higher religions, it becomes a matter for theology and philosophy only. But this view assumes that ethnology is confined to non-Western and non-modern societies alone. In fact the higher religions too form a tradition, as is shown by the limited and repeated range of metaphors with which preachers exhort their flocks. The ideas of Frazer and Tylor are thus questioned: it is improper to judge primitive religions by Western standards, and it is factually wrong to argue that they lack ideas of sin and expiation (here, Hertz cites Lévy-Bruhl and Durkheim against 'Frazer's theses on the naturalist positivism of peoples of rudimentary civilization'; Hertz 1994: 88). Similarly, missionaries' searches for such ideas among other peoples tend to produce either disappointment and a denial that they have them or an ethnocentric attribution of such ideas to them. The mere lack of words for sin and expiation does not necessarily rule out their presence as ideas. The fact that the Batak carry out cannibalism and headhunting with a good conscience, whereas the Dayak regard even faults of etiquette as serious sins, shows the lability of ideas of sin, and again that it is not just a Christian phenomenon.

What one needs, therefore, is neither the exclusive claims of Christianity to the phenomena of sin and expiation, nor the assumption of their universality throughout humanity. Instead, one must test for their presence by specific enquiry among specific populations. This was to be the task of the proposed work in respect of a distinct ethnographic area, i.e. these ideas would be studied in their full ethnographic context, other comparisons being drawn on only secondarily. The area chosen was Polynesia, an area allowing sufficient variation within a limited compass, for which there was already a sufficient literature, and which had been made famous through the concept of *tabu* – the Polynesian word, says Hertz, for a virtually universal phenomcnon. Polynesians are significant in the present context for other reasons too. Admittedly, says Hertz, they cannot be seen as absolute primitives – the ideas they have were probably developed in the course of their migrations across the Pacific – but this work is not a search for origins. The Polynesians are still sufficiently remote from us in terms of evolutionary development to aid us in testing interpretations of sin and expiation – archaic, antecedent to Christianity, etc., but not primitive (in Durkheimian terms, that is, they are not Australians).

In the fourth and final part of his introduction, Hertz faces the problem of providing universal definitions of sin and expiation in such a way as to avoid ethnocentrism on the one hand and irrelevance engendered by casting one's net too wide on the other. Producing a mere inventory of sins will not do, since it would leave out some, while others would be redundant in relation to any particular society. Identifying an essence, such as rebelliousness against moral rules, pride, etc., would not help either – this is too psychological and metaphysical and is essentially the theological explanation (i.e. in modern terms it would be considered ethnographically specific). Accordingly, Hertz proposes to start with our own, Western case, and to refine it further with the aid of history.

First of all, sins are transgressions against moral rules; their effects persist after the events that gave rise to them have disappeared, and they can only be removed with God's help, before the sinner dies. Thus sin may be defined provisionally as 'a transgression which, by the sole fact that it is carried out, tends to bring about death' (Hertz 1994: 99). Sin might be compared with sickness or with tempting fate by ignoring the doctor's advice, but in these cases the subject is likely to be pitied rather than blamed, says Hertz, and in any case this is more in the nature of a mechanical transgression against the physical world. Sin, on the other hand, transgresses 'an ideal and moral order' (*ibid.*: 101) prescribed by the divine, and faith is needed not only to restore the sinner but to endow him with the very sense of having sinned; until then, his sin does not exist.

Hertz also distinguishes between sin on the one hand and crime and offences against honour on the other. Sin is a matter between God, the Church and the sinner, with concern for the life to come. The Church offers, as an alternative to sin, the ideal of sanctity, which is transcendent. Honour, on the other hand, is concerned with the individual's dignity and worth vis-à-vis other individuals, in which a social fault leads to social isolation until honour is restored. As a matter between society and the individual, it is purely this-worldly. The Church is egalitarian, says Hertz, while honour involves hierarchy.

Crime is closer to sin in being a transgression of the law, but it is still distinct. Sacrilege remains a sin in the West but is only a crime in so far as it may threaten public order (cf. Durkheim 1898b). Unlike either sin or loss of honour, crime produces no immediate effect within the person having committed it. With crime, society eventually imposes its punishment on the criminal. With sin, on the other hand, negative effects arise when the sinner realizes his sin; this, in effect, is his punishment. There are also differential consequences after death, through which the criminal can escape punishment but the sinner cannot. Crime is necessarily action; sin can be mere intention. Here, we see Hertz once again resorting to a purely internal guilt feeling which may be engendered originally by society but whose actualization appears to be chiefly a personal matter. As so often with the Durkheimians, and despite themselves, individual psychology has to come back into the picture in order to make good the deficencies of the sociological method. Hertz attributes these distinctions partly to the development of different social groups in more modern societies and partly to the latters' scientific separation of fact from value. There may still be a degree of overlap. Church and state claim distinct sets of actions for their own jurisdictions, but something like murder is likely to fall under both. The Church, however, can only act if the murderer is repentant and willing to be saved, whereas the state acts willy nilly.

Of course, other societies too place transgressions in different categories according to who or what they offend, who is responsible (if anyone) for correcting and punishing them, their consequences, their seriousness, etc. However, the key element for Hertz would seem to be the religious dimension, as we see in his final definition of sin:

> sin is a transgression of a moral code which is considered to involve, by virtue of itself, disastrous consequences for its author, and which concerns the religious society exclusively. (1994: 108)

Even this definition is ultimately provisional. There are variations even within the Christian tradition, especially regarding the Old Testament. The distinction between sin and crime was less clear in Greece and Rome (e.g. in the case of perjury), while dishonour may necessitate death, as often in the Middle Ages. One also has to accept the possible transitoriness of modern attitudes and admit that for us, sin is the domain of the Church, which conceptually, at least, opposes itself to civil society — other societies, whether historical or contemporary, may make this distinction less. But this is not to deny the existence of a sense of sin in other societies, nor its 'universal and absolute value' (*ibid.*: 111) overall.

It is possible to say much less about Hertz's proposed definition of expiation, which only survived in note form. Expiation is a necessary part of any religious system, involving reparation by the sinner through the action of divine power, the abolition of the past and final reconciliation. However, it involves more than acknowledging the fault or appeasing God, essential though these are. It has as its objects the destruction of the sinner's sin and the elimination of evil, a destruction which at the same time 'restores the mystical integrity of the sinner and returns to him his normal place in the religious world' (*ibid.*: 112). In short,

> there is expiation when certain actions, which are generally ritualistic, are able to re-establish the state of things anterior to the transgression by annulling it and by satisfying justice, without the transgressor and those near to him being crushed thereby. (*ibid.*: 113)

THE PROBLEM OF THE REMAINING TEXT

As already noted, the rest of Hertz's proposed text only existed in note form when Mauss set about trying to reconstruct it. According to the last recorded plan, dated January 1913, there were to have been three core chapters and a conclusion in addition to the introduction we have already dealt with. The first two core chapters would have concerned respectively sin and expiation among Polynesians, especially the Maori. The first was to have carried the title 'Sin and its Consequences', with the following section headings:

1. Order and peace: an account of the system of taboos, covering those involving the chiefs in relation to their subjects, men in relation to women, such activities as sleeping, eating, cooking and working, war, cult observance, illness and death.

2. Transgressions: the notions of *tabu* and *noa* (see below), showing also that the archetype of sacrilege in Polynesia consisted in the eating of the

sacred (also the means whereby the fault is removed). Here Hertz would have introduced comparative material from the Kikuyu of east Africa. Mauss specifically mentions Hertz's intention to compare *tabu* with *mana* (1994: 117), and Hertz's own notes for his course of 1909–10 refer to the need to determine 'the religious significance attributed to the violation of a taboo' (*ibid.*: 114).

3. The effects of the transgression on the transgressor, the sacred, and the world in general. Sin amounts to the sinner himself being cursed, destroyed; physical sanctions, including illness, suicide, death.

4. The offence and its interdiction.

5. Conclusion: 'general characteristics of sin, its function in the religious world, its psychological significance' (Hertz 1994: 115).

Although Mauss, in his Collége de France teaching report for 1932–3, says that this part is recoverable from what Hertz left behind, nothing is apparently left of it now. He records being impressed, however, by 'the dualism inherent in Polynesian religions, in particular in Maori religion', which Hertz's researches had highlighted (Mauss 1969 III: 513–14).

The second chapter would have carried the title 'The Elimination of Sin', divided as follows:

1. Why expiation is imposed: lustration, expulsion.

2. Separation.

3. The leading-back of the sin to its original source.

4. Conclusion: 'general characteristics of lustration [*sic*], its function, its relation to more spiritual forms' (Hertz 1994: 115).

Here we have a little more detail, from Hertz's own teaching reports for the Ecole des Hautes Etudes (for 1908–9; reproduced 1994: 113–14, 115) and from Mauss's report for the course he taught in 1933–4 (see 1969 III: 514). Hertz's notes tell us that the violation of a taboo alters the very nature of the powers protected by that taboo, as well as condemning the transgressor to eventual death, a state which lasts until either punishment or pardon takes place. Pardon consists in the destruction of the fault without the destruction of the person, a process which may take the form of lustration or expiation. Since the sinner is in some way impregnated with his sin, pardon as defined here may clearly take the form of a rite of separation. But expulsion of the bad mystical substance that has caused the sin is not enough – it must be directed back to its origin, accompanied by a suitable rite. This element in the process often takes the form of the sinner giving something of himself, such as blood, life, or suffering through flagellation. Mauss (*ibid.*) adds the isolation of the sinner or even of his whole community, spitting, vomiting and lustration as further means whereby the removal of the sin is effected.

Hertz's reference to forms of expulsion links his treatment of sin and expiation to Durkheim's 'negative rites', under which the latter specifically groups those dealing with sin and forms of penance, and also asceticism. In a more general sense, these are rites which bring about the separation of sacred and profane, as opposed to positive rites, which allow access to the sacred. This distinction is not stressed in Hertz's published text, but it is obvious that it would have become more important subsequently.[3]

Hertz's course for 1909–10 makes particular mention of confession and of oblations concerning food in this context. His course for 1910–11 apparently concerned itself with the circumstances in which social, i.e. human sanctions come to be added to the normally pre-eminent supernatural ones in respect of sin among the Polynesians (1994: 114–15). This indicates a recognition that offences against the gods are not necessarily offences against one's fellow men (see next section).

The third core chapter would have dealt exclusively with sin in ancient Semitic religions and in Christianity. Mauss says explicitly (1969 III: 513) that it could not be reconstituted from Hertz's notes. Its title was to have been 'Redemptive Suffering', to have consisted of the following parts:

    Preamble: the problem stated.

1. Necessity of blood and life for sacred beings who have been offended.

2. Specific characteristics of expiatory sacrifice.

3. Penitential asceticism.

4. Conclusion: the theory of sacrifice of the Man-God (Hertz 1994: 115-16).

A general conclusion, consisting of a 'recapulation of the general characteristics of the ideas and rites examined', was to have followed and to have included the points that the notions of sin and expiation in Polynesian societies accord with their overall social structure (which, in Mauss's added words, was 'semi-segmentary, semi-concentrated'); and that in Christianity these notions combine to form a 'unique dogma ... of an absolute and univeral range' (1994: 116). Hertz was to end with some remarks on the future of these ideas in our own, i.e. Western societies, where the ideas of sin and expiation still have a role to play, even where religion as conventionally defined is absent (Mauss *ibid.*).

Additional points can be drawn from Lavaquery's notes of Mauss' course for 1934–5, itself based on material collected by Hertz (see Hertz 1987). These cover principally the Polynesian material, but they also give an overview of the whole project by way of introduction. Although they were, as the editors say, apparently carefully taken down (Jamin and Lupu 1987: 44), they are not always entirely clear, at least in the given context. A further problem must have been Mauss's anecdotal and otherwise idiosyncratic way of lecturing, imposing an additional filter between Hertz's original thought and the editors' transcription of Lavaquery's notes. Nonetheless, they show the variety of ideas Hertz was able to find and would have had to deal with.

The notes start with the striking comment that 'Hertz discovered confession among the Maoris' (1987: 45) and immediately saw in it an example of expiation. Hertz had, of course, started his introduction with the Christian idea of sin, as a reference point against which to compare the Polynesian case. With Christianity there is the complication of original sin, i.e. that man is born already burdened with it and that his whole life will be dedicated to its removal. But the sense of sin is no less strong among non-Christians, only less sharply defined. Their concept of *tabu* is intended to protect the soul, a protection that sin removes. What appears to be a general definition of sin and expiation then follows:

> Sin is a transgression of the moral order which entails deadly consequences for its author and concerns religious society uniquely. There is expiation when certain actions are able to reestablish the state of things prior to the transgression and to abolish it without crushing the transgressor. Pardon is a mystical operation, achieved by way of rites, which destroys sin, appeases the collectivity and the gods and, at the same time, restores the good state of the sinner. (*ibid.*)

Mauss then interpolates a passage dealing with the theory of *tabu*, drawing on works by Farnell, Robertson Smith and Ellis (already available to Hertz) and Firth and Handy (published after his death). *Tabu* means literally 'interdiction'. Mauss opposes it to *noa*, which he glosses as profane, implying that *tabu* also refers to the sacred, and says that neither on its own is dangerous, only their mixing. *Tabu* and *noa* nonetheless need each other, for they give each other meaning through their opposition. The association of these two dichotomies has been criticized by Steiner (1956: 41):

> It is a misunderstanding to apply Durkheim's notion of sacred and profane to taboo-noa contexts. Sacred-profane is a relation of tension and polarity: the profane threatens the sacred, the sacred has to be protected against the profane. These are concepts alien to the Polynesian

taboo and noa, which are better understood by recourse to the simile
of tying and untying.

For Steiner, therefore, *noa* is the absence of *tabu* rather than its opposite, the state which obtains when *tabu* has been violated, not that which
violates it, though they are nonetheless mutually exclusive (*ibid.*: 36). Mauss
too, however, points out that *tabu* is relative to an individual and not an
absolute force. Chiefs have, or are, *tabu*, an aspect of which is *mana*, which
Mauss here translates as 'soul'; it is this that maintains *tabu*. Slaves, by contrast, have no *mana*. The *tabu* of the chiefs is manifested in their own inability to touch the ground, as well as in their subjects' not being allowed to
pass behind them or to step on their shadows. Furthermore, they cannot
touch food themselves and have to be fed by others (cf. Dumont 1972: 183;
also the photograph in Jamin and Lupu 1987: 42). Their *tabu* is exceeded
only by the *tabu* of still more sacred persons or gods (i.e. it is relative). Many
other examples are listed, of varying importance and intensity, relating to
weaving, walking over another person or over that person's property, touching bodily products, touching the cooked food, boats, tools or houses of
another person, and behaviour towards affines and the dead. It is clear that
many of these examples do not particularly resemble sins in the Christian
sense but fall more into the category of personal avoidances of dangerous
substances and actions.

The next passage concerns the nature of sin, which consists essentially
in wrongly bringing sacred and profane together. Hertz describes how transgression renders the sinner impure, like one rendered impure through birth
or natural circumstance, which is how the sinner and his or her sin becomes
detectable, and also how it affects the world in general and specific divine
powers in particular. Among the Polynesians, sin consists above all in
cooking or eating the divine, which can perhaps be regarded as the mixing of
sacred with profane through the improper ingestion of the former by the
latter. To eat another's leavings is to eat a part of himself and is a great insult,
which itself makes it a sin. To eat the leavings of a chief is to eat the divine
(since the chief is divine) and is an even greater sin, presumably because the
seriousness of the sin is said to be in direct proportion to the importance of
the one sinned against. Any sin destroys life, whether of the sinner, of society
or of the gods. Generally, the sinner becomes more accessible to demons
(*atua*), though sometimes the demon may take hold of him first – in either
case, the sinner is eaten from within. This is simply the condition of sin, its
consequence; 'the notion of vengeance through the demon is secondary'
(Lavaquery's notes in Hertz 1987: 46).

Most of the rest of the account is taken up with the elimination of sin
through expiation. Not all sins can be expiated among Polynesians, but for

those that can, one can identify a moral element and a mechanical element. This distinction is ethnographically contingent: it is absent, for instance, from the notion expressed by Latin *expiare*, where the two concepts are fused. Among Polynesians the removal of sin may involve the destruction of the sinner, even of his family, as well as of his house (cf. the stoning to death of adulterers in the traditional Middle East). We are also told that the place of death of a chief is abandoned for ever, for it is now *tabu*. What this has to do with sin is probably the notion that someone, somewhere, is to blame, there being no such thing as a 'natural' death. Other Polynesian rites to remove sin are less drastic and may involve bathing or ordeal by fire (the water or fire separates the sinner from his sin, but also directly restores to him his original wholeness). Other methods may involve a more direct action on the part of the sinner, such as spitting, perhaps into a fire or into someone else's mouth, walking under an arch, tying and untying (cf. the metaphor mentioned by Steiner, above), bathing, and stepping over someone. All these rites involve separation, of sin and sinner, and also transition, from an inauspicious state to an auspicious one. The last, i.e. stepping over someone, is especially interesting, since normally it is itself *tabu*. It is obviously one example of the cause of a sin being used to remove it when one is already in a sinful state — an example, in fact, of ritual reversal, or alternatively of a subordinate level, at which one is constrained, because of one's existing sinful state, to perform an act normally considered sinful. Preventative rites are also mentioned, e.g. asperging warriors about to set off for battle and also when they return, presumably to safeguard them from, and to remove from them, the sinful consequences of their having killed. Also to be included here are such practices as offering tribute or first fruits to the gods or chiefs and making an offering to the gods of the field before cutting the soil for sowing or planting, in order to divert their anger in the future. Regarding reincorporation, one should also mention communal feasts (as in India, accepting offenders back into the caste) and rites involving hitting the sinner to bring him back within the community.

Mauss repeatedly stresses that these means of expiation are not purely mechanical but have a moral force too (cf. 1969 III: 514). A discussion of confession among Maori, Eskimo and Catholics bears on this. For the latter, confession amounts to the ejaculation of one's sins into the ears of the priest, similar in a sense to spitting or vomiting; the priest is then able to absolve one. Among the Maori, this is followed by ritual baptism. However, other offences, such as adultery or failing to prevent the death of someone in one's care, offend not against the gods or other representatives of the sacred but against other individuals like oneself or other families like one's own. Such offences may lead to demands for compensation from the offended family or clan. Such payments are labelled *utu* among the Maori and join the sinner to the sinned against, thus leading the sin back to its source. Vengeance may also be sought through violent means, killing or pillaging (significantly, the word for pillage, *muru*, also means 'pardon' here). This is more a matter, however, of balancing the loss of blood than of punishment, otherwise one would be bringing sin closer to the notion of feud, from which Hertz had so carefully sought to distinguish it. This balancing is shown by what happens in the case of a murder within the clan: since no vengeance is possible within the clan itself, an outsider's life must be taken, even though he is innocent.

In dealing with such cases, Mauss invokes the still current distinction between magic and religion. The latter applies when the vengeance is the gods', or more generally society's, acting through its priests. The former is at work when vengeance is essentially private, involving socially recognized mechanisms but administered not by the sacred or by any other manifestation of the social but by an individual, through his personal *mana*. Here, Mauss seems at first sight to go beyond Hertz, whose thesis would probably have restricted itself to the religious-cum-social dimension. However, Durkheim had also said that 'there is no sin in magic' (1915: 301), precisely because it excludes society from being its agent. Consequently Mauss places in a separate category those societies in which a payment (of goods, money, a woman) takes the place of pardon as the means whereby an offence is expunged and peace restored: 'when the offended person has been paid, he is satisfied' (Lavaquery's notes in Hertz 1987: 49). For Mauss, this is clearly a property of the 'simpler', not the 'higher' religions: 'the absence of pardon is the fundamental characteristic of paganism' (*ibid.*). Wrong-doing in such cultures is, at least in certain cases, a concern of the individual, not the society, and is then expiated by vengeance or compensation, not by punishment, nor by submission followed by forgiveness. There is, however, a parallel with sin, in that wrong-doing gives the victim power over the culprit, by whom he is owed some recognition of the fault committed and some form of recompense.

In either case, expiation leads to a reconciliation, both of which require sacrifices in Polynesia. The sinner offers something of himself, e.g. hair or blood. Sometimes criminals are sacrificed to appease the gods, presumably when they have also offended the whole community and sometimes as a precaution against the consequences of any future offences. It is through such intermediaries that expiation proper is distinguished from lustration. The grand conclusion is that religious, jural and moral notions come together in these ideas and further, that 'the anger [generated by the fault] can only be assuaged by the destruction of its object or by any destruction whatever, or, in the absence of any destruction, by a humiliation, a confession. The outcome is the notion of pardon' (*ibid.*: 51).

In his further courses after 1935, using fresh documents from Hawaii, Mauss found evidence that expiatory sacrifices had been better established there than elsewhere in Polynesia, there being 'great seasons of purification' (1969 III: 515). Above all, he came to the conclusion (*ibid*.: 516) that the Polynesians are, after all, much nearer to Semitic and Indo-European societies (he does not specifically mention Christian ones) in respect of their attitudes to sin and, more broadly, to the maintenance of a natural order through moral sanctions. Mauss explicitly distinguishes here, the notion of the right sacred and the observance of rites and interdicts, and that of the left sacred, of sin and of death, which expiation can avoid in returning to life, peace and order' (*ibid*.), a statement which comes close to summing up Hertz's whole approach and interest.

Hertz would also have introduced the notion of *hau*, a Maori word made famous by Mauss as 'the spirit of the gift' in his work on exchange (1950 [1925]: 158–9, 159 n. 1 on Hertz; cf. pp. 35–6). However, the *hau* was also the spirit of anything stolen which, like the spirit of a gift which is wrongly retained, harms the guilty party. It is thus distinct from *mana*, 'the power which the owner retains over the thing stolen' in Mauss's words (*ibid*.: 159 n.1), i.e. the spiritual force upholding the sanction against theft.

Mauss used further notes left by Hertz in the study of the effects of suggestion on the propensity to die without evident physical cause (1950 [1926]: 311–30; also mentioned by Mauss in Hertz 1987: 46). At the time, this tended to be attributed especially to so-called 'primitives', and Mauss discusses the question in relation to Australians and Polynesians, drawing on Hertz for the latter. In both cases the mere suggestion of danger arising from consciousness of one's own infringements of taboos or of the evil spells of others was enough to lead to death, but the Australians were much less actuated by the sense of sin as such than the Polynesians. Moreover, sin renders magical attacks by others more possible, though at the same time the commission of a sin causing the sinner's death may itself be the unintended result of someone else's magic. And of course what makes the sinner suffer under the weight of his infringement can be seen as 'magic', in the form of loss of *mana*. Mauss linked this theme with his uncle's study of suicide (Durkheim 1897), which concerned *inter alia* the loosening of social bonds around the individual through anomie, egoism or altruism.

LATER WORK ON SIN

The elements of Hertz's model can thus be set out as follows. Sin is the transgression of an absolute moral law enjoined by society under the guise of divine or supernatural power and authority. Transgression entails spiritual and moral death for the sinner, which must be expunged before actual death intervenes. Expiation depends first and foremost on the sinner's recognition of his fault and subsequently on the taking of ritual action to destroy the evil without destroying the sinner. This action entails separating the sinner from his sins through, for example, confession, spitting, vomiting, gift-giving, offering a sacrifice to which the sin has been transferred, etc. Since the sacrifice is typically paid for by the sinner it also involves a degree of penalty, while sharing the sacrificial meal with the community afterwards is an equally typical example of the final reconciliation between wrongful individual and wronged society or other power that Hertz says is also necessary.

Sin is thus linked with guilt, which is at once a manifestation of the action of society on the individual and the precondition for his reconciliation with society, through expiation. It is also implicitly linked to the will of the individual and, if not always to the voluntary nature of his actions – his sin may have originated in another's actions – then at least to his failure to seek redemption for them. It is thus first and foremost Christian, in accordance with Aquinas's definition (*Summa Theologica* II/1, question 71, article 6): 'The first cause of sin is in the will, which commands all voluntary acts, in which alone sin is to be found' (quoted in Ladd 1957: 458 n. 27). Whether it should therefore be considered specifically Catholic rather than Protestant is less clear. Despite the latter's doctrine of predestination, this concerns only the believer's eventual fate. Given that sins may be committed unknowingly, and further that predestination certainly gives no licence to sin, we may judge that there is little difference in outlook in this respect. What is different is that the sinner stands before God directly, not before a Church and priesthood mediating between them.

These elements should be kept in mind as we track down the occasional use made of Hertz's ideas on sin subsequently and specific attempts by others, without reference to his work, to pin down the notion of sin as either a universal or an ethnographically specific phenomenon. One perennial problem is avoiding the ethnocentrism involved in attributing essentially Christian concepts of sin to other societies. Another is to isolate sin from closely related but more general concepts such as morality, ethics and the mere violation of taboos. There is a clear sense in which the whole of Durkheimian sociology is a sociology of morality, not in the normal philosophical sense of discussing moral rules as a prescription for living but in the sense of describing, analysing and explaining the moral rules different human populations actually live by. As Madan points out (1981: 127), the idea that man is by nature moral but that it is society that gives him his specific morality goes back at least to Aristotle. For Evens (1982: 205), this is what characterizes the structural-functionalist school of anthropology, distinguishing it from more 'scientific' approaches (he singles out Barth's work as typical of the latter). There are, of course, variations even within the first approach. Bloch, writing in a *Festschrift* for Meyer Fortes (1973: 75), points out that for the honorand, the morality connected with kinship acts to restrain individual interest, whereas for Leach it masks that interest, allowing it to be manipulated.

Nonetheless, sin does tend to get buried under the weight of what anthropologists spend so much time writing about anyway, namely the nature of the social rules that constrain the individual and the means of making sure they are observed. Those writing specifically on the anthropology of morality tend to restrict themselves to identifying the specifically anthropological as distinct from, say, philosophical or theological approaches to morality, and they do not necessarily mention sin at all. Firth is a good example. He stresses that no society is wholly without moral rules, and also that morality can be considered objective, 'in the sense of being founded on a social existence which is external to the individual' (1971: 214). The sense of relativity arises only when cultures are compared, especially if the comparer is an outsider. To tackle sin as such is therefore implicitly superfluous; it is enough to mention it in passing in one's general work.[4]

Not all anthropologists have felt this way, however. One important exception is Evans-Pritchard, whose detailed examination of sin among the Nuer (1956) is valuable in showing how a sense of wrong may vary from the Christian sense of sin in a society which at first sight seems to belong, if remotely, to the same set of Semitic-influenced religious traditions. In discussing the Nuer one must also take into account the possibility of direct Islamic influence, just as when discussing Evans-Pritchard's account one is almost compelled to consider his own conversion to Catholicism, something which may have involved him in a more conscious reflection of notions of sin than if he had been brought up a Catholic. He does not mention Hertz's work on sin in his book on Nuer religion (1956), though he was probably aware of the sin article, since this was roughly the period in which he was including a lecture on Hertz every year in his teaching, and he mentions Hertz's article on right and left elsewhere in the book when discussing Nuer spear symbolism.

Generally among Nuer, any breach of an interdiction 'is thought to bring into operation directly, and often almost immediately, spiritual sanctions. We may speak of such a breach as sin' (Evans-Pritchard 1956: 177). In the background is God, or Spirit, a normally distant but ever-watchful being: 'God is far removed from man in that man cannot ascend to him. He is very near in that he can descend to man' (*ibid.*). A key concept is *thek* 'respect', which involves a whole series of avoidances, between affines, potential spouses, regarding food, use of another's property, etc. Menstruating women may not drink cows' milk, men may not milk cows. *Thek* has connotations of 'deference, constraint, modesty or shyness [or] embarrassment' (*ibid.*: 180) and keeps apart people and things, either absolutely or in certain circumstances. Faults against *thek* and their consequent misfortunes come less from the action itself (accidental exposure of one's genitals, for example) as from the disrespect that it involves.

But injunctions are not only *thek*. Serious *thek* is *nueer*, which like *thek* may be unintentional. 'The breach of a *thek* rule may be shameful and despicable, but when it is spoken of as *nueer* it is also sinful' (*ibid.*: 182). *Nueer* also means 'to kill, destroy', death being an especially likely result here. Incest is 'like' *nueer*. Adultery is a lesser sin, but it is one that harms the wronged husband. An animal is sacrificed, then cut in two with the two parties holding different ends of it. Indeed, ritual separations rather than the return of the sin to its origin seem to be the remedies here. Intercourse with one's wife while she is with an unweened child is also a serious fault.

The consequences of sin may thus bear on other persons than the one actually responsible: the husband, not the adulterer, the unweened child, not its mother or father. But all sins are 'offences against God ... who punishes them' (*ibid.*: 190). The transgressor 'is contaminated by his act', which must be 'wiped out' by sacrifice, something which links sin to states such as boyhood, virginity and death, which are similarly wiped out in life-crisis rites. Once sin is wiped out, 'God turns away.... He does not regard it any more, so it ceases to be' (*ibid.*: 191). But more than sacrifice is needed – the sinner must have the will to be rid of his sin, which, of course, also involves acknowledging it. There is thus a spiritual and moral as well as a ritual dimension.

Any fault, however minor, may be counted a sin by Nuer if it is likely to attract divine punishment. Unredeemed faults may accumulate, hence confessions are made at certain sacrifices. Sacrifices may be held to prevent misfortune coming from a known sin, or in response to a sickness that is attributed to some past but unknown sin. For Nuer, 'the sin lies not so much in the act itself as in the breach of the interdiction' (*ibid.*: 189). This is because of its consequences, something which applies to killing another man as much as to the birth of twins. One's spiritual condition, not morality, auspiciousness, not goodness – these are the foci of Nuer attention. So here we have the intervention of the divine in response to the sin, the acceptance by the sinner of his sin, and his redemption through sacrifice – which involves a transfer to the divine but also a separation of the sinner from his or her sin – and confession. At least parts of Hertz's model are recognizable here. However, for Nuer it is human weakness rather than human wickedness that it is at the root of most sin. This is perhaps true of other cultures too. Certainly the Navaho of North America regard wrong-doing as being possible only through ignorance or incompetence, not through the individual's will. According to Ladd, therefore (1957: 272), 'although psychological explanations of the absence among the Navahos of a sense of sin in such terms as "guilt" may be perfectly true, it should also be recognized that the conception of "sin" is also incompatible with their "theory".'

Fürer-Haimendorf is another who has tackled sin in its own right. In his major work, *Morals and Merit* (1967), whose main theme is social approval and disapproval in a number of south Asian societies, he does not actually mention Hertz, but he does incorporate data on what constitutes sin in particular societies where appropriate.[5] However, sin is explicitly the subject of his Henry Myers Lecture (1974), in which Hertz's work receives one of its first mentions since its issue by Mauss over fifty years earlier. Fürer-Haimendorf expressly contradicts Hertz in suggesting that the absence of any word for sin would mean that the concept too was lacking. He distinguishes sins from ritual faults, which may invoke the gods' anger but are not inherently sinful. This colours the nature of the human responses to them: the Negritos of West Malaysia studied by Schebesta make offerings not 'in a spirit of piety or contrition [but] to avert worse disasters' (Fürer-Haimendorf 1974: 543). He sees the Nuer as another example where sins and ritual faults can be distinguished, since actions that offend God are not necessarily the ones that offend fellow Nuer. Like many African peoples, Nuer seemed to him to be activated more by a sense of shame than of sin, something which stresses man's obligations to his fellows as much as, if not more than, those to God.

Turning to the concept of original sin in Christianity as an example of the widely occurring belief that the discovery of sex made death necessary, he goes on to suggest that its absence in Hinduism is made good through the doctrine of the impurity of birth. Any birth signals a degree of sin to a Hindu, as it means that the child has not yet escaped the cycle of rebirths, just as every Christian is burdened with the sin of Adam from birth. Of course, there is also sin in Hinduism that is more directly the individual's responsibility (see below). Fürer-Haimendorf suggests that in general, specific actions are more likely to be classed as sins the more they threaten the social fabric, but he ends by deciding that different categories of sin have no other specific sociological correlates and that therefore reasons for sin can only be philosophical or psychological, not anthropological. His main purpose is to debunk the idea that the concept of sin is universal, in answer specifically to the question posed by Hertz. In the process, he ends up by shifting the problem on to other disciplines that are more concerned with the individual than with society.[6]

The tribals of middle India, very familiar to Fürer-Haimendorf personally, also belong in the category of peoples for whom ritual faults may not be sins. Indeed, it is clear that these societies generally lack any concept of sin that a Hindu or Christian might recognize. Fürer-Haimendorf deals with this general theme in some detail in *Morals and Merit* (1967). Often, the consequences of an act are more important than the act itself, so that the necessary rites are propitiatory or purificatory rather than expiatory in Hertz's sense. After returning from a successful expedition the Naga headhunter must be purified, but he is not punished. The overriding concern is often with social harmony rather than with an abstract moral order. Especially among hunting and gathering groups, there may not be any social sanctions, just a sense of moral disapproval for certain actions, which does not, however, lead to socially imposed penalties. Elsewhere in the region, acts that produce pollution or supernatural danger for the whole community may be the subject of action by the community, but wrongs to individuals may be disregarded unless referred to the community, or else left entirely to individual vengeance. In the former case, excommunication must be seen as society protecting itself, not as a punishment. In the latter case feud may occur, in which case the responsibility becomes collective and is not based on individual guilt. However, this is not the same as a tribal court or religious being making judgements and receiving the submission of offenders. While a Gond malefactor stands alone before the judgement of, ultimately, his whole tribe, a Naga may lose his head, through feud, for an act committed by one of his kin.

Nor need personal misfortune be linked to the fact of having sinned: it might be connected with eschatology. In these societies it is the manner of one's death, i.e. whether it was auspicious or inauspicious (in the latter case, by suicide, accident, a tiger etc.), not the worth of one's life, that is significant. And it is significant for such matters as whether or not one will be reincarnated, not whether one will go to heaven or hell. Finally, supernatural forces, while formidable, are not necessarily linked to morality. Evil beings may be directly dangerous rather than tempting the sinner to his destruction through his own actions. Similarly, gods are more powerful than men, but not necessarily morally superior or guides to morally correct action. Ideas of sin are not everywhere absent from these tribes. The Oraon of Bihar link personal misfortune to it and the Badaga of the Nilgiri Hills in Tamil Nadu take steps to remove the burden of sin from the dead. However, in these areas the influence of Hindu or Christian notions of sin cannot be ruled out. Certainly none of these tribes regard sin as irremovable or as condemning one permanently to any sort of hell.

For the most part in these societies, then, sin is less significant than shame, guilt less significant than fear, moral turpitude less significant than ritual danger. For Fürer-Haimendorf, the situation is not so radically different when one moves to caste society. Breaches of caste rules, though serious, are generally expiable, though there are exceptions, as when a woman goes wrong with a man of a lower caste. Such breaches are not necessarily regarded as sins, which are a personal matter (but cf. Rao 1981: 193) and are basically free from guilt, though not from other emotions, such as shame. Although caste rules are axiomatic, they are so primarily for one's own caste: it is recognized that they differ widely from caste to caste. Hence there is a degree of tolerance if not exactly in attitude, then at least in practical behaviour. While there is, among Hindus, a clear idea of sin linked to the theory of *karma*, it itself is not actionable by the caste, nor by any other body, but is a matter of individual responsibility alone. Pollution offends against the caste — and that differentially — which is only a small part of humanity. Sin offends against the world and against all humanity, but not against the caste as representing society, nor against specific deities. Thus communal pollution is distinguished from individual disadvantage, and the only way of reversing the latter is through an equally individual act of merit, not through community intervention.

This neat separation has been criticized by Parry (1991) in the course of discussing Raheja's work (1988) on the relation between impurity and inauspiciousness. While Raheja had linked sin to the latter but not the former, Parry argues that 'notions of "sin" and "pollution" commonly shade seamlessly into each other' (*ibid*.: 270-1). Conversely, Madan abjures either extreme, contending that 'the permutations and combinations [of sin, impurity and inauspiciousness] are manifold' (1991: 293). Some support for Fürer-Haimendorf's position may be drawn from his experience of Buddhist Sherpas, amongst whom the community is, if anything, still less involved in curbing breaches of rules, primarily because notions of pollution are less marked. Ladd's comment (1957: 333) that 'the chief function of moral principles is to advise us how to act rather than to punish us afterwards' seems especially appropriate here. Nonetheless, he who has offended against caste still depends on reconciliation with it, through admission of his fault and expiation, in order to go on existing as a normal human being. Hertz's model is actually more applicable here, even though the offence may not constitute sin as the society defines it.

The adverse impact of a particular sin on persons apparently innocent of it may also be discerned in Hinduism, at least through its retrospective attribution when misfortune strikes (e.g. Sharma 1973). But what is only apparent may conceal a burden of previously acquired sin. What is most directly involved is bad *karma*, here a particularly bad spiritual condition which arises through the accumulation of *pap* (sins) which may have been committed in previous existences and may therefore be unrealized by the sufferer until misfortune strikes. As a cause of misfortune, *pap* is distinguished from misfortune sent by an angry deity, which may nonetheless be the result of the individual's neglect of that deity.

Ritual responses to the problem of sin and the bad *karma* it generates may be remedial or preventative. Sins may be washed away by going on a pilgrimage (Fürer-Haimendorf 1967: 166), by bathing in the Ganges (Wadley and Derr 1989: 14) or by being transferred with gifts to those whose duty it is to receive them, who include certain Brahmans, Barbers, Sweepers, members of other service castes, and wife-takers (Parry 1980, 1986; Raheja 1988, 1989). These recipients must either 'digest' the sin, i.e. deal with it themselves internally, or pass it on with increment to others. For example, a Gujar wife-taker may pass on the wedding gifts he receives from his wife-giver to his family priest or *purohit* (Raheja 1989: 95). Raheja talks of inauspiciousness (*nashubh*) rather than of sin, though this, together with *dos* faults and *kast* afflictions, is removed along with it (*ibid.*: 82). Her discussion concerns the collective removal of inauspiciousness by the dominant caste of, and on behalf of, the whole village rather than individual transgressions, a communalization of sin that makes specific sin-based and misfortune-causing incidents even more difficult to identify or to link with particular individuals who have transgressed what is right. The removal of inauspiciousness by the dominant caste is an act for the whole community but it is not directed at any particular sinner. In fact, all are sinners, in so far as they have contributed by their actions to the accumulation of inauspiciousness in the village.

Aspects of Hindu death ritual also involve removing the sins of the deceased, by means of a bull which is set free or a Brahman 'eating' the dead symbolically (Parry 1985). So long as he has made himself sufficiently virtuous through the consistent and proper observance of all his daily rituals, the Brahman is supposed to be able to 'digest' and remove the deceased's sins. This is a representation or analogue of the burning away of those sins by Yamaraja, the god of death. Thus the Brahman's action amounts to the separation of the deceased from his sins. Other parts of the death ritual concern the symbolic consumption of other parts of the deceased, in the form of *pinda* or rice balls, by the chief mourner and his wife. In this way, the wholesome parts that are left are reabsorbed by the family as the essence of a new life, which also represents a further life for the deceased.

Other actions are preventative, e.g. doing good works (feeding Brahmans, fasting, charitable donations), the purpose being to build up good *karma* through merit and thus improve one's chances of a better rebirth, or even *moksha*, i.e. salvation through escape from the otherwise endless cycle of rebirths. Above all, of course, Hindu doctrine links sin to rebirth, the sinful becoming lower forms of life in future existences until their sins are expunged. Even rebirth as a higher form of life is not wholly desirable, given the pain of any rebirth and of all earthly existence. *Moksha* and the ultimate non-state of *nirvana* are only produced by eliminating all desire, the best way of achieving which is through individual austerities. These are ideally carried out in a state of asceticism, in which one acts outside society (ascetics undergo their own death rituals and so are socially dead). Whether or not desire itself constitutes sin, the elimination of desire can be said to remove temptation and, more importantly, to place the individual in a state where sin has no hold and no consequences. The connection is nonetheless indirect. *Nirvana* does not remove sin. It itself depends on its prior removal, although since it constitutes non-existence it can also be said to remove the possibility of sinning in the future.

These tendencies are perhaps even stronger in Buddhism (see Obeyesekere 1968: 19ff.). *Nibbana* depends on entering the right path, which here sin does not prevent, though the decision, the willingness to do so, may elude one who is too much burdened with sin. Here good works do not help since one is still trapped in a cycle of higher existences, though bad actions still trap one in a cycle of lower existences. The Buddhist heaven is a true paradise, but it is not salvation. *Nibbana* depends on freeing oneself from all actions, good or bad — and desire is the root cause of them both (*ibid.*: 29).

With Obeyesekere, we come again to a restriction of the concept of sin. As he observes: 'It is obvious that if concepts like theodicy, sin, and salvation, which are rooted in Western theology, are to be used in sociology or social anthropology, they have to be redefined in order to facilitate comparative analysis' (1968: 9). One of his concerns is the link between sin and eschatology. He denies that 'preliterate' societies necessarily have a religious sanction for sin in respect of the afterlife. The afterlife may be a world free of suffering, the present life a world full of it, a view he draws from Hertz's work on death (1909a). Alternatively, the world hereafter may be structured like this one or be much more unstructured and neither especially pleasant nor unpleasant. But the social sanctions that exist in these cases are in his terms secular, not religious. Breaches of taboo may bring retribution directly or through an ancestor or deity, but the ethical dimension is absent. The literate religions, by contrast, take over morality completely and give it a religious sanction. Obeyesekere thus resembles Hertz in linking sin with divine authority and he defines sin (*ibid.*: 14) as 'a violation of the religious ethics of morality'. But he has narrowed the applicability of Hertz's thesis considerably by limiting the term 'religion' to the 'higher' religions and by divorcing morality and ethics from any religious quality as far as 'preliterate' societies are concerned.

Obeyesekere is, of course, using religion here with its everyday or perhaps more accurately Weberian meaning, not in the Durkheimian sense of something inescapably equivalent to the social. A more useful distinction might prove to be the one he draws between those eschatologies that see the other world as accessible to all, regardless of their actions in this, and those that use the other world to punish sinners and reward the good, a discrimination depending on the development of what he calls, following Weber, 'ethicization'. The problem is that even in the former case there is usually discrimination on grounds of whether the dead person has died a 'good' death (i.e. what the society defines as a normal death) or a 'bad' death (e.g. by accident, suicide, murder, etc.). The good dead achieve a normal transfer to the other world, while the bad dead are excluded from it and must typically wander unrequited in this world for ever. Thus a differential measure of spiritual quality is introduced, as with sin. The difference between the two eschatologies would then consist in the criteria of spiritual quality, not in whether or not this is important to begin with. It also reminds us that sin need not be the only such criterion. For a Hindu, interestingly, the two notions come together. The deceased is regarded as having shown willingness to be a sacrifice to the ancestors in the cremation fire, but not all corpses are suitable. In particular, the bodies of the inauspicious dead are excluded, because of the sinfulness they have attracted to themselves, whether in this life or in previous ones. Thus the inauspicious dead are also, and primarily, sinful, not simply unfortunate (cf. Das 1977b: 123).

Two authorities on Indonesia have referred explicitly to Hertz's work on sin in recent articles (Barnes 1989; Platenkamp 1990). Platenkamp offers the more complicated analysis, partly because he also wants to bring in considerations of hierarchy and exchange acquired from his association with Dumont's *équipe* in Paris in the 1980s (see pp. 85–6). He starts with the intention of using Hertz's ideas on sin as a framework for analysing a ritual to effect a marriage within what would otherwise be an exogamous group, but he ends by deciding that they are not so useful after all.

The Tobelo of Halmahera, northeast Indonesia, are divided into exogamous 'houses' of the type identified by Lévi-Strauss (1984: 189–99). Marriage between them involves asymmetry of the sort common in eastern Indonesia, where wife-givers are superior to wife-takers. Platenkamp calls this 'hierarchy'. Any marriage within such a group can only take place if relations between wife-givers and wife-takers remain equal, either through the direct exchange of spouses or by ensuring that there is no inequality in the prestations that each side gives to the other. There must also be rites to avert the socio-cosmic disaster that might otherwise ensue — preventative rather than expiatory, as Platenkamp says. But all relations in Tobelo society are hierarchical: indeed, all relations in the society have to be established as hierarchical before they can be developed further. Any equalizing tendencies offend the honour and prestige of the superordinate party, represented by the ancestral image of the wife-giver's house. But hierarchy is actually impossible to achieve in the present case, since the marriage partners belong to the same house and thus share the same ancestral image. Classic structuralism would probably have dealt with this as a matter of an illegitimate mixing of categories, the Durkheimians as an illegitimate bringing together of sacred and profane. Here, however, it is presented as an illegitimate inversion – or more exactly, perhaps, negation – of the proper hierarchical cosmic order.

To what extent is sin really involved here? Platenkamp's own references to Hertz are less than wholly accurate and even contradictory. He rightly shows Hertz distinguishing crime and breaches of honour from sin in the latter's final definition of sin itself, but he is hardly justified in suggesting that this does not apply to Hertz's definition of expiation too (Platenkamp 1990: 74). Although the definition of the latter as such only occurs in Hertz's notes, a distinction is still evident in his treatment of the problem in the body of his text – crime is punished and honour avenged, but only sin is expiated. At the end of his paper (*ibid.*: 90), Platenkamp goes even further in suggesting that Hertz denied a firm distinction between sin and breaches of honour. Hertz's comparison is actually restricted to the argument that the effects of an insult on a man of honour are similar to the effects of sin on the sinner in that in both cases the inner being suffers adversely, and he denies (1994: 103-4) that the parallel should be developed any further.

One countervailing factor in the Tobelo case is the fact that the whole of society is threatened by this rupture of the moral order. It is not a case of the individual alone being burdened with guilt or fear in the face of social or divine displeasure. Indeed, guilt would hardly seem to come into this act at all, since it is premeditated, undertaken with the agreement of several parties if not of the whole community, its possible consequences being taken fully into account. We are not dealing here with a surreptitious act of, for example, incest, which the community has to take cognizance of after the event in order to prevent disaster. At first sight, there is still a sense in which, as Hertz says, the remedy involves returning the sin (or sinned against) to its source, in combination with a penalty. Ancestral images come originally from local stretches of water, and if they are dishonoured there is a danger that the waters will destroy the world through flooding, in order to claim back what they originally gave. The solution is to return the image to the water, transformed into 'dead money', i.e. ritual wealth, through ritual action and offered as a sacrifice. The image remains dormant until three generations have passed, whereafter the sundered house becomes one again (there is a corresponding rule preventing the repetition of a marriage between two houses for three generations). Perhaps, then, it is really a matter of re-creation by going back to the origin rather than of returning the sin to its source. That 'dead money' has to do with restoring or establishing honour is shown by the fact that it also constitutes the normal payment from wife-takers to wife-givers before a marriage between them can be entertained. Platenkamp himself argues that the concept of sin as actually defined by Hertz would be out of place here (1990: 90), but it is questions of guilt and individual responsibility that are really problematic. What is actually at issue here is the possibility of a supernaturally imposed disaster for an unredeemed transgression. Only the broadest conceivable definition of sin would be appropriate in this example.

This problem is less evident in Barnes's case. While Bahasa Indonesian does have the term *dosa* for sin in the Christian or Islamic sense, more widely used is *kesalahan* 'mistake, blunder, fault', none of which suggest, says Barnes, 'an attack on a moral order prescribed by a Divine Being' (Barnes 1989: 539, translating and quoting Hertz 1922: 46 [1994: 102]). In the community of Lamalera, Lembata, eastern Indonesia, which has been Catholic since the mid 1920s, pre-Christian forms of expiation are still surreptitiously carried out. Here, *koda kiri*, the local equivalent of *kesalahan*, covers a wide range of infringements, some of which may have been committed by earlier generations or in ignorance and all of which may lead to misfortune. 'A European would label some examples as mere mistakes or social blunders, while regarding others as heinous crimes' (*ibid.*: 539). When misfortune strikes, a soul-finder is brought in to determine the cause, even though it may lie in an infringement committed several generations back. Such searches are called *méi nafa*, which literally means 'blood-soul' but in fact refers to the return of 'hot blood' (perhaps a vessel or metaphor for the wrong) to the person suffering the misfortune and with whom the sin, even if vicariously, originated. Pigs and other foods are used, depending on the specific rite being undertaken, to take the faults out of the village or household. The confession of faults is a vital element. Faults confessed to vary widely and include the defilement of sacred places, murder, and failing to hold a *méi nafa* previously. The significance of the latter is that unredeemed faults accumulate, making disaster more likely. Despite the arrival of Christianity, ancestors continue to be important in punishing or supporting their descendants as well as in 'passing on misfortunes caused by their own past [unredeemed] transgressions' (*ibid.*: 539). Being, apparently, the guardians of the moral and cosmological order, they provide the religious element demanded by Hertz. At the same time, there is the separation of sin and sinner through confession and the taking of the sacrifice out of the village, which also involves a material penalty in the livestock and other foods which are also removed from the village. The English glosses for *kesalahan* (which Barnes took from a standard Indonesian-English dictionary, incidentally) clearly impoverish the notion of transgression in this community.

Fürer-Haimendorf's negative answer to Hertz's query concerning the universality of a sense of sin thus seems justified. Even our short survey here has shown the variation in attitudes to wrong-doing, however universal the existence of a moral code as such might be. Faults may or may not be intentional; they may involve pollution, danger or ethics; and they may or may not bring about direct divine or supernatural retribution and/or jural action by the society. Sanctions range from feud to excommunication, and shame is as likely as guilt. Mediation rather than reincorporation into the society is the usual response to feud. Not even Hertz's considerably wide interpretation manages to take all possible factors into account. Hence definitions of sin must ultimately be narrow and ethnocentric.

It is apparent from the notes he made for the body of his thesis that many of the faults Hertz would have discussed were really ritual rather than purely ethical in nature. The relation between morality and pollution was taken up again by Mary Douglas (without reference to Hertz) in her well-known *Purity and Danger* (1966), her main concern being to rescue magic from the status of non-moral residue to which the Durkheimians had tended to relegate it and to turn it into part of a structuralist model of symbolism and ritual action generally. To begin with, one can discern a stark break between the Old Testament and Pauline Christianity in that sin became 'a matter of the will and not of external circumstance' (*ibid.*: 60). While the shedding of blood could defile a church as much as the Temple, it was now the sin involved in its deliberate shedding (this representing an intention to defile) that did so, not the blood itself. Similarly the physiological wholeness of the supplicant no longer mattered, only his internal preparedness – any worthy cripple could approach the altar. This internalization of accountability for wrong-doing must have had a lot to do with promoting the idea of guilt as a social category. It will also have started a shift towards individual responsibility, which in the West has culminated in the idea of crime as primarily a matter of inter-personal relations, not the violation of a sociocosmic order, though it is still normally subject to the state's enforcement of social peace. We have seen that certain other religions, such as Hinduism and Buddhism, have embarked on a broadly similar but in detail separate evolution. Elsewhere, as Douglas also points out, a connection between pollution and morality can often be made, though not invariably. Pollution beliefs may reinforce morality, especially when the latter proves insufficient by itself. But where pollution is easier to remove than moral faults, wrong-doing may actually be encouraged. Pollution beliefs do not prevent Bemba adultery, for example (*ibid.*: 137, after Audrey Richards). Conversely, what counts as pollution — largely a matter of contact — may be clearer than what counts as morality, as is shown by the moral dilemma posed by killing in self-defence (*ibid.*, Ch. 8). Of course, contact does not necessarily produce pollution: luck may also be transferred by it (*ibid.*: 112).

In a general way, of course, a vast amount of work on ritual dealing with transgression and its consequences has entered the literature and been analysed on broadly Durkheimian lines without any reference to Hertz. This is true even of France, where Makarius could devote a whole book to the topic, yet only mention Hertz's work in passing in a footnote (1974: 65 n. 1). This is no doubt due in the first instance to the incompleteness and relative obscurity of Hertz's work on sin hitherto. However, it also reflects the commonality of the ideas of the *Année* generally and the status of their work as a sociology of morality. Although Hertz emphasised the negative aspects of these ideas specifically, they were not ignored by others in the group. The insistence on the autonomy of the social and its virtual equation with religion were taken over by Hertz from his colleagues, while the idea of the liminality of the sinner, as of expiation itself, as something involving a ritual separation (of sin and sinner) were publicized in a more general way by van Gennep.[7] What remains perhaps more particularly Hertz's own is the connection of sin with guilt, i.e. the argument that there can be no sin and therefore no expiation without the sinner's recognition of it, though even this depends ultimately on the standard Durkheimian formula of society's ultimate control over the individual. His view of the necessity of separating the sinner from his sin often becomes in practice a matter of separating the sinner from its consequences, while talk of returns to origins and sources probably has more to do with processes of re-creation than with returning sin back whence it came. For all these reasons, his work on sin has been less used and less developed than the two articles for which he is best known.

Plate 1   The rock of St Besse and its sanctuary (Robert Parkin 1990)

Plate 2   St Besse as a Christian soldier about to be martyred by being thrown from the rock (from a shrine on the rock: Robert Parkin 1990)

Plate 3   Cross at the top of the rock dating from 1933 (Robert Parkin 1990)

Plate 4   Portrait of St Besse being auctioned after the ceremony (Robert Parkin 1990)

CHAPTER SEVEN

St Besse and the Analysis of Myth

INTRODUCTION

In the summer of 1912 Hertz spent six weeks (20th July to 1st September) in the Cogne valley in Aosta, north-west Italy, a trip that counts as the *Année*'s only productive stint of fieldwork. Hertz's purpose was to study the cult of St Besse, a Roman legionary soldier who had been converted to Christianity and was subsequently martyred and beatified. The result of his visit was a long article entitled 'Saint Besse: étude d'un culte alpestre', first published in the *Revue d'Histoire des Religions* in 1913 and reissued by Mauss in 1928 along with other works of Hertz's in *Mélanges* (reissued 1970). More recently, the article has been translated by Stephen Wilson and made the banner article of a collection edited by him entitled *Saints and their Cults* (Wilson ed. 1983).[1]

Hertz's article — which Mauss referred to as 'his delightful *St Besse*' (1923–4: 24) and 'his charming *St Besse*' (1994: 55) — is indeed a marvellous blending of legend and history, with a very modern concern for meaning. By today's standards the description of the ritual is no more than perfunctory, but Hertz's main concern was to show, *contra* the usual historical interpretation, that there is no single correct version of the legend: competing versions have equal validity for their particular proponents, and their differences can be explained with reference to the particular social groups that hold them. Thus while at one level this is an examination of the relation between myth and ritual, at another it treats history as a created text, while at yet another it shows how a ritual which brings social groups together for an apparently common purpose can actually come to be the subject of contested meanings and disputes over its custody. The second and third of these levels have come to mean as much in the 1980s and 1990s as the traditional structuralist analysis of ritual in terms of the symbols by means of which it conveys meaning (see respectively Tonkin *et al.* eds. 1989; Boissevain ed. 1992), though the latter approach still flourishes too (see pp. 85–6).

But also this text, in one way so Durkheimian, was in another way a departure, not only in being a monograph based on fieldwork but also in its concern with myth rather than with ritual process. It must have been written up very quickly to have been published in 1913, especially since the sources Hertz used were literary as well as ethnographic. It appears to us as his third major publication, after the articles on death and right and left, even though Mauss calls it just a 'pastime' (Mauss *ibid.*), a piece of relaxation from his work on his thesis. Of course, everything takes on a narrower focus than in his other articles, where he had the whole world's ethnography at his disposal. Yet even here, documents are not left aside. This was not fieldwork as we would recognize it today and one often feels that, although essential to what he had to say, the data he collected in the field were merely supplementary to his literary researches. Indeed, many of his informants were from the local literate elite, clerical and lay, with whom he corresponded as well as visited, though he also talked with the shepherds from the hills while in the area. Still, for its early date it is a considerable advance on the usual separation of fieldwork and sociological interpretation in France at the time, though not invariably approved of by his contemporaries, even in the *Année* (see pp. 12, 163–5). And the study does contain much sociological analysis, in contrast to the stories and songs Hertz took down at the front from his men just before his death, which lack all but the barest commentary.[2]

The cult area is divided into two distinct parts. Apart from a two-day visit, Hertz did not work in the Val Soana (in the province of Turin) but relied on local correspondants (the chemist at Ronco and some local professors and learned monks) and Valsoanians living in Paris for data about the valley. Otherwise most of his trip was spent over the mountains in Cogne, in the province of Aosta. He cannot have had any language problems in this all too short burst of fieldwork. Aosta had always been French-speaking, though dialectically it leaned towards Occitan, and Hertz clearly knew Italian, at least to read. Originally part of the Etats de Savoie, Aosta was joined to Italy, though without the usual plebiscite, in 1861, at the time that Savoy itself was permanently joined to France. Since the first world war it has become more open to settlement from other parts of Italy, yet it retains a degree of separate identity, recognized officially by its being a separate though small province within the Italian state. Political activity is directed towards autonomy rather than separation (Stephens 1978: 508–9). Today, it is a tourist area summer and winter, Cogne especially having changed into a jumping-off point for the Gran Paradiso National Park. However, in Hertz's day, although Cogne itself attracted some tourists, it was still not linked to the outside world by motorable road (unlike the Val Soana),[3] and the Italians tended to regard the whole area much as some Americans regard the Appalachians – backward, and inhabited by people made mentally retarded by persistent inbreeding (Stephens *ibid*.).

HERTZ'S TEXT

The cult of St Besse, or San Besso in Italian, is centred on a shrine in the mountains at the head of the Val Soana, which meets the Val Orco at Pont Canavese, the nearest small town. The chapel itself rests at the foot of an enormous rock, at the summit of which stands a cross and a small shrine. The four villages of the Val Soana proper – Campiglia, Valprato, Ronco and Ingria – are in northern Piedmont and were Italian-speaking even in Hertz's day. But it is not only they who follow the cult: over the mountains, in French-speaking Aosta, the village of Cogne is also involved, the saint being the protector of all five villages. Despite the mountain barrier and disputes between Cogne and the Valsoana villages over its custody, Hertz clearly regards the cult as bringing these five villages together as a unit. The mountains are ultimately less of a barrier than the shared hostility towards the plains, despite the relative ease of access to the south. Only in the previous twenty years had the Valsoanians been linked by a proper road from the valleys. They called the plainsmen *maret* and blamed their illnesses on the dark clouds that arose from the plains. They maintained an *occlusion morale* through their own dialect and traditions of armed resistance to interference from the plains, ensuring even then that their economic dependence on the latter did not affect their identity. Even in Paris, where some of the men worked as glaziers during the winter, they stuck together wherever possible, the women, who stayed behind in the valley, ensuring that traditional values were maintained. Cogne, with its lack of a proper road, shared this general attitude, though it had its own differences with the Valsoanians.

Hertz has no real explanation for all this beyond talking of 'the obstinate particularism, the gregarious instinct, the passionate attachment to local tradition' of the people (1983: 58). His intention is rather to study the role of the cult in the present-day life and ritual of the saint's devotees, the organization of the cult and the legends on which it is based. Specifically, he was asking what was the meaning of the cult for its participants – from whom he expected no more than rationalizations – and what was the actual reason that motivated them to be there. We can already see that the answer to the latter is the very identity that they maintained marking themselves off from the plains. Yet the plains too had an interest in the cult, at least the local bishopric of Ivrea and the main church in the village of Ozegna, which San Besso shares with Maria Nascente. And these were not just plainsmen, but the local clerical and literary elite. There was thus rivalry over the ownership of the cult, not only among the mountain villages, but between them and the plains, between authority and ordinary folk, and between the literate and the illiterate. This has given rise to conflicting traditions of the cult's origin. Hertz set out to show historians that history was a created text, not a set of scientific facts, and that this creation was a social act whose result might vary with the social identity of those making it.

In Cogne the origins of the cult are unclear to its devotees, but its present importance is evident enough in its 'great powers' and 'many miracles' (1983: 59), especially as regards healing. Those with a favour to ask of the saint go to the chapel on August 10th each year and promise to return the next, or for the next nine years thereafter, if cured (the number nine is significant for other reasons too, as we shall see). This practice of votive offerings, i.e. ones made after the request has been satisfied rather than as a means of bringing about this satisfaction directly, is typical of Catholic Europe. The cult is effective against malevolent powers and people as well as against illnesses, whether in man or beast. The saint also protects soldiers (obviously, one might think, in view of his hagiographical origin as a Roman legionary soldier), who, if going to war or merely being called up, go to the festival and carry a stone away from the site with them for protection. Many Cognians had fought for the French Empire, and none had been killed, so far as was remembered. Since the introduction of military service, the saint is said to have become more important in ensuring good luck in the drawing of lots. Wilson points out (1983a: 37) that this aspect of Besse's power, i.e. the preservation of people from conscription, gives him a rather anti-military character when compared to battling saints like St George, whose prowess ensured victory on the field of battle itself. Hertz treats the military aspects as secondary.[4]

The annual visit to the shrine is the most important event connected with the cult. The saint is the more honoured the greater the numbers of people attending. Vows made during the rest of the year, by which one obtains grace in advance, as it were, in no way replace the obligation to visit the shrine at this time. Debts to the saint incurred during the rest of the year are paid and grace for the coming year renewed (sometimes a priest is paid to make the journey instead during the course of the ensuing year). The journey is itself a sacrifice, says Hertz, given that it deprives the villagers of a couple of days of the short summer when they could be working in the fields. The climb is long, eight to nine hours from Cogne, though only two from Campiglia, and steep and hard; some do it barefoot.[5] Those from Cogne come up the day before (the 9th), stay in the hostel built on to the chapel or out in the open on one of the plateaux near by, attend the celebrations on the 10th, and go down the same evening. Along the way are other small chapels.

The main celebrant and cult organizer is a lay person of good reputation and fortune. There is a mass and an invocation lauding the saint's qualities, but the main activity is the procession around the rock, in which people are 'grouped according to sex, age and religious dignity' (1983: 61). The more devout, and those with vows to fulfil, climb the rock on which the chapel stands in order to complete their recitation of the rosary. Those from Cogne do this the night of their arrival (i.e. the 9th), after nine circuits of the rock on which the chapel stands, kissing the iron cross at the summit after each rosary.[6] There are two essentials accompanying the procession: the *fouïaces*, connected originally, or at least traditionally, with blessed bread consumed afterwards by the celebrants, but in 1912 having more the image of a military triumph or trophy, preserving just the ribbons that used to cover the bread;[7] and the statue of St Besse, in the uniform of a Roman legionnaire and carrying the palm of martyrdom. The *fouïaces* were carried by young girls on their heads, the statue clockwise around the rock by four or eight young men. Hertz makes no comment on this obvious piece of dualistic symbolism, despite his article on right and left, as a modern anthropologist might well have done. After the statue is returned to the chapel, the faithful prostrate themselves before it and kiss its feet. Offerings are made to the saint in the form of clothes or livestock which are sold on afterwards in an auction held by the lay organizer, sometimes back to the original owner.[8] In this way, the devotee deprives himself of a precious object for a while and leaves something of its value with the saint even on receiving it back. Hertz thinks this particularly significant: 'Giving up the spirit in order to keep the substance, is this not, in the last analysis, the very basis of religious sacrifice?' (1983: 62). Devotional items are also sold at the church door.

The rock has healing properties. Although Hertz himself did not observe it, he was told (though by his intellectual friends, not by the hill-dwellers, who professed ignorance of it) that men and women rub their backs against it to cure themselves of back pain or sterility.[9] When the cross at the top of the rock was made of wood, people would scratch powder off it for keeping. This cross eventually fell down in a storm and was replaced with an iron one (the present one, also of iron, dates from 1933). Now they chip away pieces of the rock instead, using a ladder behind the altar in the chapel for the purpose. These are considered saintly relics: the saint's spirit is incorporated in the rock and animates it. But this spirit can also be incorporated into the saint's devotees, since water containing grains of rock is swallowed as a cure for illness. In this way, says Hertz, the saint is always with his devotees, whose devotion brings forth blessings just as the clouds bring the necessary rain from the plains.

Hertz ends his description by making the very Durkheimian and obvious remark that if the cult were not kept up, St Besse would cease to exist (cf. Durkheim 1915: 344, 346, 347). This is no van Gennep-type account, with different stages in the rite, from original condition, through liminality, to renewal for the coming year; just a very flat description, with scant attention to detail, and little sense of either structure or dynamic process, compared with Hertz's work on death.

The five parishes are jointly responsible for the upkeep of the cult and its buildings and traditionally took turns to arrange it each year, with the right to nominate the lay organizer and the bearers of the saint and the *fouïaces*. Even before Hertz's visit, changes in its administration were taking place.[10] Cogne claims that its turn came every seven years, but Hertz puts this down to the mystique of the number seven pushing out the ability to calculate properly. There is anyway jealousy, even conflict, over the custody of the rite between the different parishes, which Hertz describes at some length, relating the tales of an old Cognian of the fights he had been involved in as a youth with the Campiglians. Much of this conflict indeed seems to have centred around Campiglia's attempts to convert its claims to priority into a monopoly over the cult's organisation. The attitude of Cogne is especially noteworthy. Its remoteness over the mountain and the Francophone identity of its inhabitants tend to set it apart from the rest. The Cognians tend to conceal their identities while at the shrine, says Hertz, and never cross the mountain now for any other reason, such as commerce, though the situation may once have been different (see below). No more than about twenty people attend the cult from Cogne in most years, though this figure rises to one or two hundred when it is the turn of Cogne to arrange it. Nonetheless, the annual presence of even a few individuals preserves the rights of Cogne in the cult. Campiglia, though by far the smallest village, has in some ways the best claim to it, since the shrine is located in its parish and it was traditionally the first village in the valley to be converted. Many of its men are called Besse. Nonetheless, the tradition seems to Hertz to be dying, and he predicts that the cult will either disappear in the future or degenerate into a picnic, or else end up completely in a cathedral, probably Ivrea. In fact, it has done none of these things but still flourishes very much as Hertz described it.

Ivrea, the local see — beyond the Val Soana, though the valley is part of it — claims the saint's relics, and although the cathedral itself is dedicated to the Virgin Mary, Besse shares with two other saints (Tegulus and Sabinus) the honour of 'co-patron' of the diocese. Here the saint's festival, which is first mentioned in records dated 1338, takes place on 1st December. The saint is also honoured, jointly with the Virgin Mary, at Ozegna, southeast of Ivrea. Otherwise Besse is unknown in Christianity, and only the church in Ozegna and the cult chapel in the mountains bear his name. Hertz therefore decides that the same saint is involved, but which version has given rise to which? *Contra* one historian (Fedele Savio), Hertz thinks that it originated in the mountains, since Ivrea is the local city and bishopric, and it is unlikely to have started there and spread to so few parts of its see. Campiglia, because of its proximity to the cult centre and the early date of its conversion, is the most likely origin point, especially since Cogne is apparently ignorant of the traditions regarding the cult's origins and has been attached to the diocese of Aosta, not Ivrea, since at least the twelfth century. Only in Campiglia does Besse exist as a (male) personal name, nowhere else in Europe (though it is encountered in southern France, Switzerland and Italy as a family name). Presumably because of the undignified connotations of some similar words in the local dialect (such as *bess* 'imbecile'), it is often replaced by 'Laurent', through 'shame', whenever Campiglians go out of the valley.

The official tradition has a number of features that could be regarded as structural in the sense that they appear in similar relationships to one another in other traditions of the same kind. It starts with the attempt by a group of 'pious robbers' (Hertz 1983: 68) from Monferrat, south of Ozegna, to steal the saint's relics from its shrine in the mountains during the ninth century. They were taken to Ozegna, where the robbers spent the night in an inn, but the relics revealed themselves to the innkeeper, who stole them back; later, the inn became the church of San Besso in Ozegna. In the eleventh century the relics were transferred to Ivrea on the orders of King Ardouin, except for one of the saint's little fingers, which had to remain in Ozegna before the cart carrying the relics to Ivrea would move (cf. the shedding of limbs on ritual journeys in the Himalayas, Allen 1978). There was a further interruption on the bridge over the Dora when they reached Ivrea, which was only overcome through a promise that the saint be laid to rest in a crypt under the main altar in the cathedral. Hertz points out that the theft of relics and their resistence to being moved are common themes in medieval hagiography, as is their discovery and stealing back.

Since Ardouin had made Ivrea the capital of Italy, its bishopric endowed him with the status of the originator of the cult. But despite having most of the relics, Ivrea also recognized the importance of Ozegna and the Val Soana in the cult's legend. Historically the valley came under the control of Ivrea in 1213. This may have led to the consolidation of the cult in its various places, while the claims of Ozegna were reinforced by its position as a crossroads and commercial centre, and by its feudal possession by the see of Ivrea from 1094 to 1337. Thus historical fact, legend and the diffusion of the cult are concordant, says Hertz, the implication being that it is wrong to privilege any one over the others in trying to assess its authenticity or present meaning. But nor is there any attempt to confuse them conceptually, as a historian might do: in particular, legend is distinct from the historical reconstruction of the facts, and both are distinct from the facts themselves.

So the cult organization and its practice can be described separately from the legends that support it and can therefore be analysed separately. But the legends themselves differ, according to those that put them forward and the social context in which they originate, be it Ivrea, Val Soana or Cogne. The first difference is the date on which the rite is held. At Ivrea, this is the 1st December, when the mountains are under snow, not the 10th August, for which the official saint is Laurent.[11] The Valsoanians regard the 1st December as the true date, which was changed by decree of the archbishop in Ivrea (presumably to avoid it being held in the mountains in winter). The Cognians, however, do not know of this.

The identity of St Besse is another source of difference. In the official, ecclesiastical, literary version of Ivrea, Besse was a Theban legionary soldier put to death on the Emperor Maximian's orders in AD 286 after escaping to the Campiglia area and converting the local inhabitants. He was stabbed or beheaded by the soldiers who had come to find him, in some versions after being thrown from a rock by local shepherds whom he had discovered thieving. In some but not all the written versions, the rock from which he was thrown is said to be that connected with the chapel in the mountains, the chapel being the site of his eventual burial by his devoted followers. In the oral version of the Val Soana, he was himself a shepherd who died after being thrown from the rock, a representation entirely absent from the written versions, which the Val Soana otherwise accepts. In Cogne there are yet other versions. In one, Besse is supposed to have been martyred through merely falling from the rock, having gone to live in the Val Soana only *after* living at Cogne. In another, he was a shepherd who was known for praying and having good sheep who did not wander off and get lost and who got fat of their own accord. He was accordingly thrown from the rock by jealous shepherds, his body being found intact under snow by the people of Cogne after they had seen a miraculous flower growing there. Hence the chapel was built there, the exact spot being that from which present-day believers take fragments from the rock. Cognians use these versions to claim that it is they, having discovered the saint's body, who have the prior right to the cult, not the Valsoanians or the bishopric of Ivrea. Nonetheless, says Hertz, no one in Cogne knows, or cares, where his body is now.

The first Cognian version is, says Hertz, merely a garbelled version of the official one. The second is the one Cognians mainly subscribe to, but in seeing Besse as a shepherd it conflicts with the story of Besse as a soldier, despite this image being on the medallions associated with the cult and the fact that Besse is a patron saint of soldiers. There is little attempt by Cognians to reconcile this contradiction, which they do not care very much about. Hertz attributes this to their reluctance to accept anything coming from the plains. In their version Besse is a shepherd like themselves, whereas the official version tends to moralize and lecture to them, and even to represent them as thieves and murderers.

Hertz declares theirs to be the original version. Church hagiography is mostly uniform, only the name of the saint distinguishing one legend from another. We have seen that the official version of the Besse legend is no exception. The Church wants to separate Besse from the shepherds who supposedly brought about his martyrdom. Moreover, he could not just be allowed to die simply by falling from the rock: he had to be properly martyred by imperial, pagan soldiers so that the Church could remind its followers of its dual importance as both opponent and successor of the pagan Roman Empire. At the same time, and not without contradiction, attempts were made to identify him as an early bishop of Ivrea. The centre of the cult in the official version is therefore at Ivrea, not in the mountains. The rock of Besse's martyrdom need not actually have been that near Campiglia, though as the site where the saint's body was laid to rest it could be allowed a status as a place of holiness. The Cognians, however, want Besse for their own. For them, he is a shepherd and a power rather than a person of spiritual and moral excellence. And the circumstances of his martyrdom mean that it is the rock that is important for them, for it *is* the body of the saint, who fell into one of its crevices: what happened to the real body doesn't matter. For the Church, however, it does matter, especially since it can secure the body in a way that it cannot secure the rock. Thus it is not only in legend that St Besse appears differently in different, essentially social traditions. The place in which his spirituality continues to reside is also different, the rock for the mountain dwellers, the cathedral at Ivrea for the clergy.

Hertz is not the first to cast doubt on the official version. Baldesano, at the start of the seventeenth century, had tried to prove that Besse had not been a bishop of Ivrea and wanted to restore the version of the hills as historically correct. Hertz reports that he has been successful in so far as the image of Besse as bishop is now largely forgotten, but he regards the attempt to convert the hills version from legend into history as over-correction. Although historians are typically concerned with establishing which is the correct version — perhaps out of several which differ for narrow 'political reasons' — for the sociologist this is beside the point. Although the various versions may not help to reconstruct the actual history of St Besse, they do tell us a lot about the construction of different traditions by different groups around the same theme. This is especially significant since the different versions are not simply those of different political factions, of a sort historians are used to dealing with, but of different social classes. Through Hertz, therefore, the voice of the generally unheard and disregarded makes itself felt in unmistakeable terms. In the 1990s this all sounds very modern. In another way, it is a demonstration of what Durkheimian sociology had to offer the intellectual world of around the turn of the century, even in an unaccustomed field study of this sort. It must be one of the earliest demonstrations in anthropology that history is social construction, not scientific interpretation, but it also implies that sociology is a true science, in a way we are generally less confident about today.

Hertz poses three questions following this exegesis. First, why the participation of Cogne in the rite? Secondly, why is the rock involved? And thirdly, what is the origin of belief in its efficacy? Each of the two main legends gives an answer which satisfies its respective proponents. Is there a third version which is more genuinely historical? Hertz conducts his search for one by answering each of these three questions in turn.

1) Ronco, Valprato and Ingria were originally in the parish of Campiglia, before becoming separate parishes between 1280 and 1750. Cogne, says Hertz, was never in this parish, but nonetheless it seems to have been attached exclusively to the Val Soana at one time, since the route from Aosta is later and tradition has it that Cogne was peopled from the south, in particular by Campiglians using the meadows there as summer pastures. Trade too was at first carried on exclusively with the south, where at Cuorgné, just southeast of Pont Canavese, there was still a market named after Cogne in Hertz's day. Even after Cogne began to gravitate economically and politically towards Aosta, especially after mining was started there, it retained its religious connections with the Val Soana. The Cognians are still different from the Aostans in custom, costume and physical type.[12]

2) The rock cult goes back beyond Christianity. In France, the Christian priesthood tried to force it out entirely, but in the Alps it was simply Christianized. Hertz tries to prove this further by tentatively connecting the name Besse with regional toponyms signifying rocks. In all rock cults, the ritual is consistent from one to another, though the explanatory legends are not. The Durkheimian insistence on ritual rather than myth or belief in sociological explanation comes out clearly here, and although Hertz identifies some common elements in Christian hagiography, it was left mainly to Lévi-Strauss to standardize mythical structures much later.

3) The rock has no inherent spirit. The spirit is exterior and superior to it and animates the rock by incorporating itself with it. This spirit turns out to be not the saint but the life of the community, the rock itself being 'the emblem and focus of their [the Cognians] collective existence' (1983: 86). Though *mana* is not mentioned, we see here both the Durkheimian community representing itself to itself, superior to each individual within it, and the downplaying of the idea of a spirit favoured by the intellectualists. St Besse and his rock form a pure collective representation.

In conclusion, Hertz opines that religious life reaches deep into the collective consciousness of a people. The hagiography of Ivrea was stuck with its written records until he showed how other material could be used to cast light on it. The cult of St Besse offers a rare opportunity to unravel the popular tradition from the literary because it is still followed in Cogne in its 'pure', original form. This form is not concerned with either historical truth or Christian morality but is indifferent to both. It has a purpose and a coherence of its own, which the literary tradition has distorted for its own ends. The latter is therefore not the reliable record of popular traditions that the historian likes to think. Hertz thus shows us his opposition to the debasing of popular legend in standard historical accounts. The people of Cogne represent a part of Europe's oldest religious traditions, with only a thin veil of Christianity, but the cult is not a survival nor a set of superstitions but a true, living, meaningful ritual — and it is not alone in this in Europe.

THE SIGNIFICANCE OF HERTZ'S STUDY

It is only relatively recently that this text has come to be properly situated in its anthropological and sociological contexts, both Durkheimian and more generally. The work of Maître (1966), Isambert (1982, 1983) and Chiva (1987) has been especially relevant here. The latter's attempts to associate Hertz's approach to the study of ritual with van Gennep's has more resonance as regards the death article than the present one, where the focus is more on the creation of tradition (but see Chiva 1986). His brief appraisal (1987: 17) comes in the course of a disquisition on the creation of an ethnology of France and is not concerned with theories of ritual as such. Nonetheless he supports the view of the other two writers that Hertz's article stands at the interface of folklore and Durkheimian sociology as a particular ethnographic case to which are applied the more general notions of reciprocity — seen in the rotation of responsibility for the cult and of the tasks connected with it — and the total social fact.

This brief spurt of direct enquiry may have been one of the reasons for the disquiet with which this text was received by some of the Durkheimians, especially, it seems, Hubert (see p. 12), although as Maître points out (1966: 60), Hertz treated fieldwork as 'only one sort of information among others'. Isambert gives as one possible reason for this disquiet 'Hertz's attempt to integrate his views on folk religion into an overall theory of mythology' (1983: 165 n. 23), and he also hints at the awkward place of any search for origins or 'relics' in the new sociology, in which 'to explain a phenomenon [was] basically to assign it a function in a society conceived as an organized whole' (*ibid*.: 153). In this respect, it is instructive to compare Hertz's experience with that of another junior Durkheimian, Czarnowski, author of a thesis on the cult of St Patrick (1919). Although Czarnowski's supervisor Hubert was evidently not happy with his fusions of the roles of saint and hero in Patrick (see Isambert 1983: 164), the hero, like the legend of St Besse as peasant, marks a specifically popular counter-tradition and represents 'the incarnation of those values in which the community recognizes itself' (*ibid*.: 169 n. 29). Here too, there seems to have been disagreement over the question of origins:

> For Czarnowski, explaining the legend of St Patrick consisted in discovering its origin.... For Hubert, the origin is not essential to the sociologist, whose subject is the creation of the hero ... by folk practice, even if the raw material on which this creation is based is itself of a scholarly nature (*ibid*.: 165).

This may have been a source of Hubert's dissatisfaction with Hertz's St Besse article too, given the fact that its last section is taken up precisely with speculations as to the cult's origins. This is something Hubert himself was well placed to discuss critically, given his own interest in European prehistory and in the pre-Christian origins of European religion (e.g. 1950 and 1952 on ancient Celts and Germans respectively, both published posthumously). This may suggest that his objection was actually less to such work in principle than to some failure of fact or method, or that it lay somewhere else entirely. It is, of course, the very idea of 'relics', of the historical and here also prehistorical tradition, that is crucial in enabling one to see clearly the geneses of different traditions relating to the rite (*ibid*.: 171, 172; Maître 1966: 61, 66; Chiva 1987: 7). Hertz himself seems to have been more concerned that his text did not offend the inhabitants of the valley, especially his informants,[13] and none of the existing correspondence from his colleagues, to many of whom he sent copies in proof form, is critical.[14]

MacClancy has more recently argued (1994) that it was this particular emphasis on different traditions in Hertz's paper that was the source of the trouble, since it tended to give the lie to the standard Durkheimian view that ritual represents the high point of social identity and social unity, the one occasion on which the consciousness of the individual is wholly absorbed in

the mass, on which the fissive tendencies in society can decisively be coun-
tered. This is certainly another possibility, though it is doubtful that Hertz
actually had the intention of rocking the boat in any sense. To begin with, he
seems to have been more interested in the purely Durkheimian problem of
demonstrating that it was the *conscious collective*, not the properties of the
rock or the spirit of the saint, that forms the basis of the cult: only later did he
come to see the possibilities presented by the different accounts of the
legend.[15] It can also be questioned whether what Hertz had discovered necessarily makes the standard position untenable. Much turns on what constitutes a society or community. It is clear that rituals often bring together
several communities which regard themselves and each other as distinct,
whether or not they are necessarily well-disposed towards one another. We
might follow Baumann here (1992) in talking about different 'ritual constituencies', each with its own interest in a particular rite and its own view of
the traditions attached to it, which may or may not come into conflict (see
further below).

    In any case, the objection of Hertz's colleagues could not have been to
the study of popular religion as such. Isambert also deals briefly (1983:
159-60) with the concentration of the Durkheimians, including Hubert, not
simply on religious orthodoxy — the word of the book in the mouth of the
priest — but also on its interplay, both antagonistic and syncretic, with
popular observances. This leads to the general point highlighted by Maître
(1966: 59; also *ibid*.: 66), that 'the practice of the rites imposed does not
imply any adherence to the beliefs imposed': i.e. it is sociality, not belief, that
is the reason for the rite, a reminder of the debate with the intellectualists.
Judging from Hertz's interpretation, all these groups appear to be aiming at
oneness with the sacred, despite having different traditions of or charters for
the rite, different 'beliefs' concerning it. Their conflicts concern most obviously the custody of the rite, both physically and morally. Certainly, differences in tradition, doctrine and ritual observance interact with disputes over
precedence, providing the latter with both a possible cause and a means of
being rationalized. Yet there are no obvious grounds for arguing that the
central reason bringing people to the shrine on August 10th differs crucially
with the 'constituency' to which they belong. In Durkheimian terms it is still
the search for the sacred that impels people to ritual action, however differently that may be defined by different groups, even in respect of the same
rite and shrine.

    Thus whatever position Hertz's colleagues took on this point, one
might equally argue that his paper provides a demonstration of how different
views of the same tradition, although they may conflict, ultimately tend to
reinforce one another. In Isambert's words:

> The most important element for us is the circuit, analysed along the way, which goes from the local tradition to its elaboration by the urban clergy, and back again to be reinvested in the local tradition where the new images feed into the popular feast. (1983: 171; also *ibid.*: 172)

As an example of the last-mentioned stage in this process, the image of Besse as a soldier, though alien to all the popular traditions, nonetheless enters them from the official version in the guise of the protector of conscripts.[16]

Diversity and unity can thus coexist. Faced with the attempts of the Church to monopolize the tradition, the ordinary believers neither succumb nor cease to believe. They develop or continue a counter-tradition of their own, one which draws on pre-Christian beliefs and observances but which meets the official tradition halfway while remaining essentially distinct from it. Like all ritual foci, St Besse is regarded as a transcendental figure, offering access to the sacred through the further mediation of the Church. Although in the essential rites the ordinary believers have to accept this mediation, their possession of their own tradition, together with their own extensive involvement, allow them to subvert it to some extent. The Church is thus faced with a permanent reminder that it has yet to incorporate its believers fully into itself and that its claims over them are always contingent and negotiable.

This situation is by no means unusual where a religion has a developed scriptural as well as 'vernacular' dimension (cf. James and Johnson 1988). Wilson (1983a: 38–40) mentions cases of different social groups having different hagiographies in relation to the same saint from all over Europe. Pina-Cabral is concerned with a similar question regarding the peasants of the Alto Minho, Portugal (1980, 1986; he mentions Hertz on St Besse specifically, 1986: 206). Here, while some of the older priests remain complaisant towards the foibles of their flock, the younger ones, often from or influenced by a more bourgeois background, are less tolerant concerning cults and local superstitions. One example is the conflict over how to deal with a corpse that has proved to be uncorrupted on exhumation prior to the rite of secondary burial. The priest's whipping of it, in order to reincorporate it into the Church, is resented by the laity, for this is only consistent with the assumption that the corpse is that of a sinner. The laity, on the other hand, incline to the view that it must be the corpse of someone saintly to have been able to resist corruption under the earth for so many years. On this first occasion the corpse is usually reburied on the Church's insistence, but if on a subsequent exhumation it again proves not to have decayed, the Church is normally obliged to submit to popular pressure and allow a cult to develop. In the case of St Besse the tension seems to be less marked, but the Church nonetheless has to accept much that lacks scriptural authority, such as devotion to the rock and the observances connected with it.

Another aspect of the use of time in tradition has been highlighted by Pina-Cabral elsewhere (1992: 59), where he cites the cult of St Besse as an example of the way in which non-scriptural, 'vernacular' elements in religious experience are relegated to a past of inferior value. 'What was different became anterior. Thus, pagan survivals are the products of a struggle for power between the religious creativity of the masses and the Church's need for control.' Time is thus a means of establishing distance from an inferior other (cf. Fabian 1983). This is, of course, an elite process. Although the Church's use of history is far from being unproblematic, it does find a place in its rationalizations. The peasants, by contrast, are hardly concerned with history at all: indeed, their world-view is virtually entirely atemporal. Thus does history, supposedly 'objective', even 'scientific', become a tool of discrimination. Yet there is another reason for the Church's dominance. Only it offers transcendence for the entire community of believers that it summons together, united by its own claims to speak for universal humanity. It is, in short, ultimately nearer the sacred even for the peasants. Local communities, with their particular religious traditions, can be allowed a place, but only at an inferior ideological level. These traditions partake of the Church's activity, but although the Church might incorporate them, selectively, it does not concern itself with their maintenance. The relationship is one-sided, the opposition recognizably hierarchical in Dumontian terms (cf. pp. 85–6).

It is not that these peasants are the objects of any sort of ideological manipulation: they have their own sociality, and they exploit it in support of their own identity. Ultimately, however, they form a common tradition with the Church and the intellectuals. What we have here is therefore a society divided into groups, each with its own identity, but with enough in common to be able to discourse with one another. It is this that gives Hertz's study an added sophistication within the Durkheimian corpus, based on what Isambert calls his 'particular aptitude for grasping the disorganized in religion' (1983: 167). Of course, sociologists of religion study traditions rather than facts (except in the form of 'social facts'), which are the domain of the historian. Nonetheless, they are entitled to take account of the latter to shed further light on the former. This is precisely what Hertz does, nothing more.

This particular treatment of tradition makes Hertz's study a perfect candidate for Appadurai's critique (1981) of the Malinowskian view of history as a charter for action in the present. Hertz's study can quite easily be seen in this light, of course, granted only that this 'history' is largely if not entirely a creation, not an exact representation of what really happened. At this epistemological level, myth and history easily shade into one another, as any of the

legends Hertz recorded will serve to show. But it is not so much this that constitutes the problem as the sheer plurality of legends associated with the rite.
If ritual is the expression in the present of the events recorded in the myth,
what happens when each group with an interest in the ritual brings its own
myth to the performance?

Appadurai starts by opposing Malinowski's view to a second approach,
one which exploits the fact of different ideas of time and duration (e.g. Bloch
1977; Leach 1961). But there is a third approach, one which looks at ways in
which those holding rival interpretations debate 'pasts'. This is clearly linked
more to Malinowski than to Bloch, but there is a connection via Leach's
recognition (1954) that there may be not a single charter making for stability
but several charters competing with each other. The corollary of this is that
social disequilibrium if not actual conflict may result, rather than that the rite
creates unity out of the diversity of 'ritual constituencies'. This is precisely
the sort of question raised by Hertz's study. The example Appadurai choses
concerns a temple in south India whose control is regularly disputed by
groups of Brahmans, priests, Untouchables and so on, as well as by the State.
This being a Hindu environment, we are again in the presence of a religion
which has both literate and popular dimensions, one that incorporates not
just different viewpoints but real antagonism on occasion. Nonetheless, here
too the different discourses have to occupy a degree of common ground in
order to be able to communicate their disagreements with each other. In any
such situation, 'for an authoritative past utterance to have the maximum
value as a charter, it must encode the maximum number of features relevant
to the charters of other groups' (Appadurai 1981: 211). In the case of the disputes surrounding this temple, the overlap is provided partly by the Tamil
Prabandham corpus of medieval devotional poetry and partly by a series of
High Court decisions made in modern times. In the case of the communities
of Cogne and the Val Soana and the local Church and intellectual hierarchies,
it is provided almost entirely by St Besse himself.

A ritual bringing together different groups need not, however, generate conflict: it may unite them in favour of an identity which they can all
assume. Bowman (1993) shows how, in response to the Israeli occupation,
the ostensibly Christian shrine of Bîr el-Saiyideh at Beit Sahur on the
Palestinian West Bank has acquired meaning for both Christian and Moslem
Palestinian groups as a symbol of Palestianian nationalism. Associated at first
with a visitation by the Virgin Mary, the local munipality provided the site
with a shrine which accommodates Christian as well as Moslem symbols and
worshippers (aided by the Virgin's own importance to Moslems) and which
is deliberately designed to act as a unifier of Palestinian nationalism, regardless of religion. In this example, the rite brings together not the popular and

hierarchical wings of a common religious tradition but two quite separate traditions whose relations are normally antagonistic. Their unity on this occasion is brought about by minimizing religious differences in favour of a non-religious identity generated by their common opposition to the Israeli presence. It is also mediated, if not manipulated, by the secular local authority. Despite the difference from St Besse, therefore, Bowman is still able, in citing Hertz, to mention not only the different groups that have been brought together by the rite (*ibid*.: 432), but also 'the dialectical process through which social groups reify their sensed community in monuments and markers on the landscape they occupy, and in turn recognize the spirit and power of that community when looking on those edifices' (*ibid*.: 453–4). The shrine is the equivalent of the rock of St Besse, Palestinian nationalism the equivalent of the community of believers in the Val Soana.

What is perhaps most interesting in this situation is the position of the local authority, those responsible for the form the rite presently takes. The rationale of creating a social whole out of a disparate population is clearly discernible in their action, though it is a whole which incorporates only the participants in the rite itself — the Israeli occupiers, against whom the rite is just as clearly directed, are of course excluded. This last element aside, the rite is therefore actually very Durkheimian. But more generally, the circumstances of its modification suggests that no one is going to create or modify a rite expressly with the *intention* of dividing those taking part in it from one another. It is only later that conflicts may arise, as different groups of people associated with the rite come to view it differently, developing different agendas, some of them perhaps seeking to establish a claim to be involved that was ignored or rejected initially, and so on. Of course, none of these developments are in themselves inevitable, nor do they exclude the entirely separate possibility that the ritual is aimed at a specific group of outsiders, as in the Palestinian case.[17]

Wright's account of ritual regeneration in north-east England (1992) shows what may happen when conflictual messages are deliberately designed into a ritual from the outset. At the time, she was acting as a rural community worker in this economically depressed former mining and ship-building area of England. In other words, she was herself involved, with colleagues, as an actor in the events she describes — this was most definitely not a case of the anthropologist as observer and recorder alone. She and her colleagues decided to incorporate what she calls a 'critical history' of the area into their re-creation of a miners' ritual from the past, which in large measure meant a stress on the history of local working-class struggles against the owners of industry and both local and national politicians. However, this proved too conflictual for many who attended, who preferred to see the event simply as a family day out, in which political speeches of any sort were unwelcome. Eventually, local politicians took it over and sanitized it by converting it into an event for the whole community, though evidently with the acquiescence of many of the local population. The attempt to create meaning by challenging rather than encouraging the sense of a shared community simply did not work. The process outlined above as typical, of a shift from uniformity to conflict, was completely reversed. The ritual became more Durkheimian as time went on.

Although Hertz's article is ostensibly about a particular rite, his ultimate purpose is not to describe the rite as such, whether as a dynamic process or as a simple confirmation of identity and belonging. He too is much more interested in the social meaning the rite has for the various participant groups and in how they relate this to their own views of the tradition. As an early study of myth, it is very much sociological rather than symbolic in its treatment of the topic. But Hertz's essay can also be linked to more modern anthropological discourses on the creation of tradition, as exemplified by the recent collection *History and Ethnicity* (Tonkin *et al.* 1989). What one misses with Hertz is the ethnic dimension that these and many other modern studies are primarily concerned with. It was open to him to discuss this too, given that francophone Cogne had certain different traditions to those of the Val Soana. His silence may have reflected contemporary political realities – at the time, the 'problem' minorities were those like the Poles, Czechs and Irish, who had no independent nation of their own, not the French of Aosta, who did have one, though on the wrong side of an international frontier. In fact, French claims to German-speaking Alsace and Lorraine, on historical rather than ethnic grounds, may have precluded too much attention being drawn to the situation of the Aostans, though they themselves were already campaigning in defence of their language, a campaign which Hertz supported (see his letter, 1912c). What was open to Czarnowski in his studies of Ireland and later Poland, i.e. religion as an aspect of nationhood, had less relevance to Hertz in north-west Italy (see Isambert 1983). Today, however, when so much of the anthropological study of Europe is the study of minorities, one would be more inclined to take ethnicity into account.

Another difference is Hertz's use of history. Both he and modern scholars interested in such matters recognize that history is both fact and interpretation and that the latter tends to shade into myth or tradition at a popular level (and sometimes at a scholarly level too). The differences are in emphasis. The moderns tend to begin and end with tradition and its creation, reflecting on 'real' history only for the sake of occasional clarifications. For Hertz, musing on the creativity of tradition is not enough in itself: he feels he has to turn to real history in order to complete his analysis. Although many of his suggestions can only be speculative, there is no doubt that this greatly enriches the overall picture. The spirit is positivist, not relativist. It arises, of course, out of attempts to make sociology a science in its own right, one with its own particular view of history as of every other aspect of human cultural life, a view which covers the uses to which it might be put as well as what it is. Here the argument is developed against both folklorists and historians, but by using their own types of sources.[18]

The creation of tradition is not the only possible way of interpreting Hertz's paper, though it is perhaps the most salient. MacClancy (1994) has preferred to stress the element of pilgrimage, seeing in Hertz's account a little-noticed forerunner and counter-weight to Turner's better-known treatment of pilgrimage as an example of 'communitas' (e.g. 1974a: Ch. 5). This aspect was certainly stressed in the officiating priest's invocation to the saint in 1994 (MacClancy and Parkin n.d.), and was considered justified by the difficulty of the climb. Although Hertz himself frequently calls the saint's devotees 'pilgrims', especially those from Cogne, i.e. from over the mountains, he does not define pilgrimage or distinguish it from other forms of ritual — which, as we have seen, he is anyway less concerned with. On the other hand, if the interpretation is accepted, it means that St Besse provides, at least in some respects, another counter-example to Turner's view of pilgrimage, one which has often been found problematic.

Turner can be followed in seeing pilgrimage as something different from everyday life to which everyone returns. For him it involves, like any other manifestation of communitas, a temporary change of situation for the community of participants, through a kind of spontaneous coming together and feeling of oneness. A sense of community continues to exist, but in a different form, both it and the ritual occasion constituting an anti-structure opposed to the social structure that exists normally. It is as if Turner had taken over Durkheim's effervescence and adapted it as a mechanism for subversive or at least alternative forms of social life. In time, however, communitas itself becomes routine and more like a structure, which Turner calls 'normative communitas'.

Yet as MacClancy points out, there is typically no permanent change in status for the participants in a pilgrimage. In addition, what has struck many observers is the conflict that pilgrimage frequently entails, like many other rituals, for that matter.[19] It is here, most obviously, that the St Besse data challenge Turner's model, given the different traditions and claims to the rite that Hertz wrote so extensively about, even between different villages, and the fights over precedence that he was told about. But this is not invariably the case. Although there was no great sense of integration among the pilgrims of north-east Brazil that Gross studied (1971), he found no conflict between them either. Instead, given its aim of fulfilling vows made to the saint, the pilgrimage to the shrine of Bom Jesus da Lapa seemed rather to be a replication of the patron-client relationship characteristic of the secular society. Although social structure does not in any sense depend on the pilgrimage, it 'finds ideological support in it' (*ibid.*: 146). Thus pilgrimage is not always characterized by conflict, but nor can we identify it exclusively with communitas. Many pilgrimages merely take the form of a coming together in space and time, and in a common interest in the ritual, but not in any other sense.

Perhaps Hertz provides us with a possible way of mediating between Durkheim and Turner on this theme. Both tended to see ritual as appealing to a united mass, but for the former, pilgrimage, being a type of ritual, would still have been structure, whereas for the latter it was a form of anti-structure. In Hertz, ritual is treated as basically Durkheimian in the sense that it has a unifying function, but in the St Besse paper one is led forcefully to the realization that a number of competing groups may be involved. In such cases any unity will be that of each participating group, of each 'ritual constituency' separately, which may dispute matters of precedence and interpretation with the others but which nonetheless shares with them a common interest not merely in being present at the event but also in ensuring its successful outcome and its repetition on future occasions. There may be cases where the very existence of the ritual may be threatened by conflict, especially if this originates from outside. On the whole, however, disputes typically centre around its custody and matters of interpretation, not whether it should be held at all. Even in circumstances such as these, therefore, a rite might still be an opportunity for discourse and mutual definition within a larger whole.

CHAPTER EIGHT

Conclusion

In the course of the previous chapters Hertz's work has been introduced and discussed item by item, with reference especially to the reactions of others to his ideas and the developments they themselves have seen fit to introduce. It is now time to attempt an overall assessment of his all too brief career and its significance. This has already been tried previously, by Evans-Pritchard (1960) and Needham (1979b), though both tend to focus on the essays on right and left and on death in making their assessments, to the exclusion, relatively speaking, of Hertz's work on sin and on St Besse.

Hertz followed Durkheim's doctrine of social control of the individual closely, but he did not always adhere rigidly to other aspects of the master's message. His decision to concentrate on the more negative aspects of social life was on the whole complementary rather than antagonistic to the mainstream of Durkheimian studies, though the work on St Besse created problems even here. He had occasion to revise or develop other points more explicitly. Thus in the article on right and left, he distanced himself somewhat from Durkheim and Mauss's doctrine of the foundation of symbolism in social forms. Although the notion of polarity itself, as a symbolic form, is seen as having a social origin, with primitive dual organisation as its archetypal expression, it is not rooted in the morphology of any particular sort of society but is rather regarded as a basic principle of collective human thought from which not even modern man has entirely been able to free himself. Similarly, the study on death did as much to identify and isolate notions of transition and process as to develop understanding of the social significance of death as such, a transition that affected the corpse, the soul and the mourners equally.

Needham has argued (1979b: 296) that this concern 'to detect certain abstract features of collective representations and social conduct underlying ... particular institutions' entitles Hertz to be regarded as 'a methodological successor to his teachers Durkheim and Mauss'. The appeal of this for Needham clearly lies in the fact that his own work has tended more and more towards the search for primary factors of human thought and experience,

173

factors which have to be couched in very abstract terms to have any comparative relevance. Even then, some such notions, such as opposition, may prove to be excessively varied in type and therefore recalcitrant to any sort of universality or standardization (cf. Needham 1987). At the same time, Needham has also been led to deny the relevance of at least one of the factors he finds in Hertz's work, namely the homology of terms in a system of dual symbolic classification. On the positive side, it can be said that in generalizing dualistic thought and fixing it to the phenomenon of opposition, Hertz so modified Durkheim's archetypal distinction between sacred and profane as to increase considerably its ethnographic relevance and applicability.

Needham has also made the interesting point 'that Hertz makes no doctrinaire disjunction between social facts and inner states' (1979b: 297). In other words, although it is still the sociology of religion that is his main concern, Hertz did not feel intimidated by one of the questions the Durkheimians had originally posed themselves, namely the relation between individual psychology and social facts. While Hertz would have agreed with the Durkheimian doctrine that a social phenomenon such as a ritual may control and even generate emotions as well as assuaging them, he does not move from this to arguing that the classification of emotions is itself socially determined. Rather, he recognizes that ritual and symbolism may be emotionally satisfying in themselves, whatever their origin in specific social conditions, and whether one is dealing with death rites, the expiation of sin, the collective celebration of community identity or the recognition that every positive value has a counter-balancing negative one. Durkheim and his colleagues have often been accused of ultimately resorting to a psychological reductionism of their own in order to circumvent the inadequacies of the sociological method. Needham's remarks help us see how what has often seemed like special pleading might more fruitfully, in Hertz's work, be regarded as a positive and less rigid aspect of that very method.

In ritual too, Hertz developed something of a distinctive voice in his two studies which bore most directly on the problem, those on death and St Besse. The intellectualists, above all Frazer, had contented themselves with classifying different rites according to the associations that were supposed to be operative in them (e.g. homeopathic as opposed to contagious magic). For the Durkheimians generally, the importance of ritual resided mainly in its role as the generator of collective feelings and remover of social fissions. Hubert and Mauss's joint analysis of sacrifice (1899) was primarily concerned to show this as the high point of ritual, the point at which the suppliant attained oneness with the sacred through the sacrifical object. Hertz contributed two modifications to this static view of ritual as producing conformity. One was the demonstration in the article on St Besse, underplayed by

Hertz but undeniable, that ritual occasions could generate competition and even conflict. We have argued that the objection this implicitly contained to Durkheimian orthodoxy is not necessarily unanswerable, but it does provide a wider perspective of the model they put forward. The study also linked ritual to myth, seen here in the form of tradition and history.

The other modification, in the article on death, showed conclusively that ritual was a process rather than just an occasion at which social cohesion was promoted, a process, moreover, which in certain circumstances permanently changed the status of the leading participants. They were not simply oscillating between ritual time and normal time, returning to the latter in the same state as they left it except for being uplifted by the effervescence they had experienced. They were undergoing what have come to be called life crises which are ritually marked. The stage was set for the identification of such rites separately from either rites of healing (more personal still, and assimilable to much of what was still being called 'magic') or rites for the whole community (e.g. rites of renewal, agricultural rites etc.), as well as for the supplementation of the mere classification of rites with an analysis of the underlying structure common to them all. Both, of course, were brought to fruition in the work of van Gennep, whose treatment by the Durkheimians almost suggests that they saw in him a rival of importance.

Like his colleagues, Hertz tended to treat rival disciplines almost as part of the data requiring explanation, rather than having any explanatory value in their own right. This is particularly evident as regards theologians in the essay on sin and historians in that on St Besse, but it could also be applied to folklorists and ethnologists, like Frazer. This was part of the attempt to establish sociology as an autonomous discipline, one, moreover, which was superior to others in recognizing that even academic representations were socially determined. In establishing a certain distance between itself and its data, Durkheimian sociology was claiming a pre-eminence over other disciplines that went back to Comte.

Hertz shares with Mauss in particular something of the character of a proto-structuralist that Mauss later became so well known for, in that the social phenomenon being studied was not isolated from other social facts but was seen, indeed explained, in relation to them. The relation itself was also to be found in numerous other societies, apart from those that were currently being examined. Causality did not lie in the predominance of one social fact over another but, if anywhere, in the total social environment in which the phenomenon being described existed. Causality was anyway not as important as it had been in certain other schools of sociology and anthropology: it was enough if a pattern with relevance to a number of societies could be demonstrated to exist underlying the ritual or other social phenomenon under discussion. This could sometimes lead to a reduced emphasis on difference in the interests of a more integrated comparison. Evans-Pritchard remarks:

> In his study of second burials [Hertz] drew attention to the large number of different forms disposal of a corpse takes in different societies but pointed out that these differences need not be taken into account in the making of a sociological analysis, since the procedures have the same purpose and function. (1960: 13)

Linked with this is Hertz's place in the Durkheimians' peculiar form of evolutionism. Generally speaking, they were at best agnostic about the value of evolutionary reconstructions, they were always sceptical about linking evolution with 'progress' in the manner of Tylor or Frazer, and they were relatively disinterested in the search for human origins. Nonetheless, they could hardly ignore the fact that the picture of 'primitive' society that emerged from ethnological materials was radically different from their own experience as representatives of modernity, and that this needed explaining. Sometimes, the difference was seen as a typological dichotomy rather than an evolutionary sequence, as largely with Durkheim's distinction between mechanical and organic solidarity, which is also one between segmentary social systems, where each segment is essentially identical to any other, and the interdependence of the division of labour (Durkheim 1984). This meant, *inter alia*, that each segment would perform all the functions that were distributed among several interdependent groups in a division of labour. However, this conflation of functions could also be seen as separating out in the course of history. This sort of evolutionism was also applied to concepts seen as initially merging aspects which became separate later in history. This is especially visible in some of Mauss's work, for example *The Gift* (1954), in which early society merges the notions of disinterested gift-giving and of exchange, which ultimately become separated as gift and commercial transaction. Similarly, the essay on the person (1938) traces the development of the concept from an initial stage involving roles and the occupation of a series of bodies through a series of reincarnations to the modern notion of the autonomous individual personality distinct from other such personalities and from society. Finally, the early joint article with Durkheim (Durkheim and Mauss 1963 [1903]) on primitive classification sees the classification of nature as originally embedded in the classification of men, from which it subsequently frees itself, developing eventually into a value-free and socially neutral scientific classification.

Hertz paid lip service to this approach to evolutionism without ever constructing his articles around it in the way Mauss had sometimes done. The article on sin recognized the separation of church and state, and of sin and crime, in modern (or at least 'non-primitive') societies (e.g. 1994: 108–10). In the article on death can be found passages suggesting that historical changes have led to the decoupling of the fates of the corpse, soul and mourners that Hertz had identified, through, for example, conflation of the first and second burials or the tokenization of the latter (1960: 40-1, 75-6). Similarly, Christian theology postpones salvation for every soul until the Day of Judgement, regardless of immediate disposal of the corpse and the limited period of mourning (*ibid*.: 78-9). The article on right and left, finally, acknowledged that in modern society the two notions have a mostly spatial meaning, devoid of the different values with which non-modern societies invariably infuse them (1973: 11-12). It was clearly always this initial stage that interested Hertz: although he applauded the arrival of ambidextrous learning, for the most part later stages are only of interest in providing antitheses to what obtained in humanity's original state.

Hertz's style was not so dry as Durkheim's was wont to be and has plenty of dramatic or otherwise apt phrases to help the flow of argument. His writing on sin is particularly florid at times, and his dramatic opening to the article on right and left immediately engages the reader's attention:

> What resemblance more perfect than that between our two hands! And yet what a striking inequality there is! (1973: 3)

The article on St Besse is studded with similarly evocative passages, such as the opening again, and the famous sentence where he praises 'those precious instruments of research, a pair of stout shoes and a walking-stick' (1983: 87), necessary at least in the Alps. This style may perhaps be said to reflect Hertz's expansive personality, but also, Durkheim's subordinates could afford to be less dogmatic than he himself, who had been forced to concentrate on establishing the subject, both academically and institutionally, in the face of hostility from better-established disciplines such as philosophy, psychology and law. Once the initial battles had been won, the chairs and other posts secured, his students and colleagues could afford to indulge themselves a little more in their work. Certainly their writings are on the whole less technical, more concerned with extending the new perspective to other themes than with establishing fresh methodologies. Coming later, they also had somewhat better and fuller ethnographic materials to work with.

Mauss said of Hertz (1994: 116), he 'was a scholar, not just a philosopher', by which he meant that he used facts not just to illustrate his theories but actually to work them out. Some of Hertz's letters to his friend Pierre Roussel gives us insights into his views on methodology. An early one describes his joy at discovering 'inductive research' when in London,[1] and he was later to praise the Fabians for their use of 'the inductive method ... starting from the facts' (1911b). And an excellent place to find facts was ethnography:

> ... comparative ethnography gives us, after a certain period of time, the
> desire to study facts which are more directly graspable and intelligible,
> which are made more 'explicit' through the very consciousness of the
> people who have lived them, in other words, which are capable of
> being studied historically, even philologically.[2]

But one also needs hypotheses:

> In effect ... it is a matter of proving the hypothesis that was proposed at
> the start ... by examining if, and how, and to what extent the conse-
> quences which one can logically draw from this hypothesis agree with
> the facts.[3]

Yet there is no doubt that Hertz also shared many of his colleagues'
methodological faults, including basic reasoning. Evans-Pritchard (1960:
21ff.) lists especially the sweeping generalizations that they often fell into the
temptation of making on the basis of a narrow range of facts and their ignoring of negative instances or their recourse to the principle of evolutionary
change to explain them. Examples of the latter in Hertz's own work have
been pointed out in the preceding chapters, and *pace* Needham (1979b:
296), he cannot really be absolved from this particular offence of method.
One can also doubt whether the inductive method was always applied so rigorously, especially once innovation began hardening into dogma: the models
and hypotheses often seem to be driving the data rather than the other way
round. Indeed, Hertz must take his share of the blame as well as the credit in
having helped perpetuate the drawbacks and advantages of Durkheimian
methodology to later generations of scholars.

That Hertz had a mind of his own is clear not only from his academic
writings but also from his desire to use his intellectual abilities for the better-
ment of his fellow men. Although he found a possible answer to the problems
then facing society in Durkheimian sociology, his involvement with the latter
was undertaken at the cost of having to give attention to purely academic
problems whose relevance was not always immediately apparent to him. In
his treatment of those problems, he did not deviate markedly from the orthodoxy of the school he had chosen. His contribution was distinctive, in that it
addressed the nature of the social primarily from the point of view of the negative forces that regularly threaten it. His point of departure was always
Durkheim's sociology, but in developing his chosen themes he confirmed
Durkheim's overall position while supplementing it with new insights in
some repects and modifying it in others. Only once did a modification come
to seem like a challenge to that position, and that was probably unintended.

The personal difficulties Hertz faced in producing his work were in
the last resort not intellectual but linked to the contradiction of being a pure
scholar in a society that was badly in need of reform. One way of coping

with this was to choose topics that allowed him to examine the consequences of social breakdown and the means of overcoming them. Another was to hope that all this activity might lead to a regular post in teaching, which he saw as a social relevant profession. It was his experience of war that finally led him to contemplate giving up purely academic research to concentrate on problems in education. Whether or not he would ultimately have taken this step, posterity has reason to be grateful that he stuck at the task Durkheim encouraged him to follow for as long as he did, for it is ultimately here that his impact has been felt. What he produced has long outlived the society whose problems were of so much concern to him and which died with him in the first world war.

Notes

NOTES TO CHAPTER ONE

1. Durkheim 1916: 116; Bourgin 1970: 484; FRH, Hertz's birth certificate, Stammblatt; Antoine Hertz, personal communication. The exact date on which Adolphe Hertz was killed was 4th August (FRH, Stammblatt). A maternal uncle founded the Paramount film company in the United States, but committed suicide after being ruined in the Wall Street Crash of 1929. Robert's younger brother Jacques became a surgeon at the Hôpital de Rothschild in Paris.

2. FRH, Diplôme de Bachelier de l'Enseignement secondaire classique, dated 15/7/1898; Diplôme de licencié ès lettres, dated 26/11/1900; Livret Scholaire. Durkheim 1916: 116. Durkheim's view is confirmed by Hertz's Livret Scholaire (i.e. school reports), which regularly show him achieving high places and receiving glowing reports from his masters on everything except physical education, at which he was consistently mediocre. Quick to learn things, he appears to have been especially gifted at languages, one teacher remarking that he knew ancient Greek better than French. In addition, he certainly knew Latin and English (Antoine Hertz, personal communication), and could clearly at least read Italian, German and Dutch, given that he reviewed books in all these languages. Another indication of his precociousness is that he completed his *baccalauréat* early (at Janson de Sailly; Antoine Hertz, personal communication).

3. FRH, 'Lettres du service militaire de Robert, 1900–1901'; also his Certificat de Bonne Conduite, dated 24/8/1901, which must have been issued on or shortly after his discharge. Other documents indicate 12th November 1900 as his call-up date and that he was subsequently recalled in July 1903, September 1906 and May 1909 to his unit's depot in Reims for further military training. On Hertz's dislike of his time as a conscript, his view of the wastefulness of conscription, its bad influence on those that go through it etc., see his letter to Frederick Lawson Dodd, 21/10/1901. As we shall see, once war came, his attitude to military life was to change dramatically.

4. Durkheim 1916: 117; Alice Hertz 1928: ix; FRH, Certificat d'Agrégation. On the ENS and its connection with secondary teaching, see Clark 1973: Ch. 1. It became part of the Sorbonne, and therefore of the University of Paris, in November 1903, in Hertz's last year there (Clark *ibid.*: 29, 40).

5. Hertz to Dodd, 8/12/1897.

6. Durkheim 1916: 117. According to Mauss, Lucien Herr, librarian of the ENS, recommended Hertz and others to Durkheim (Fournier 1994: 203 n. 1).

7. Besnard 1983. Clark points out (1986a: 63–4) that the ENS and the Sorbonne were politically allied to a large extent, both having been pro-Dreyfusard and therefore opposed to the more conservative Collège de France, where the psychologically grounded sociologist Gabriel Tarde had just been given the chair in modern philosophy. See also Lukes 1973: 304.

8. See Lukes 1973: 195ff. Clark (1973: 17–18) sees this as the outcome of the take-over of Cartesian and positivist thought by the Napoleonic and later bourgeois

181

state, which it combined with the control and even suppression of dissent, thus leading opposition almost of necessity to take a violent form; unlike in England, it was difficult for political parties and similar associations to form a bridge between state and people. One result was that the universities tended to be much more closely entwined with the societies that supported them: other sociologists, such as the Le Playists, and not just the Durkheimians, were also concerned with social stability and harmony (*ibid.*: 105, 109, 217).

9. Cf. Durkheim 1915: 427–8; Lukes *ibid.*: 546.

10. Cf. Durkheim *ibid.*

11. Durkheim 1916: 116; Mauss 1925: 23–5; letter, Durkheim to Mauss, 22/4/1915 (reporting Hertz's death). Hertz first got to know Mauss in 1902, when he invited him to give a talk on cooperatives to a meeting under the patronage of *La Prolétarienne* (Fournier 1994: 308–9). Fournier (*ibid.*: 308ff.) describes their relationship at some length.

12. E.g. Simiand for economic sociology, Hubert and Mauss for religious sociology; see Besnard 1983: 27; Lukes 1973: 291.

13. I owe caution on the latter point to Philippe Besnard (personal communication), who specifically denies the common assumption that the group as a whole was entirely or mostly of Jewish origin: in fact, only Durkheim, Mauss and Hertz are known to have been of Jewish family. This view may therefore be of some significance in accounting for Hertz's special relationship with Durkheim, but it can hardly account for the genesis of the group as a whole. Durkheim's rejection of the religious side of his origins is, of course, well known, as is, conversely, his support of Dreyfus and his ever-present consciousness of his Jewishness in non-religious ways (see Lukes 1973: 44, 332ff.; Pickering 1984: 14–18). As we shall see, this was broadly Hertz's attitude too.

14. See letter from Fauconnet to Bouglé dated 26/2/1907, published in *Revue Française de Sociologie* 20/1 (1979), p.44.

15. See Jamin 1988: xi–xii. Mauss used Hertz's published and unpublished writings extensively in his own teaching and writing in the inter-war period (on the latter, cf. Mauss 1950: 158, 315). On Hubert's attitude, see pp. 12, 163–5.

16. The words are Mauss's, 1994: 53; also Mauss 1924: 24.

17. Mauss's words, 1925: 24; 1994: 53; cf. Jamin and Lupu 1987: 44. In a letter to Hubert of 1905, written when he was in London with Hertz, Mauss describes both Hertz and his wife as 'a little too serious but altogether nice' (quoted by Fournier, 1994: 310).

18. Bourgin 1970: 482–2.

19. Alice Hertz 1928: x.

20. Hertz to Pierre Roussel, 19/8/1905. The article is listed in the bibliography below as Hertz 1907a. Roussel was an old school friend of Hertz's with an interest in ancient Greece. He spent six years in Athens (1904–1910) and was eventually to become director of the Athens School (Alice Hertz 1928: xiii n.i; Hertz to Roussel, 19/7/1908, 4/6/1910).

21. Hertz to Roussel, 27/4/1907. Publication of the article on death was already imminent.

22. Hertz to Roussel, 27/4/1907.

23. Hertz to Roussel, 19/7/1908. He was clearly working on sin already, since he tells Roussel that this aspect of his work has 'hardly advanced' this year, though Mauss's request to talk on it in the autumn at the Ecole Pratique des Hautes Etudes will concentrate his mind somewhat. Two earlier letters to Roussel (9/10/1907; 13/11/1907) hint that he is continuing to write on a Greek subject, and the first mentions that Salomon Reinach had asked him for a contribution

for *Revue Archéologique*. This may be a reference to what was to become a paper on the myth of Athena (see below and Mauss 1925: 24-5), now presumed lost.

24. Mauss 1994: 54-5. A letter from Hertz to Pierre Roussel, dated 21/3/1905, tends to confirm this: 'imagine', says Hertz, 'that I have had the feeling (*entirely illusory,* perhaps, but real) of discovery. Finally coming to know inductive research has been a genuine revelation to me, a joy, after so many hair-splitting discussions [*tout de bavardages et de ratiocinations*]' (first emphasis in the original). A similar sentiment is found in a letter to Roussel written two years later (dated 27/4/1907). Cf. Mauss (1983: 146), writing around 1930 of himself and Hubert: 'Discoveries and novelties were a delight to us', enabling the boredom of repetition to be avoided.

25. Alice Hertz 1928: x. Hertz himself felt that his treatment of the subject had been philosophical rather than scientific in nature, though he acknowledged that he had managed to isolate some hitherto unrealized aspects (letter to Roussel, 27/4/1907).

26. This was normal practice for those placed first (Clark 1973: 39).

27. Hertz to Dodd, 31/4/1904; on Durkheim's visit to Germany, see Lukes 1973: 85, 86-95.

28. Durkheim 1916: 117; Alice Hertz 1928: ix; Mauss 1994: 54; FRH. The dates given by Jamin and Lupu (1987: 43) for Hertz's visit to London, 1905-7, are wrong.

29. Hertz to Roussel, 19/8/1905.

30. Hertz to Roussel, 19/8/1905; Halbwachs to Alice, 23/4/1915; Chevalier to Alice, 11/6/1915. Mauss, at least, was also there to study at the British Museum (Fournier 1994: 310).

31. Especially 17/12/1904, 21/3/1905 and 19/8/1905.

32. Hertz to Roussel, 17/12/1904.

33. Hertz to Roussel, 19/8/1905.

34. Alice Hertz 1928: ix-x.

35. Hertz to Roussel, Reims 20/9/1906; Hertz to his mother, London 31/7/1906, Letchworth 27/8/1906. This second trip took place in July and August 1906, between Hertz's teaching in Douai in the academic year 1905-06 and his recall to Reims for further military training in September 1906 (the dates of his second trip therefore cannot have been 1905-06, *pace* Mauss 1922: 3). There was a third visit to the British Museum in the autumn of 1910 (Hertz to his mother, 10/10/1910).

36. On Durkheim's personal and political closeness to Jaurès, which dated from their years together at the ENS, see Lukes 1973: 44-5, 77, 320, 350. Durkheim is credited with turning Jaurès's attention more to social problems, Jaurès with helping Durkheim break with Judaism (*ibid.:* 44 nn.1, 2). Jaurès was assassinated just before the outbreak of war in 1914. On Clemenceau and his relish for conflict, see Zeldin 1973: 698ff.

37. On these activities, see Lukes 1973: 327 ff.; Clark 1968b: 82-4; 1973: 188. On Durkheim's personal dislike of involvement in politics and his belief that academics made bad politicians, see Lukes *ibid.:* Ch. 17. Even he, however, made an exception for the Dreyfus case. The only deviations at this time in the political orientation of the group were Bouglé, who was more radical, and Gaston Richard and H. Muffang, who were evidently less so. Both Richard, Durkheim's successor at Bordeaux and a lukewarm socialist at best, and Muffang, who had opted to stay neutral rather than come out in support of Dreyfus, split from Durkheim early on (see Besnard 1983: 24-5). Another eventual defector was Hubert

Bourgin, loyal during Durkheim's lifetime but an adherent of the far right and something of an anti-semite in the inter-war period (see Lukes *ibid.:* 321 n. 4).

38. The ENS had become a stronghold of socialism by the 1890s and remained so until 1905, when there began a Catholic and nationalist reaction against the republican and Dreyfusard dominance which had prevailed hitherto (see Clark 1973: 188, 215). Hertz was thus a student there towards the end of the earlier period, and he was already organizing meetings on socialist issues (see above, note 11).

39. On Jaurès, see above, note 36. Blum became leader of the Popular Front governments of the late 1930s. On Herr, who died in 1926, see the *Dictionnaire de Biographie Française,* Vol. 17, pp. 1118-19; also the biography written by his friend and fellow socialist Charles Andler (1977, originally 1932); and Clark 1973: 187-8. Politically originally a *possibiliste,* Herr is also known for his translation of the correspondence between Goethe and Schiller into French (Paris, Plon, 1923); for introducing Frazer's work to Durkheim (Mauss 1927: 9); and for helping pave the way for the replacement of the Dupuy government by Waldbeck-Rousseau's, which ordered Dreyfus's retrial (a letter of Herr's complaining of police brutality had been quoted in the Chamber of Deputies; see Clark *ibid.,* pp. 190, 188 n. 66). According to Andler (*ibid.:* 217), Herr was especially close to Mauss, but the nature of his relationship with Hertz is unknown. Mauss makes Herr share the credit with Durkheim for Jaurès becoming a socialist: 'if it was Lucien Herr who, in 1886-1888, converted Jaurès to socialism, it was Durkheim, in 1885-1886, who had turned him away from the political formalism and the hollow philosophy of the radicals' (1971 [1928]: viii). He adds the intriguing information (*ibid.:* ix) that both Guesde and Jaurès accepted Durkheim's definition of socialism.

40. See Durkheim 1916: 118.

41. Hertz to Dodd, 10/10/1897, 8/12/1897, 19/7/1899, 14/10/1899. The first letter sums up his position at this time: '... I am not a socialist, or rather, not a collectivist: I do not believe that the good of society depends on a general reorganization of institutions but on the better and more equitable functioning of those we have at the moment.' This view becomes progressively less dogmatic, and by the third of these letters he is definitely prepared to work with the socialists if need be.

42. Cf. Hertz to Edward Pease, 21/2/1912 (written in English): 'You know that I am a thorough Fabian.' The passage cited in the previous footnote, which is a translation of Hertz's original French, comes from an early letter in what was already becoming an established correspondence which lasted until Hertz's death. Soon Hertz would be writing to Dodd in English, which progressively improved to real fluency.

43. See Hertz to Dodd, 14/6/1911; also 3/5/1913, where he complains that the three-year law of conscription, about to be introduced in France in order to counter the threat from Germany, will prevent any further social reconstruction.

44. Bourgin 1970: 481. This qualifies Karady's opinion (1983: 82), that the Durkheimians neglected 'social problems' in favour of a purely intellectual approach. Given their greater activism, this was less true of the acolytes than of Durkheim himself (see above).

45. Bourgin 1970: 481-2. Years later, Bourgin reported that he himself had been 'brought to collaborate [with the Durkheimians] some years later [i.e. after his own time at the ENS] by a friend who surpassed almost all of them ...' (1925: 45). Was this Hertz?

46. Hertz 1911b.

47. See Durkheim 1916: 117; Bourgin 1970: 482. Two of Hertz's letters to Roussel, who had evidently expressed some doubts about Durkheim's approach, confirm this. In one, dated 20/9/1906, he is explicit about socialism being the answer to the 'anarchy' and 'egoism' of contemporary France. The second, of 22/6/1907, shows how Durkheimian his socialism had become: 'You see why am resolutely Durkheimian. The practical part of sociology, which formerly had repelled me too, is what appears to me now as the most obvious, the most certain, the most urgent. Durkheim concluded his course for this year at the Sorbonne by affirming the need for a public cult, and I subscribe entirely to this seemingly bizarre view. It is necessary that society periodically reminds individuals of itself, recreates itself in them, imposes itself upon them, so that they believe in it; and in doing so, on such [illegible] days, it invades their consciousness ..., removes their individual desires from them, raises them above themselves. The task of we sociologists is precisely, it seems to me, to show what must survive from a past (which is thought to have been condemned by 'progress') because it is essential, necessary for the life of society in general.'
48. Lukes 1973: 328 nn. 34, 36; Clark 1968b: 82-3 and n. 19.
49. See Paul Lapie's letters to Célestin Bouglé, dated 18/2/1900 and 11/7/1900 (published in Besnard 1983: 67).
50. Hertz to Pearse, 21/2/1912. Hertz claimed that Fabian principles were already influential in France, even with Jean Jaurès himself, and that they therefore needed no further organization. Although the GES explictly linked itself to the French Socialist Party, it is not clear whether it had any official status within it. The words 'citizen' and 'comrade' appear frequently in correspondence between members. Hertz himself lectured on the Fabians to the Ecole Socialiste (see below; also Bibliography, Hertz 1911b). In addition to the other sources cited, this and the next paragraph are based on GES records in the FRH. For an account of the GES, see Parkin (forthcoming).
51. Durkheim 1916: 118; FRH. According to Bourgin (1925: 85-6; 1970: 481-2), it was Simiand who was the brains behind both ventures, Hertz their soul, their inspiration. This view is not supported by the fact that it seems to have been Hertz who did most of the work for both, as secretary, treasurer, editor, and even translator on occasion (see below; also Fournier 1994: 680).
52. This was *What Syndicalism Means* (1912), published as *Examen de la doctrine syndicaliste*, Cahiers no. 14/15 (i.e. a double brochure) in 1912. The initiative for the translation, which appears to have been done by Hertz himself, came from Sidney Webb (letter to Hertz, 6/8/1912). It proved to be far and away the most successful brochure in the series (FRH, GES committee report for 1912). Webb also refers in his letter to Hertz having translated the Webbs' 'The Prevention of Destitution' (1911), though according to the title page this was actually done by H. La Coudraie (*La lutte préventive contre la misère*, Paris: Giard & Brière, 1912). A subsequent letter (Webb to Hertz, 26/8/1912) gives final permission for the second translation and asks for a complete set of the Cahiers for the London School of Economics library in return.
53. On the GES's troubles in 1913, see Hertz to Dodd, 12/10/1913; GES committee report for 1913. However, this report was regarded as overly pessimistic by some members. Certainly the GES's last known meeting, which took place in May 1914 and was addressed by Henri Gans ('Le problème financier: les mesures fiscales qui s'imposent'), was described in the ensuing circular as 'one of the best attended and most animated we have had for a long time'. Mauss tried to revive the Cahiers as a monthly in 1936, but could not raise the capital (Fournier 1994: 680).

54. The Ecole Socialiste ran initially from 1899 to 1902, having been set up by the Groupe de l'Unité Socialiste to instruct workers in socialist principles. As well as Hertz, Mauss, Simiand, Emmanuel Lévy and Paul Fauconnet also lectured there, as well as Edgar Milhaud, expert on nationalization. The Ecole – which Fournier describes as a 'popular university of the fifth arrondissement' (1994: 208) – was revived in 1910. See Andler 1977: 193, 218; Besnard 1983: 25.

55. See Hertz 1910p, 1911b, for the first two. The paper on the prevention of destitution does not appear to have come down to us, but we know that Hertz talked on the topic from one of his letters to Dodd (30/1/1912). He may have based it on the Webbs' brochure, with which he was probably already acquainted (see note 52). Manuscripts of the other two talks are in the FRH. Hertz says that he was not intending to publish the one on Fabianism, though it had gone down well with the audience (letter to Dodd, 17/1/1911). The intention of a paper on the political fortunes of the English working-classes, of which the final part survives in the FRH (see Bibliography below, Hertz no date), is not known. Hertz may have given other talks, here and/or elsewhere, that we know nothing about. See pp. 51–7 for his political writings.

56. See Lukes 1973: 329 n. 38; the letter is in Durkheim 1975 (II): 459–60. Hamelin had been one of Hertz's lycée teachers (Hertz to Roussel, 24/4/1907; Hamelin to Hertz, 1/9/1904).

57. Heilbron 1983: 14 n. 4; Clark 1968a: 46; 1973: 165. Notes of meetings apparently taken by Hertz in and around May 1914 are sufficiently detailed to indicate that he may have been secretary of this too for a time (FRH).

58. 1994: 53.

59. Undated letter, probably summer 1910. The book appeared in 1911, two years after Rauh's death, under the title of *Etudes de morale*. A whole team, consisting of his students and others who had attended his lectures, collaborated in their reissue, using notes apparently taken by Georges Davy and René Hubert as a basis. Some of the collaborators did the actual editing, while others checked their work later. Hertz's assigned task was to check the third course, on 'La Justice', together with Henri Wallon (who may have initiated the project, since he also wrote the book's preface).

60. Letter, Maxime David to Hertz, undated (probably around October 1913, since it also thanks Hertz for a copy of 'Saint Besse'; cf. below, Ch. 7, note 15). Apparently Darlu had criticised all such work (i.e. the courses of Hertz on the topic, and also those of Davy, who had freely copied from them) as not really being about 'la morale' at all but about the problem, in Davy's words, of 'forming the kids' consciences' – i.e. it concerned moral education, not the scientific study of morality.

61. Durkheim 1916: 117. Hertz himself is unequivocal about the disapproval of Durkheim, Mauss, etc. on this matter, a point also made by a colleague at Douai, the historian Conard (Hertz to Roussel, 27/4/1907). Hertz also hints at his 'having something to live off in Paris'. Hertz's and Alice's financial circumstances after they married were somewhat straightened to begin with (Antoine Hertz, personal communication), although there are occasional hints in his letters (e.g. to Dodd, 3/5/1913) that he and Alice were comfortably off, and they were at least able to afford nurses for Antoine (Hertz to Dodd, 4/6/1910; 8/8/1911). However, this may have been later: Hertz's going to England had depended on his receiving a scholarship (Hertz to Dodd, 31/4/1904).

62. Clark 1973: 9, 38.

63. In a letter written from Douai, dated 10/11/1905, (cited by Fournier, 1994: 311); also Mauss 1994: 53; Durkheim 1916: 117.

64. Hertz to Roussel, 11/2/1906, 3/9/1906, 27/4/1907.

65. Hertz to Dodd, 1/10/1911.

66. Hertz to Dodd, 3/5/1913. The letter continues with a passage about the future belonging to the young (though Hertz was still only 32) which ends with an outburst of what Mauss would have recognized as his pessimism: 'What a blessed institution is death!'

67. Hertz to Dodd, 12/10/1913.

68. Hertz to Roussel, 27/4/1907. The fact that Hertz took leave rather than resigned must have something to do with the standard undertaking extracted from Normalians that they would serve the state education system for ten years (see above). We know that he also took the following year off (Hertz to Roussel, 13/11/1907), and the year 1913-14, for which he received 100 francs (FRH, Certificat de congé d'inactivité). His 'leave' would seem to have become a permanent arrangment, for there is no record of him actually returning to *lycée* teaching in Douai or anywhere else.

69. The chief sources for Alice Hertz are Mauss 1928; Durkheim 1916: 117; Antoine Hertz, personal communication; FRH, anonymous dedicatory speech on the renaming of her Petite Ecole (rue de la Source, Paris) the Petite Ecole Alice Hertz (2/11/1929; other schools she was involved in included the Moulin Vert and the Collège Sévigné).

70. The exact date was 28th November. Her father was Abraham Albert Bauer, merchant, her mother Irma Meyer, 'of no profession' (FRH, copies of Alice's birth and marriage certificate; Stammblatt). A photograph (FRH) indicates that she was attending the Lycée Racine in 1892–3.

71. FRH, copies of Alice's birth and marriage certificate; the place of honeymoon is indicated by some photographs in the FRH. They had met through her brother Paul, a fellow student of Hertz's at the ENS (Antoine Hertz, personal communication).

72. Antoine Hertz, personal communication. Her having been secretary of the Froebel Society is evident from an unused letterhead carrying her name in the FRH.

73. FRH, anonymous dedicatory speech on the renaming of the Petite Ecole after her (2/11/1929). Hertz himself initiated the purchase of the site for this school through a *promesse de vente* and arranged an architect friend of his, one Auburtin, to build it; the purchase was eventually completed by Alice in 1921. It has since been rented to UNESCO by Antoine Hertz (Antoine Hertz, personal communication).

74. On Hertz as a student at the Ecole, see Fournier 1994: 298, 299 n. 1, 311-12. No record exists of Hertz actually having been Chargé de Cours at the Ecole (Philippe Besnard, personal communication), but both Mauss and Alphandéry state unambiguously that he taught there and, according to Mauss, that some of his lectures still existed in draft form in the 1920s, which Mauss himself used to teach from (Mauss 1925: 23; also 1994: 55, 113ff.; Alphandéry 1919: 337-8). According to Antoine Hertz, his father was Maître de Conferences, not Chargé de Cours (personal communication). On his lecturing on morality, see FRH, undated letter (probably around October 1913), Maxime David to Hertz (see also note 60). His students included Henri Beuchat, Stefan Czarnowski, Georges Davy and Jean Marx, all minor Durkheimians (Fournier 1994: 312).

75. Mauss 1994: 113; Karady 1983: 77.

76. Nos. 8-12, covering the years 1903 to 1912, though they were usually published in the year following the last cover date. Hertz's own reviews for the journal date from between 1905 and 1913.

77. See Lukes 1973: 293–4. His wife is said to have helped him with proof-reading and other editorial tasks.
78. Cf. Durkheim 1916: 118. Nonetheless, the requirement to write reviews seem to have put Hertz's thesis temporarily on the back burner at certain periods (see Hertz to his mother, 3/2/1910; Hertz to Dodd, 18/6/1912). Complaints about the amount of reviewing Durkheim expected from his collaborators are not infrequent in their surviving correspondence with one another; see Besnard 1983: 31.
79. Mauss 1925: 24; 1994: 54–5. On Mauss's difficulties with writing, see Jamin and Lupu 1987: 43. Hertz nonetheless credited Mauss with training in the technical aspects of conducting research, e.g. in using index cards (Hertz to Mauss, 29/11/1905, cited in Fournier 1994: 298).
80. It is obvious from the letters and photographs in the FRH that the Alps were a favourite holiday destination of the Hertzes for many years, despite the tragic death of Hertz's father in a climbing accident (see above). An early letter from Hertz to his friend and future brother-in-law Edmond Bauer (8/8/1901) lauds 'the wild life' (*la vie sauvage*) that can be found there, and he told Dodd that mountaineering was '*the* thing for me', better than the sea for a holiday, which did not provide a great enough change after spending the rest of the year in the city (letter, 18/6/1912; also 3/5/1913). On the length of these holidays, see Hertz to Dodd, 12/10/1913. The FRH has a typed account of a walking holiday from Chamonix to Vevey in autumn 1902, presumably composed by either Hertz or Alice.
81. Alice Hertz 1928: x–xii; Hertz 1970: 111 n. 1. Hertz was accompanied on this trip, as on others to the Alps, by Alice and his son Antoine (Hertz to his mother, Cogne, 29/8/1912; Antoine Hertz, personal communication). One can infer from other correspondence (Casanova to Hertz, 30/8/1912; A. Farinet to Hertz, 1/10/1912) that they spent the September of that year at Menthon Saint Bernard, Haute Savoie.
82. Hertz 1913a. This disregards Paul Lapie's early *Civilizations tunisiennes* of 1898, based on 'empirical research' carried out while teaching at the *lycée* of Tunis in 1893–6 (see Cherkaoui 1983: 219 n. 10), but as one of Durkheim's earliest associates he appears to us now as a sympathetic colleague rather than a converted acolyte. There was one other pre-war effort, by Henri Beuchat, who died of cold and hunger in 1914 on Wrangel Island, Alaska, following a shipwreck while carrying out fieldwork among the Eskimo; his notes and other research materials went down with the ship. The only other research trip recorded was a three-week visit to Morocco that Mauss made years later, in 1929, to study a cultic dance (see Mauss 1925: 20; Jamin and Lupu 1987: 44, 52 n. 8).
83. 1928: xii. In the FRH is an envelope containing a medallion of the Saint and Virgin Mary, and a small piece of rock, which Hertz clearly obtained at the site of the cult. In a letter to his mother (dated Cogne, 29/8/1912), he says that he and Alice are also proposing to take away with them 'statues of the Virgin and the saints, plates of tin and copper, old wooden goblets, bonnets and pearl necklaces, like those children wear, etc.', though they expected problems with Italian customs in getting all this to France.
84. Alice Hertz 1928: xii–xiii and n. 1; Durkheim 1916: 118. Hertz's letter to Hubert, of 16/7/1913 (published in *Etudes Durkheimiennes* 11, 1985, p. 2), also makes allusion to this text. A number of letters of May 1913 in the FRH, to and from Hertz, show that he was in correspondence with a number of people at this time, especially in France, concerning place names referring to jumping. Two letters to Dodd (dated 11th and 18th May) ask about the Devil's Jump in Surrey,

though judging from what survives, none of these efforts produced any useful information from his correspondents.

85. See Mauss 1994: 52; letter to Radcliffe-Brown, dated 6/12/1924 (published in *Etudes Durkheimiennes* 10, 1984), p. 2. Although Needham, in his encyclopedia entry on Hertz (1979b: 296), mentions two different texts, it is pretty certain that there was only one – i.e. the text mentioned by Mauss, despite the different title he gives it, is the same as that mentioned by Alice and Durkheim. Neither they nor Mauss mention the existence of two papers on what is discernibly a single theme. A further reference to it by Mauss, in which he calls it 'an important comparative thesis on Greek mythology' (1925: 24–5), brings it closer to Durkheim's description and thus places the matter beyond reasonable doubt.

86. Mauss 1994: 111, 115.

87. 1925: 24–5; 1994: 55; see also Mauss's letter to Radcliffe-Brown (note 85, above), pp. 2–3, where he mentions Durkheim's, Mauss's and Hubert's 'very strong reservations' concerning the paper on the myth of Athena. Georges Davy told Alice that the monograph on St Besse had been well received in England (letter, 7/5/1915), which can hardly have been much of a recommendation to his colleagues at this time.

88. 1916: 118.

89. Dated 13/7/1913; published in *Etudes Durkheimians* 11 (1985), p. 2.

90. Or perhaps they saw in him something of a rival. Cf. Lukes 1973: 524 n. 35.

91. Cf. Karady 1979: 79 and n. 63; 1983: 80–1. The problem is discussed further, pp. 163–5.

92. See Parkin 1992b: 21 and Appendix. A letter from Paul Farinet to Hertz, of 26/1/1914, asks him for references in support of a further brochure he is preparing.

93. The chief published sources on Hertz's death (Durkheim 1916: 118–19; Alice Hertz 1928: xiii–xiv) do not tell the whole story. The FRH has a file of letters from Hertz at the front, mostly to Alice or his mother. Two further letters, from E. Vermeil and Henri Lévy-Bruhl to Alice, both dated 28/4/1915, give details of his last hours and the circumstances of his death, as then known, respectively.

94. Letter to Alice, 21/8/1914. This was the 44th Territorial Infantry Regiment, 2nd Company.

95. Letter to Alice, 10/8/1914.

96. 14/3/1915. His actual 'baptism of fire', of which he made light, had actually come some four months earlier (letter to Alice, 1/11/1914).

97. See Alice Hertz 1928: xiii–xiv.

98. His friend from school days, the English Egyptologist Alan Gardiner, also remarked on Hertz's love of being in a crowd, which he felt inevitably made him a socialist (Margaret Gardiner, personal communication). In Hertz's own words, 'this war is the most formidable experience of collectivism' (letter to Alice, 24/12/1914); and further: 'The individual no longer counts: the troop is unity' (letter to his brother-in-law Léon Eyrolles, undated, but early November 1914). Durkheim himself could not have expressed better the anonymity of serving in a mass army.

99. A fellow officer, Adjutant G. (?) Michineau, seems to have helped Hertz, or at least took an interest in this work (Michineau to Alice, 12/6/1915). He was wounded in the same attack in which Hertz was killed.

100. On or before 26/3/1915 (letter to Alice of that date; also Vermeil to Alice, 28/4/1915, who had spoken to Hertz about the matter on 2/4/1915).

101. The offical decision was taken on 3rd April 1915 (FRH, Extrait de l'ordre général, no. 59, dated 7/4/1915); a covering letter indicates 8th April as the

effective date of appointment (these two facts are confirmed by Hertz's letter to Alice, 10/4/1915). See also Durkheim 1916: 119; letter, Henri Lévy-Bruhl to Alice Hertz, 28/4/1915. According to Michineau (letter to Alice, 12/6/1915), Hertz actually transferred to his new unit, the 17th Company of the 330th, some months earlier, in November 1914. Hertz himself explains to Alice that the 330th is the reserve regiment of the 130th, so that he is still not in an active unit (letter of 3/11/1914).

102. See especially Lt. Trocmé to Alice, 4/7/1915, on the final moments before the attack, scheduled to take place at 2.50 pm: 'He [Hertz] encouraged his men by freely joking with them, saying to them, "come on, get ready, we're going to a celebration". We can still feel the impression his calmness and courage made on us, at a time when the least perceptive of them [sic] could appreciate the terrible difficulty of the task before them, the almost certain death to which they would have to march at the appointed hour.' Trocmé apparently did not take part in the attack himself, and he succeeded to the command of the 17th afterwards.

103. FRH: Hertz's death certificate; Notice de Guerre, Lt. Jean Pollet; letter, Sgt. Moisant to Alice, 4/7/1915; account and plan of the action (possibly in Alice's handwriting). Pollet was the lieutenant leading the attack, Moisant the company adjutant. Another sergeant, Marcel Voriot, was killed immediately afterwards while going to the aid of the fallen officers (newspaper cutting, FRH). Partridge later helped Alice visit the scenes of her husband's death and burial (Antoine Hertz, personal communication). Hertz was 33 when he died (not 35, *pace* Mauss 1922: 1; Jamin and Lupu, 1987: 43).

104. On 23rd June 1920 (FRH). The citation reads: 'Having been transferred at his request from a territorial regiment into an active regiment, he gained the admiration of his superiors through his high appreciation of patriotic duty. Was killed on 13th April 1915, before Marchéville, while leading his section in an attack on a strong enemy position under a violent artillery barrage and bursts of machine-gun fire. Was mentioned in dispatches.' Certificate of 130th Infantry Regiment. Obituaries of Hertz were written by Durkheim (1916), Mauss (1925), Paul Alphandéry, editor of *Revue de l'Histoire des Religions* (for which Hertz reviewed a number of books; Alphandéry 1919) and Salomon Reinach, editor of *Revue Archéologique* (1915). Bourgin also talks about him at length in much later writings (1925: 85–6; 1970 [1938]: 480 ff.).

105. Alice to Dodd and his wife, 22/4/1915. Alice had learned the news only the day before this letter was written.

106. Antoine Hertz, personal communication; FRH, Stammblatt; Mauss 1928. A letter from Alice to her sister-in-law, Cécile Eyrolles, of 31/4/1915, mentions work as a cure for her despair, which her late husband would not have wanted her to feel on his account. Durkheim visited her soon afterwards and reported her 'perhaps excessive stoicism', but also the 'exaggerated detachment' with which she read out some of Hertz's letters to her (Durkheim to Mauss, letter dated end April, 1915). Alice also had to suffer the temporary loss of her brother Edmond Bauer, a sergeant in the 24th Infantry who was wounded on 22/8/1914 in the battle of Anderlues, near Charleroi. He seems to have recovered quite rapidly, but was taken prisoner and spent the rest of the war in various German prisoner-of-war camps, and latterly as a clerk in a library at Leipzig (FRH; Antoine Hertz, personal communication). In 1919, he became the rector for natural sciences of Strasbourg University, in tandem with Pierre Roussel, rector for humanities and social sciences there at this time.

107. Halbwachs to Alice, 23/4/1915. Hertz's letters from the front were privately printed after the war, for limited circulation within the family (Antoine Hertz,

personal communication; letter, Robert Hertz's sister Fanny to Alice, 29/11/1917). The FRH has both typed and typeset versions of some of them (the latter in proof).

108. Isambert 1983: 166; cf. Mauss 1925: 24; 1994: 53. Hertz's remark to Dodd on the 'blessedness' of death (see above, note 66) may also be relevant here. When Durkheim was collecting material for his memorial of Hertz (Durkheim 1916), Pierre Roussel told him of Hertz's tendency towards emotional excitement and pessimism. According to Roussel, in Durkheim's words, 'there seemed to be something a little barmy [*braque*] about him — grand gestures, violent demonstrations, boisterous shouting, aggressive practical jokes on new [illegible; students?].' But then Durkheim adds: 'How can we recognize Hertz in all this' (letter, Durkheim to Mauss, 6/12/1915). In a letter to Mauss of the 14th, Durkheim calls Hertz 'a very noble soul, but ... a little woolly-headed [*fumeux*].'

109. Vermeil to Alice, 28/4/1915.

110. Halbwachs had informed Hertz of Bianconi's death (card dated 21/3/1915).

111. Hertz to Alice, 26/3/1915.

112. Dated 15/5/1918. Chiffert had witnessed the battle, without at first realizing that Hertz had been killed.

113. In fact, Hertz had qualified as a section commander (sub-lieutenant or adjutant) as far back as 1903 (FRH, Certificat d'aptitude, Reims 14/8/1903). On what he himself felt to be his lack of aptitude for the practicalities of military life, see his letter to Alice of 21/8/1914. Because of it, Chiffert had tried to dissuade him from seeking more active service (Hertz to Alice, 25/9/1914).

114. Hertz to Eyrolles, 17/10/1914, 18/10/1914, 2/11/1914, undated (but early November 1914); Gorodiche to Hertz, 12/10/1914; Cécile Eyrolles (Hertz's sister) to Hertz, 24/11/1914. (Léon Gorodiche was the husband of Hertz's sister Fanny.)

115. On the latter point, see Hertz to Alice, 3/11/1914. He also gives his pre-war army career as one of his reasons for volunteering in a letter to Alice of 25/9/1914, adding the information that the call for volunteers was based on the lack of any sergeant in his new unit from the class of 1899, which he calls his own class. However, according to official records, his initial period of military service started only on 12th November 1900 (see above, note 3). The possibility of his becoming an interpreter (in either English or German) was not dropped entirely (see letters to Alice, 29/12/1914, 6/1/1915), but further attempts were made directly through his unit where he was stationed; they had no greater success.

116. E.g. 25/9/1914: 'I live in the hope of a new France in a new Europe'; also 4/12/1914.

117. Antoine Hertz, personal communication.

118. Original emphases. In a later letter (13/12/1914), he says that he always acknowledges his Jewishness to those who ask him if he is from Alsace, as well as his German origins through his father.

119. Durkheim 1916: 120 and passim.

120. See Clark 1968b: 90; Lukes 1973: 321 n.4.

121. Bourgin 1970: 480–4 (quotation from *ibid.*: 481).

122. Bourgin 1970: 484. It is not clear how Bourgin acquired this view, but it may have been from Hertz's correspondence with Alice and/or discussions with her rather than from Hertz directly. The existence of Hertz's letter to Alice of 3/11/1914 prevents us from simply dismissing the account as a figment of Bourgin's by then embittered and partly anti-semitic imagination. In any case, the picture he presents was confirmed to me in its essentials by Hertz's son Antoine, who added the information that his father was very keen to be French,

yet considered that the Jews owed debts to France. The war provided an opportunity to pay them, the probable origin of the story of Hertz's premonition that he would not return. Alphandéry (1919: 336) and Durkheim (1916: 119) were clearly also aware of the circumstances, but were less explicit in their own memorials.

123. Letter to Alice, 23/2/1915. A further letter of 2/11/1915 makes reference to Alice's 'boredom' with 'folklore'.
124. FRH: Mauss's letter of condolence to Alice, 7/5/1925.
125. See Dumont 1979: 816 n. 14.
126. Translations of Mauss's *The Gift* (Mauss 1954) by Ian Cunnison and of Durkheim and Mauss's *Primitive Classification* (Durkheim and Mauss 1963) by Needham belong to this same period and milieu.
127. Michel Izard, personal communication. Hertz also has a street named after him in La Butte Rouge, a suburb south of Paris, where it runs off Place François Simiand, in parallel with Rue Emile Durkheim.
128. This is still not a topic that has been treated comparatively to any great extent. A recent exception is Carmichael *et al.* (eds.) 1994, which, not surprisingly, makes no reference to Hertz.

NOTES TO CHAPTER TWO

1. The literature on the Durkheimians and religion is vast, and no attempt will be made here to do much more than highlight those aspects of their common approach which seem to have a particular bearing on Hertz's own contribution. This chapter owes much to previous accounts of this aspect and period of anthropological history, in particular Evans-Pritchard 1965, Goody 1962 (Chs. 2, 3), Lukes 1973 and Morris 1987, and to a reading of Durkheim's own *Elementary Forms of the Religious Life* (1915) and others' commentaries on it. In the latter category I would draw attention especially to Jones (1977, 1986), who stresses the importance of studying Durkheim's work within its proper historical context; Isambert (1982), who has examined the relation between the notions of sacred and *mana* in Durkheimian thought generally; and Pickering, who, in a very thorough and readable study (1984), emphasizes the pervasiveness of the concern with religion in almost all of Durkheim's writings and points out that, despite the very real developments in his thoughts on religion, there was much continuity in his basic view of it and its place in his overall scheme. Other significant references are given in the text.
2. Cf. Evans-Pritchard 1965: 68. Besnard argues (1983: 17) that this might have been a deliberate ploy, designed to convince opponents and potential supporters alike that psychology in some form (i.e. 'social' psychology) would be retained in the new sociology.
3. Pickering shows that the relationship between belief and ritual in Durkheimian thought is actually quite complicated (1984: Ch. 20), and he argues that 'in the last analysis Durkheim holds that beliefs have primacy over ritual, although in many places he appears to give ritual and belief equal importance' (*ibid.:* 65). One should not forget, however, that although in Durkheimian thought beliefs certainly have their place in uniting the individual with society, it is society that is the source of them, even in those moments of 'effervescence' in which some creativity is to be expected. Ritual, conversely, is important as the mechanism whereby, through its use of symbols, society strengthens both awareness and acceptance of beliefs in individual minds. Ritual thus gave Durkheim the social

mechanism he needed to deny the intellectualists the validity of their grounding of a social phenomenon like religion in the perceptions of the individual and the beliefs he supposedly built on them. This view of ritual as society's chief inte-grating mechanism is challenged by the frequent observation that modern society is underritualized (cf. Pickering *ibid*.: 350, 365). Mauss later expressed the view (1969 II: 144, originally 1933) that in the early days he and his col-leagues had stressed ritual and action too much at the expense of mythology and thought.

4. For another, longer list of anthropological supporters and opponents, see Pickering 1984: 143ff.

5. Renouvier was one of Durkheim's own teachers at the ENS (Pickering 1984: 166). Hamelin, a close personal friend of Durkheim's, taught Hertz at school (FRH, letter, Hamelin to Hertz, 1/9/1904).

6. See Pickering 1984: 231 ff., who amongst other things casts doubt on the authenticity of the famous phrase 'God is society' as a statement by Durkheim himself.

7. MacClancy (1986) broadly supports Keesing as regards Vanuatu. A much earlier challenge to the suitability of the concept, again in part with respect of the ethnographic area in which it originated, was mounted by Hocart (1914).

NOTES TO CHAPTER THREE

1. Cf. Hertz on St Besse (below, Ch. 7). On the other hand, Hertz does evince a concern for origins in notes for an unpublished lecture on 'La religion des primitives' (1911c), where he maintains that ethnography, i.e. 'the study of primitive peoples', can tell us more about ancient beliefs and the origins of religion than archaeology can. 'All the past of our own race is present on the surface of the globe', though at the same time there is as large a gulf between original man and the primitive Australians – who at least have fire – as between the latter and ourselves. Like the intellectualists, Hertz accepted the basic unity of contemporary mankind as well as the existence of different stages in its development.

2. The political side of the group's work, and of Hertz's place in it, was reviewed briefly in Chapter 1. An early work on the condition of the rural population in Germany, listed under Hertz's name in Nandan's bibliography (1977: 331), is almost certainly spurious. The article exists, but its early date (1900, the year of Hertz's admission into the Ecole Normale Supérieure, when he would have been only eighteen or nineteen years old), plus the fact that it is signed simply 'Hertz', without any first name, makes it very unlikely that he wrote it. See Parkin 1992b for a fuller discussion of the matter.

3. Although Hertz himself had only one child, this may have been due to Alice's difficulties with conceiving; Antoine's birth was anyway difficult (letters, Hertz to Frederick Lawson Dodd, 15/6/1910, 17/7/1910; Hertz to Pierre Roussel, 27/4/1907, 27/1/1909). Hertz himself, however, was one of five children.

4. On the first, see p. 12. On the second, see FRH, Hertz to Dodd, 16/10/1900.

5. Hertz to Dodd, 1/10/1910, my emphasis.

6. Hertz to Dodd, 15/6/1910.

7. The manuscripts of these talks are in the FRH (see below, Bibliography, under *Unpublished manuscripts*). None of them appear to have been published, though some may have received notice in abstract form in the circulars of those organizations to which he delivered them. There is especially reason to think

this is the case for the talk on the Fabians (1911b), of which two different typed summaries exist, one of six pages and one of ten pages, the latter having been sent to Hertz specifically to shorten for publication (FRH, letter, E. Fontrel [? — a member of the committee of the Ecole Socialiste] to Hertz, 18/1/1911). Publication proper of this talk itself Hertz seems not to have been interested in (letter to Frederick Lawson Dodd, 17/1/1911).

8. All citations here are of Hertz's words.

9. Hertz's critique is, not surprisingly, close to Durkheim's as set out in *Le Socialisme* (see Durkheim 1971).

10. This was precisely the sort of group Hertz had recently set up in France (i.e. the Groupe d'Etudes Socialistes; see pp. 7–8; also Parkin (forthcoming) for the activities of the Groupe as a whole).

NOTES TO CHAPTER FOUR

1. Schwartz's work is intended specifically as an extension of Hertz's, but into the vertical rather than the lateral domain. Though anthropological sources are freely used as evidence, the perspectives are rather those of sociology and social psychology. Schwartz locates the ultimate basis for vertical classification in the parent-child relationship.

2. Miller (1972) traces the predominance of the left hand among the Zuñi, Towa and possibly Hopi to the influence of another Pueblo group, the Keres, who are supposed to have switched to left-handedness deliberately in order to distinguish themselves from the normatively right-handed Tewa, from whom they also apparently differ in giving priority to female over male. This part of the argument is based on the example of the Yunami Delaware of New Jersey, who are supposed to have adopted left-handedness during the Delaware Prophet movement of the eighteenth century as part of 'a desire to appear different in all respects from the whites' (Kinietz 1940: 118). Kinietz's suggestion is very tentative, however, and hardly enough to decide the issue for a totally separate group for whom historical records are totally lacking (Miller *ibid.:* 647).

3. This formula is to be read 'left is to right as man is to woman'; similar ones will appear frequently in this chapter.

4. Granet regards the sleeping position as an exception to the rule of male being associated with the left, but this would appear to be a mistake. North is the direction associated with death, so when asleep one should have one's feet pointed away from the north and towards the south. The woman should be to the west of her husband, which leads Granet to say that he is therefore to her right. In fact, however, he is on her real left (i.e. seeing the matter from her point of view), and so in line with the normal Chinese symbolism (1973: 52). Demiéville claims (1968: 181, 186) that Granet's general account, though correct in itself, only really applies to the last four centuries before Christ, especially the third and fourth centuries BC. According to him, values changed with dynasties: under the Ts'in and Han (3rd century BC to 3rd century AD), right-handedness predominated, whereafter left-handedness returned and remained (apart from the Yuan period, 1260–1367) until the 1911 revolution. This suggests that the emperors were able to decree such things, which may have been true of state ritual, for instance, but hardly seems feasible where more general values were concerned.

5. Kruyt himself took his doctorate at Utrecht in 1913 (van Boetzelaer 1949: 145) and apparently had no connection with Leiden. The two departments were evi-

dently rivals into the 1930s, when Schulte Nordholt remembers being 'educated in the Faculty of Indonesian Studies at the University of Utrecht in a program that was distinguished by being politically and scientifically anti-Leiden' (1980: 232).

6. The theoretical and methodological objections made by Needham in the introduction have themselves been subjected to critical scrutiny by Allen (1994).

7. Erchak's assumption (1972) that Needham relies on the presence of a system of dual symbolic classification to prove the existence of asymmetric prescriptive alliance in a society is therefore false (cf. King 1980: 16ff.).

8. This ignores feminist-inspired correctives, which *inter alia* have led the journal *Man* to revert to its old gender-neutral title of *Journal of the Royal Anthropological Institute.*

9. A monograph by the present author discussing these further developments in detail is in fact currently in preparation. As well as focussing on hierarchical opposition, it will also offer more extended coverage of Needham's position in these debates. Preliminary accounts can be found in Parkin 1992a and 1994.

NOTES TO CHAPTER FIVE

1. In a near-contemporary letter to Pierre Roussel of 9/12/1907, Hertz admits, in evident reply to a previous objection from Roussel, that cremation is a problem for the theory of there being a delay between death and the final rite, because everything is over so quickly. Hertz gives three possible options: a) the temporary sojourn of the soul on earth and the period of mourning have nothing to do with the state of the body; b) there is still a double rite, but the second takes place as if the first had not mattered; c) the second rite is reduced to 'a simple appendix to the cremation', as in the Hindu rite – i.e. there is a very short but still perceptible interval. Hertz prefers the third option, but then has to admit that there is no necessary conjunction between the length of mourning and the soul's wandering on earth, nor between these and the state of the body – it is just a strong tendency. For example, the rite converting the Hindu *preta* or ghost into a *pitar* or ancestor takes place a year after death. Actually, this may be considered a final rite, in which the *pinda* or rice-balls representing the ancestors take the place of the exhumed bones. Evolutionism is also invoked: 'For me, the easiest hypothesis is still to consider cremation as taking its place in an older system.' And further, 'in effect, it might well be that the final rite and the return to normality [*défunestation*] do not (*or no longer*) take place on the same day' (my emphasis).

2. Similarly, couvade, found especially in South America, in which a man participates in the state of his wife during pregnancy (cf. Riviere 1974: 1974), can be seen as analogous with a widow's participation in her deceased husband's condition (above).

3. Goody (1962, Chs. 2, 3, used extensively in what immediately follows here) is especially good on these debates as they affect death specifically.

4. Cf. his letter to Roussel of 9/12/1907 (FRH), where he tells Roussel that 'the existence of a collective ceremony for the dead ... does not necessarily prove anything as to secondary funerary rites' and attributes this confusion to an earlier author, Rohde. This and an earlier letter of 13/11/1907 mention evidence for double funerals in Greece and the Balkans, leading to a suggestion from Hertz that Roussel, an expert on Greek archaeology, write something similar for Salomon Reinach's *Revue Archéologique.* Roussel apparently never acted on

this suggestion (see FRH, Hertz to Roussel 19/7/1908), which Hertz seems to have made in order to deflect a persistent request from Reinach away from himself.

5. Harrisson also suggests (1962: 30–1, n. 19) that Hertz drew most of his data on the death article initially from Roth's digest of 1896, an assumption based on Hertz's supposed poor understanding of his sources and the fact that he mentions only one reference after that date that is not in Roth. Certainly Hertz did use Roth, which contains summaries and translations of a large number of relevant texts, but this was infrequent and always indicated by Hertz himself in his footnotes. This suggests that he consulted the original sources wherever possible but resorted to Roth for those he could not find. This is true of all editions of the text, so that Harrisson is at least right in assuming it is not any carelessness by the Needhams' that is at work. Cf. Needham himself on Hertz's scholarship (1979b: 296): '... he got his references right.'

6. This is also true of the Gadaba of central India (Claudia Gross, personal communication).

7. According to Maurice Bloch, however (personal communication), Huntington erred in translating the Bara word as 'order' instead of as 'building up'. This in its turn suggests that Huntington's 'vitality' should rather be 'breaking down'.

8. As Metcalf and Huntington have subsequently made clear (1991: 8–9), this treatment of the problem amounts to denying homology to the terms in each column.

NOTES TO CHAPTER SIX

1. A letter from Hertz to Pierre Roussel, dated 27th April 1907, gives a sketch of his ideas in his own words: 'At the moment, I am sounding out regions of *sin:* representations relating to error, to moral and natural *law* (these two notions being solidary, sin being essentially the infraction of a sacred law) and rites of expiation, especially confession. On this last point, I have begun an (ethnographic) study which might yield something' (original emphases).

2. Cf. Hertz's letter to Frederick Lawson Dodd of 2nd July 1911: 'If I was a Roman Catholic, I would certainly be with Pio [*sic*] X against the modernists. Those people are ashamed of having a religion: they try to beg their pardon from the intellectual people and the freethinkers; they take as humble and 'reasonable' an attitude as they can; and they lose what is the essence of religion, the emotional power, without winning intelligibility' (English original, with minor changes of punctuation). On Durkheim's very similar attitude, see Pickering 1984: 98.

3. See Durkheim 1915: Book III, Ch. 1. Entering an ascetic life is classed as a negative rite because the ascetic's concern, like the guilt-ridden sinner's, is to separate himself from the profane, though he is merely paving the way for the positive rites he will engage in subsequently (*ibid.:* 311).

4. Evil has had a similar raw deal, despite some well-known exceptions (O'Flaherty 1976; D. Parkin ed. 1985). It is possible to hear similar remarks about ethnicity. Since anthropology is anyway all about the characteristics different human populations use to identify themselves and to distinguish themselves from others, do we need it? This impression of superficiality may have been reinforced by the modern association of the concept first and foremost with Europe, where it has proved more difficult to locate the sorts of radical unfamiliarity that a more traditional anthropology has concerned itself with, such as exotic myths, kinship systems, rituals etc.

5. The same is true of others' contributions to the *Festschrift* dedicated to him and focussing particularly on *Morals and Merit;* see Mayer ed. 1981.
6. The similarity in argumentative technique here with Evans-Pritchard's (e.g. 1956) and with that in some of Needham's later work (e.g. on unilateral figures; 1980: Ch. 1), is striking. Needham himself is even more decisive in seeing sin as not universal, arguing that it is peculiar to Christianity (1981: 82).
7. The latter only mentions the use of flagellation and of beating generally to expel evil spirits and impurities, and their use also in rites of incorporation on occasion, not in connection with sin as such; see 1960 [1909]: 174.

NOTES TO CHAPTER SEVEN

1. The passages from Hertz's essay that I quote here are from this translation. The translation restores the map that was omitted from the French reissue of 1970, but neither of these editions contains the photographs of the rock with its chapel and of Besse himself which were included in the first edition of the text (Hertz 1913) and in *Mélanges* (Hertz 1928: 140). The translation also omits the fifteenth-century Latin manuscript on the legend of St Besse which appears as an appendix in all the French versions (see Wilson's note added to Hertz 1983: 93 n. 36). See MacClancy and Parkin n.d. for an account of the cult today.
2. 'Contes et dictons' (Hertz 1970 [1917]: 161–88). They were published postumously direct from the notebook he filled up at the front and would probably have been written up properly had he lived.
3. A letter from Hertz to Dodd, dated 19th May 1912, mentions that a road was currently being built.
4. It would appear that this aspect is more important for the Cognians than the Valsoanians, and that even so, it is really just one example of a collective way of marking the age of majority which is found all over the region (Alexis Betemps, personal communication). In 1994, girls as well as boys were identified as *conscriti* (MacClancy and Parkin n.d.).
5. Two points of difference from Hertz's reporting found in 1994 were the absence of people climbing barefoot, and the information that the climb from Cogne took only four hours, including a meal break (MacClancy and Parkin n.d.).
6. In 1994, the party from Cogne circled the rock only three times, with one ascent of the rock included in the third circuit. In contrast to the procession with the statue the following day, these circuits took place anti-clockwise.
7. Hertz identifies other examples from the Canavese (1983: 90 n. 16), and a similar one from the feast of St Vincent (22nd January) at Mussy, Aube, southeast of Paris ('Contes et dictons', 1970 [1917]: 176). Enquiries in 1994 revealed no knowledge of them in connection with St Besse (MacClancy and Parkin n.d.).
8. Sanchis (1983: 278) reports something similar from Portugal, and Hertz notes its occurrence elsewhere in the Aosta valley (1983: 91 n. 18). It is common at other patronal festivals in the Val Soana (MacClancy and Parkin n.d.).
9. Hertz cites the doctor at Ronco and Professor Francesco Farina, of Turin, for this piece of information (1983: 91 n. 19). An undated letter to Hertz from Pierre Giacosa, of the same university, confirms the practice for women and girls. This is clearly one point where popular and intellectual discourse diverges.
10. There is some confusion in Hertz's text as to how the cult was actually organized at the time of his visit. The principle of rotating the honour of carrying the statue seems already to have been abandoned in favour of auctioning it. By 1994, the idea of rotating the organization of the cult between the five villages

had long been abandoned, though a lay organizer, for some years past a Parisian glass factory owner with family connections in Campiglia, was active in holding both auctions. See MacClancy and Parkin n.d.

11. In recent years, at least, there has also been a celebration on the mountain on this date, though much smaller in scale than the one held on August 10th (MacClancy and Parkin n.d.). As to the name, Laurent is felt to be equivalent to Besse in Campiglia, as we have seen, and enquiries in 1994 revealed a clear association between the two saints. According to official hagiography, Laurent (Italian Lorenzo, English Lawrence) was a deacon martyred in Rome at the end of the third century.

12. Alfonso Farinet also pointed to the similarity of surnames between Cogne and the Val Soana, which Hertz did not mention in his article (letter to Hertz, 21/10/1912).

13. This impression comes chiefly from a draft or copy of a letter which Hertz evidently sent or intended to send to one of his correspondants (it is unclear to whom) along with a proof of the published text (dated 28/4/1913). While admitting that 'we are dealing here with a purely historical work that is bound to disagree to some extent with local belief', he assures his correspondant that the article will only reach a scientific readership. Perhaps he was also concerned that the text should not prove in any way detrimental to the campaign in support of the French language in the valley that was being undertaken simultaneously (see Hertz 1912c; Parkin 1992b).

14. FRH. Among those who wrote thanking him for their copies were Halbwachs, Meillet, Fauconnet, Hubert Bourgin, Maxime David (all associated with the *Année*), Sir James Frazer and Hertz's friend Jean Chevalier. The most interesting comment is perhaps Chevalier's, who had been conducting similar research in Spain and the Pyrenees: 'You have done well ... not to be too precise, as Durkheim was, since our representations are always inferior in this respect to the sense of reality which you and I share ...' (letter dated 6/10/1913). He and David (letter undated, but probably contemporary) were particularly delighted by the final pages of Part VI, where Hertz attributes the existence of the cult to the feeling of community, not to the rock itself (1983: 86–7). It is interesting to compare this passage with a letter to his mother, written while he was still doing research in Cogne (dated 29/8/1912), in which he calls Besse 'a bizarre and ludicrous (*falot*) saint, who is only there to give some justification to the cult rendered to a sacred rock, situated at an altitude of 2,100 metres, and venerated long before the name of Christ had penetrated the mountains.' Bourgin, in his letter, doubts whether the disappearance of the cult will really turn the rock with which the saint has been associated into something 'vulgar and material', but otherwise he is politely appreciative (letter dated 5/10/1913).

15. This is the conclusion to be drawn from a comparison of the two manuscript versions of the article in the FRH. One was evidently the version used by the printer and is essentially (i.e. apart from minor changes made at proof stage) that which was published. The other manuscript, obviously earlier, omits a number of passages that are in the final version, including the whole of Section IV ('St Besse in the Plain'). These omissions are not accidental but are true to the structure of this version, as can be seen by comparing it with the later one, basically a typed version of it with later additions and changes in Hertz's handwriting. The added passages deal with the differing versions of the legend held by the Church hierarchy of the plains and the local intellectuals respectively, i.e. they are those that discuss the historiography of the cult.

16. *Ibid.:* 171 n. 33. The only pictorial representations I could find during my own visit in August 1990, whether at Ivrea or in the mountains, show Besse as a legionary soldier, an aspect of the official version. The medallion of the saint brought back by Hertz (FRH) shows him in the same guise.

17. The development of conflict out of the revival of a ritual in modified form is evident from a number of the contributions in Boissevain (ed.) 1992, especially Cowan's study of ritual regeneration in a town in Greek Macedonia and Boissevain's own account of a similar situation on Malta. Other papers in that collection, however, indicate a perceptible unity among the rite's participants. See especially Cruces and Díaz de Rada 1992: 71–2 on a valley in Estremadura, in a passage that would surely have delighted Durkheim (though a footnote indicates that not all is quite as it seems even here). Poppi's study in this same volume is also relevant in the latter context, at least of the village he describes, though the festival itself is at least partly directed against outsiders. The relevance of Boissevain's arguments regarding the revitalization of European rituals in the late twentieth century to the case of St Besse is discussed critically in MacClancy and Parkin n.d.

18. In his notes for a slightly earlier unpublished lecture (1911c), Hertz makes a clear distinction between myth and history, even in literate societies. Peel (1989) has recently advocated a return to recognizing 'real' history as well as created tradition, even in this context.

19. For example, among different groups of Hindu ascetics (see Sax 1991: 12; Morinis 1984; also Sallnow 1981, on Andean pilgrimage).

NOTES TO CHAPTER EIGHT

1. Hertz to Roussel, 21/3/1905.
2. Hertz to Roussel, 27/4/1907. The reference to philology is presumably to be explained by Roussel's classical interests.
3. Hertz to Roussel, 9/12/1907.

Bibliography

A. Complete list of the works of Robert Hertz (for Alice Hertz, see part B)

Articles and Pamphlets

[1900. Les populations rurales en Allemagne, *Revue d'économie politique* 14, 197-212. Listed by Nandan (1977: 331), but almost certainly spurious; see Parkin 1992b: 22.]

1907a. Contribution à une étude sur la représentation collective de la mort, *Année Sociologique* 10, 48-137.

1909a. La prééminence de la main droite, étude sur la polarité religieuse, *Revue Philosophique* 68, 553-80.

1910a. *Socialisme et dépopulation*, Paris: Librairie du Parti Socialiste (Cahiers du Socialiste, 10).

1913a. Saint Besse, étude d'un culte alpestre, *Revue d'Histoire des Religions* 67/2, 115-80.

1917. Contes et dictons recueillis sur le front parmi les poilus de la Mayenne et d'ailleurs (Campagne 1915), *Revue des Traditions Populaires* 32/1-2, 32-45; 32/3-4, 74-91.

1922. Le péché et l'expiation dans les sociétés primitives [Introduction only], *Revue de l'Histoire des Religions* 86, 5-54. Includes editor's Introduction, Conclusion and Notes (by Marcel Mauss, pp. 1-4, 54-60). Reissued Paris: Michel Place, 1988, with an Introduction by Jean Jamin.

1928. *Mélanges de sociologie religieuse et de folklore*, Paris: Presses Universitaires Françaises. Reissued under the title *Sociologie religieuse et de folklore*, with a Preface by Georges Balandier, Paris: Presses Universitaires Françaises, 1970. Contains Hertz 1907a, 1909a, 1913a, 1915, and full version of 1913c (see reviews); also Alice Hertz 1928; Mauss 1928.

1987. Le péché et l'expiation dans les sociétés inférieures: mise au point des recherches inédites de Robert Hertz. Cours de Marcel Mauss. Notes du cours de Marcel Mauss au Collège de France en 1935, prises par Paul Lavaquery, établies, présentées et annotées par Jean Jamin et François Lupu, *Gradhiva* 2, 45-52. Lavaquery's notes of Mauss's course, itself based on notes left by Hertz.

English translations of Hertz's work

1960. *Death and the Right Hand* (translated Rodney and Claudia Needham), London: Cohen & West. Translations of Hertz 1907a and 1909a, with Introduction by E.E. Evans-Pritchard.

1973. The Pre-eminence of the Right Hand: A Study in Religious Polarity, *in* Needham (ed.) 1973. Translation of Hertz 1909a (slightly revised version of translation in Hertz 1960).

1983. St Besse: A Study of an Alpine Cult (translated Stephen Wilson), *in* Wilson ed. 1983. Translation of Hertz 1913a.

1994.   *Sin and Expiation in Primitive Societies* (translated Robert Parkin), Oxford: British Centre for Durkheimian Studies, Occasional Papers no. 2. Translation of Hertz 1922, including Mauss's notes.

Reviews (* = signed 'R.H.')

1902.   Office du Travail, *L'Apprentissage industriel: Rapport sur l'apprentissage dans l'imprimerie, 1899–1901, Notes Critiques, Sciences Sociales* 3/19, 270-1.

1903.   Karl Kautzky, *Politique et syndicats, Notes Critiques, Sciences Sociales* 4/21, 30-1.

1905a.* George Simmel, The Sociology of Conflict, *Année Sociologique* 8 (1903-4), 181-2.

1905b.* Irving King, Influence of the Form of Social Change Upon the Emotional Life of a People, *Année Sociologique* 8 (1903-4), 196-7.

1906a.* R.-H. Nassau, *Fetichism in West Africa, Année Sociologique* 9 (1904-5), 191-4.

1906b.* Carlo Puini, *Il Tibet secondo la relazione del viaggio del P. Ippolito Desideri, Année Sociologique* 9 (1904-5), 225.

1906c.   H. Gomperz, *Die Lebensauffassung der Griechischen Philosophen und das Ideal der inneren Freiheit, Année Sociologique* 9 (1904-5), 272-3.

1907b.* P. Ehrenreich, *Die Mythen und Legenden der südamerikanischen Urvölker und ihre Beziehungen zu denen Nordamerikas und der alten Welt, Année Sociologique* 10 (1905-6), 328-9.

1909b.   H. Hubert and M. Mauss, *Mélanges d'histoire des religions, Revue de l'Histoire des Religions* 60, 218-20.

1909c.   Frank Byron Jevons, *An Introduction to the Study of Comparative Religion, Revue de l'Histoire des Religions* 60, 220-2.

1909d.   A.C. Kruyt, *Het Animisme in den Indischen Archipel, Revue de l'Histoire des Religions* 60, 352-60.

1910b.* W.H.R. Rivers, *Totemism in Polynesian and Melanesia, Année Sociologique* 11 (1906-9), 101-5.

1910c.* Le P.A. Jaussen, *Coutumes des Arabes au pays de Moab*; and A. Musil, *Arabia Petraea III: Ethnologischer Reisebericht, Année Sociologique* 11 (1906-9), 160-3 (continued 1910j).

1910d.* H. Windisch, *Taufe und Sünde im ältesten Christentum bis auf Origenes, Année Sociologique* 11 (1906-9), 169-73.

1910e.* E. Doutté, *Magie et religion dans l'Afrique du Nord, Année Sociologique* 11 (1906-9), 194-8.

1910f.* W. Schrank, *Babylonische Sühnriten besonders mit Rücksicht auf Priester und Büßer III, Année Sociologique* 11 (1906-9), 210-11.

1910g.* F. Bennewitz, *Die Sünde im alten Israel, Année Sociologique* 11 (1906-9), 266-7.

1910h.* L. Hobhouse, *Morals in Evolution: A Study in Comparative Ethics, Année Sociologique* 11 (1906-9), 276-7.

1910i.* J. Roscoe, *The Bahima: A Cow Tribe of Enkole in the Uganda Protectorate, Année Sociologique* 11 (1906-9), 307-9.

1910j.* Le P.A. Jaussen, *Coutumes des Arabes au pays de Moab*; and A. Musil, *Arabia Petraea III: Ethnologischer Reisebericht, Année Sociologique* 11 (1906-9), 323-7 (continuation of 1910c).

1910k.   J. Warneck, *Die Religion der Batak, Revue de l'Histoire des Religions* 62, 59-60 (cf. 1913d).

1910l.   Edward Sidney Hartland, *Primitive Paternity: The Myth of Supernatural Birth in Relation to the History of the Family*, Revue de l'Histoire des Religions 62, 220-33.

1910m. Ed. Westermarck, *The Origin and Development of the Moral Ideas*, Revue de l'Histoire des Religions 62, 233-8.

1910n.   L. Lévy-Bruhl, *Les fonctions mentales dans les sociétés inférieures*, Revue de l'Histoire des Religions 62, 356-63.

1911a.   F.B. Jevons, *The Idea of God in Early Religions*, Revue de l'Histoire des Religions 64, 123.

1912a.   Georges Foucart, *Histoire des religions et méthode comparative*, Revue de l'Histoire des Religions 66, 253-9.

1912b.   J.G. Frazer, *The Golden Bough: A Study in Magic and Religion*, Revue de l'Histoire des Religions 66, 385-97.

1913b.* *Aus der deutschen Südsee: Mitteilungen der Missionare vom heiligsten Herzen Jesu, I;* P. Jos Meier, *Mythen und Erzählungen der Küstenbewohner der Gazelle-Halbinsel*; P.G. Peekel, *Religion und Zauberei auf dem mittleren Neu-Mecklenburg*; and George Brown, *Melanesians and Polynesians: Their Life Histories Described and Compared*, Année Sociologique 12 (1909-12), 124-7.

1913c.* K.K. Grass, *Die russischen Sekten: I Die Gottesleute oder Chlusten; II Die Weissen Tauben oder Skopzen*, Année Sociologique 12 (1909-12), 181-6. Edited by Durkheim. Full version published in Hertz 1928a.

1913d.* W. Volz, *Nord Sumatra*; Joh. Warneck, *Die Religion der Batak*; and E.H. Gomes, *Seventeen Years among the Sea Dyaks of Borneo*, Année Sociologique 12 (1909-12), 273-6 (cf. 1910k).

1913e.* Le P.W. Schmidt, *Grundlinien einer Vergleichung der Religionen und Mythologien der austronesischen Völker*, Année Sociologique 12 (1909-12), 280-2.

1913f.* Le P.P. Schmoll, *Die Bußlehre der Frühscholastik: Eine dog mengeschichtliche Untersuchung*, Année Sociologique 12 (1909-12), 305-6.

1913g.* Guttfried Simon, *Islam und Christentum im Kampf um die Eroberung der animistischen Heidenwelt*; and Joh. Warneck, *50 Jahre Batakmission*, Année Sociologique 12 (1909-12), 313-15.

1913h.   Georg Gerland, *Der Mythus von der Sintflut*, Revue de l'Histoire des Religions 67, 85.

1914.* Carl Meinhof, *Religionen der schriftlosen Völker Afrikas*, Revue de l'Histoire des Religions 70, 87.

Unpublished manuscripts (extant, Fonds Robert Hertz)

No date. La crise ouvrière en Angleterre (suite): l'affaire Osborne. Handwritten manuscript, 16 pp. Undated, but 1910 or 1911.

1910p.   Saint Simon et les Saint-Simoniens. Talk presented to Ecole Socialiste, 13/12/1910. Typed, 5 pp.

1911b.   Le socialisme en Angleterre: La société fabienne. Talk presented to Ecole Socialiste, 13/1/1911. Two typed 'resumés analytiques', of 6 and 10 pp. (former shortened by Hertz for publication; latter secretary's summary).

1911c.   La religion des primitives. Talk presented to La Ligue d'Enseignement de Versailles, April 1911. Handwritten manuscript, partly in note form, 12 pp.

Unpublished and projected work (presumed no longer extant)

1. Mythe d'Athene (see Mauss 1925: 25) and/or
2. Légendes et cultes des roches, des monts et des sources (see Alice Hertz 1928: xii–xiii). (These two titles, though different, almost certainly refer to the same paper.)
3. Paper on kites in Polynesia (see Mauss, 1968-9 II: 466).

Letters (published)

1912c.   Open Letter to Paul Farinet, dated 12/9/1911, in *La vallée d'Aoste pour sa langue française: Numéro unique publié sous les auspices du Comité pour la protection de la langue française dans la Vallée constituée à Aoste, le 17 novembre 1909*, Aosta 1912. Reissued as Appendix in Parkin 1992b: 23-4 (cf. ibid.: 21).
1913i.   Letter to Henri Hubert, 16/7/1913, published in *Etudes Durkheimiennes* 11 (1985), 2.

Translations by Hertz

[1911].   Sidney Webb, *La base néréssaire de l'organization sociale*. Handwritten manuscript, 40 pp. (apparently never published in translation, but read by Hertz to Groupe d'Etudes Socialistes, 28/11/1911).
[1912].   Sidney and Beatrice Webb, *Examen de la doctrine syndicaliste*, Paris: Librairie du Parti Socialiste (Cahiers du Socialiste, nos. 14-15, 1912; original title, *What Syndicalism Means*; read in translation by Hertz to Groupe d'Etudes Socialistes, 8/10/1912).

B.   Other works mentioned in the text

Allen, N.J. 1978. A Thulung Myth and Some Problems of Comparison, *Journal of the Anthropological Society of Oxford* 9/3, 157-66.
... 1982. A Dance of Relatives, *Journal of the Anthropological Society of Oxford* 13/2, 139-46.
... 1986. Tetradic Theory: An Approach to Kinship, *Journal of the Anthropological Society of Oxford* 17/2, 87-109.
... 1989a. The Evolution of Kinship Terminologies, *Lingua* 77, 173-85.
... 1989b. Assimilation of Alternate Generations, *Journal of the Anthropological Society of Oxford* 20/1, 45-55.
... 1994. Primitive Classification: The Argument and its Validity, *in* W.S.F. Pickering and Herminio Martins (eds.), *Debating Durkheim*, London and New York: Routledge.
Alphandéry, Paul 1919. In Memoriam, *Revue de l'Histoire des Religions* 79, 328-75.
Andler, Charles 1977 [1932]. *La vie de Lucien Herr*, Paris: François Maspero.
Appadurai, Arjun 1981. The Past as a Scarce Resource, *Man* (n.s.) 16/2, 201-19.
Augé, Marc 1979. *The Anthropological Circle: Symbol, Function, History*, Cambridge: Cambridge University Press.
Barley, Nigel 1981. The Dowayo Dance of Death, *in* S.C. Humphreys and Helen King (eds.), *Mortality and Immortality: The Anthropology and Archaeology of Death*, London etc.: Academic Press.
... 1983. *Symbolic Structures: An Exploration of the Culture of the Dowayos*, Cambridge and Paris; Cambridge University Press and Maison des Sciences de l'Homme.

Barnes, J.A. 1971. The Righthand and Lefthand Kingdoms of God: A Dilemma of Pietist Politics, *in* T.O. Beidelman (ed.), *The Translation of Culture: Essays to E.E. Evans-Pritchard*, London: Tavistock Publications.

Barnes, R.H. 1974. *Kédang: The Collective Thought of an Eastern Indonesian People*, Oxford: Clarendon Press.

... 1985a. The Leiden Version of the Comparative Method in Southeast Asia, *Journal of the Anthropological Society of Oxford* 16/2, 87-110.

... 1985b. Hierarchy Without Caste, *in* R.H. Barnes, Daniel de Coppet and R.J. Parkin (eds.), *Contexts and Levels: Anthropological Essays on Hierarchy*, Oxford: JASO (JASO Occasional Papers 4).

... 1989. Méi Nafa, a Rite of Expiation in Lamalera, Indonesia, *Bijdragen tot de Taal-, Land- en Volkenkunde* 145/4, 539-47.

Barraud, Cécile 1990. Wife-givers as Ancestors and Ultimate Values in the Kei Islands, *Bijdragen tot de Taal-, Land- en Volkenkunde* 146/2-3, 193-225.

Bataille, George 1988 [1938]. Attraction and Repulsion, I and II, *in* Denis Hollier (ed.), *The College of Sociology (1937-39)*, Minneapolis: University of Minnesota Press.

Baumann, Gerd 1992. Ritual Implicates 'Others': Rereading Durkheim in a Plural Society, *in* Daniel de Coppet (ed.), *Understanding Rituals*, London and New York: Routledge.

Baumann, Hermann 1955. *Das doppelte Geschlecht: ethnologische Studien zur Bisexualität in Ritus und Mythus*, Berlin: Dietrich Reimer.

Beattie, John 1968. Aspects of Nyoro Symbolism, *Africa* 38/4, 413-42.

... 1976. Right, Left and the Bunyoro, *Africa* 46/3, 217-235.

Beck, Brenda 1973. The Right-Left Division of South Indian Society, *in* Needham (ed.) 1973.

Beidelman, T.O. 1973. Kaguru Symbolic Classification, *in* Needham (ed.) 1973.

Besnard, Philippe 1983. The 'Année Sociologique' Team, *in* Philippe Besnard (ed.), *The Sociological Domain: The Durkheimians and the Founding of French Sociology*, Cambridge and Paris; Cambridge University Press and Maison des Sciences de l'Homme.

... 1989. Two Letters from Marcel Mauss to Henri Hubert (1898 and 1905), *Etudes Durkheimiennes* (new series) 1/1, 12-14.

Bloch, Maurice 1971. *Placing the Dead*, London and New York: Seminar Press.

... 1973. The Long Term and the Short Term: The Economic and Political Significance of the Morality of Kinship, *in* Jack Goody (ed.), *The Character of Kinship*, Cambridge: Cambridge University Press.

... 1977. The Past and the Present in the Present, *Man* (n.s.) 12/2, 278-92.

... 1982. Death, Women and Power, *in* Bloch and Parry (eds.) 1982.

Bloch, Maurice, and Jonathan Parry (eds.) 1982. *Death and the Regeneration of Life*, Cambridge etc.: Cambridge University Press.

Boetzelaer van Asperen en Dubbeldam, Baron van, 1949. Albertus Christian Kruyt 1869-1949, *Bijdragen tot de Taal-, Land- en Volkenkunde* 105/2, 143-6.

Boissevain, Jeremy (ed.) 1992. *Revitalizing European Rituals*, London and New York: Routledge.

... 1992. Play and Identity: Ritual Change in a Maltese Village, *in* Boissevain (ed.) 1992.

Boulay, Juliet du 1974. *Portrait of a Greek Mountain Village*, Oxford: Clarendon Press.

... 1982. The Greek Vampire: A Study of Cyclic Symbolism in Marriage and Death, *Man* 17/2, 219-38.

Bourdieu, Pierre 1977. *Outline of a Theory of Practice*, Cambridge: Cambridge University Press.

Bourgin, Hubert 1925. *Cinquante ans d'experience démocratique*, Paris: Nouvelle Librairie Nationale.

... 1970 [1938]. *De Jaurès à Léon Blum: L'Ecole normale et la politique*, Paris: Gordon & Breach.

Bowman, Glenn 1993. Nationalizing the Sacred: Shrines and Shifting Identities in the Israeli-Occupied Territories, *Man* 28/3, 431–60.

Caillois, Roger 1939. *L'Homme et le sacré*, Paris: Gallimard.

Carmichael, David L., Jane Hubert, Brian Reeves and Audhild Schauche (eds.) 1994. *Sacred Sites, Sacred Places*, London and New York: Routledge.

Casajus, Dominique 1984. L'énigme de la troisième personne, *in* Jean-Claude Galey (ed.); *Différences, valeurs, hiérarchie: textes offerts à Louis Dumont*, Paris: Editions de l'Ecole des Hautes Etudes en Sciences Sociales.

Chelhod, J. 1973 [1964]. A Contribution to the Problem of the Pre-eminence of the Right, Based upon Arabic Evidence, *in* Needham (ed.) 1973.

Cherkaoui, Mohammed 1983. Education and Social Mobility: Paul Lapie's Pathbreaking Work, *in* Philippe Besnard (ed.), *The Sociological Domain: The Durkheimians and the Founding of French Sociology*, Cambridge and Paris; Cambridge University Press and Maison des Sciences de l'Homme.

Chiva, Isac 1986. Aujourd'hui, les rites de passage, *in* Pierre Centlivres and Jacques Hainard (eds.), *Les rites de passage aujourd'hui: Actes du Colloque de Neuchâtel 1981*, Lausanne: Editions de l'Age de l'Homme.

... 1987. Entre livre et musée: Emergence d'une ethnologie de la France, *in* Isac Chiva and Utz Jeggle (eds.), *Ethnologies en miroir: la France et les pays allemands*, Paris: Editions de la Maison des Sciences de l'Homme.

Clark, Terry N. 1968a. Emile Durkheim and the Institutionalization of Sociology in the French University System, *European Journal of Sociology* 9, 37–71.

... 1968b. The Structure and Functions of a Research Institute: The *Année Sociologique, European Journal of Sociology* 9, 72–91.

... 1973. *Prophets and Patrons: The French University and the Emergence of the Social Sciences*, Cambridge, Mass.: Harvard University Press.

Coppet, Daniel de, 1970. Cycles de meurtres et cycles funéraires: esquisse de deux structures d'échange, *in* J. Pouillon and P. Maranda (eds.), *Echanges et communications: mélanges offerts à Claude Lévi-Strauss*, Paris and The Hague: Mouton.

... 1981. The Life-giving Death, *in* S.C. Humphreys and Helen King (eds.), *Mortality and Immortality: The Anthropology and Archaeology of Death*, London etc.: Academic Press.

Cowan, Janet 1992. Japanese Ladies and Mexican Hats: Contested Symbols and the Politics of Tradition in a Northern Greek Carnival Celebration, *in* Boissevain (ed.) 1992.

Craig, John E. 1983. Sociology and Related Disciplines Between the Wars: Maurice Halbwachs and the Imperialism of the Durkheimians, *in* Philippe Besnard (ed.), *The Sociological Domain: The Durkheimians and the Founding of French Sociology*, Cambridge and Paris; Cambridge University Press and Maison des Sciences de l'Homme.

Cruces, Francisco, and Angel Díaz de Rada 1992. Public Celebrations in a Spanish Valley, *in* Boissevain (ed.) 1992.

Cunningham, Clark E. 1973 [1964]. Order in the Atoni House, *in* Needham (ed.) 1973.

Czarnowski, Stefan 1919. *Le culte des héros et ses conditions sociales: Saint Patrick, héros national de l'Irland*, Paris: Félix Alcan.

Damon, Frederick H. 1989. Introduction, *in* Frederick H. Damon and Roy Wagner (eds.), *Death Rituals and Life in the Societies of the Kula Ring*, DeKalb: Northern Illinois University Press.

Danforth, Loring M. 1982. *The Death Rituals of Rural Greece*, Princeton: Princeton University Press.

Das, Veena 1977a. On the Categorization of Space in Hindu Ritual, *in* Ravindra K. Jain (ed.), *Text and Context: The Social Anthropology of Tradition*, Philadelphia: ISHI (ASA Essays in Social Anthropology, 2).

... 1977b. *Structure and Cognition*, Delhi: Oxford University Press.

... and Jit Singh Uberoi 1971. The Elementary Structure of Caste, *Contributions to Indian Sociology* n.s. 5, 33–43.

Demiéville, Paul 1968. Gauche et droite en Chine, *in* Raoul Kourilsky and Pierre Grapin (eds.), *Main droite et main gauche: norme et lateralité*, Paris: Presses Universitaires Françaises.

Dieterlin, Germaine 1968. Norme et lateralité en Afrique occidentale, *in* Raoul Kourilsky and Pierre Grapin (eds.), *Main droite et main gauche: norme et lateralité*, Paris: Presses Universitaires Françaises.

Douglas, Mary 1966. *Purity and Danger: An Analysis of the Concepts of Pollution and Taboo*, London and Henley: Routledge & Kegan Paul.

Douglass, W.A. 1969. *Death in Murelaga: Funerary Ritual in a Spanish Basque Village*, Seattle: The University of Washington Press.

Dumont, Louis 1972 [1966]. *Homo Hierarchicus: The Caste System and its Implications*, London: Paladin.

... 1979. The Anthropological Community and Ideology, *Social Science Information* 18, 785–817.

... 1982. On Value [Radcliffe-Brown Lecture 1980], *Proceedings of the British Academy* 66, 207–41.

... 1986. *Essays on Individualism: Modern Ideology in Anthropological Perspective*, Chicago and London: The University of Chicago Press.

... 1991. *Homo Aequalis II: L'idéologie allemande, France-Allemagne et retour*, Paris: Gallimard.

... 1992. Left versus Right in French Political Ideology: A Comparative Approach, *in* John A. Hall and I.C. Jarvie (eds.), *Transition to Modernity: Essays on Power, Wealth and Belief*, Cambridge etc.: Cambridge University Press.

Durkheim, Emile 1888. Suicide et natalité: Etude de statistique morale, *Revue Philosophique* 26, 446–63.

... 1897. *Le suicide: étude de sociologie*, Paris: Félix Alcan.

... 1898a. La prohibition de l'inceste, *Année Sociologique* 1, 1–70.

... 1898b. L'individualisme et les intellectuals, *Revue Bleue* (4ième Serie) 10, 7–13.

... 1899. De la définition des phénomènes religieux, *Année Sociologique* 2, 1–28.

... 1903. Review of Géza Révész, *Das Trauerjahr der Witwe*, *Année Sociologique* 6, 361–5.

... 1913a. Review of Lucien Lévy-Bruhl, *Les fonctions mentales dans des sociétés inférieures, Année Sociologique* 12, 33–7.

... 1913b. Review of E.S. Hartland, *Primitive Paternity, Année Sociologique* 12, 410–14.

... 1915 [1912]. *The Elementary Forms of the Religious Life: A Study in Religious Sociology* (translated J.W. Swain), London: George Allen & Unwin.

... 1916. Nécrologie, Robert Hertz, *L'Annuaire de l'association des anciens élèves de l'école normale supérieure* 1916, 116–20.

... 1951 [1924]. *Sociologie et philosophie*, Paris: Félix Alcan.

... 1971 [1928]. *Le Socialisme*, Paris: Presses Universitaires de France.

... 1975. *Textes*, Paris: Editions de Minuit (3 vols.).

... 1984 [1893]. *The Division of Labour in Society*, London: Macmillan.

... and Marcel Mauss 1963 [1903]. *Primitive Classification* (translated Rodney Needham), London: Cohen & West.

Elkin, A.P. 1961. Review of Hertz 1960, *Oceania* 31/3, 230-1.

Ellen, Roy 1986. Microcosm, Macrocosm and the Nualu House: Concerning the Reductionist Fallacy as applied to Metaphorical Levels, *Bijdragen tot de Taal-, Land- en Volkenkunde* 14/1, 1-30.

Elwin, Verrier 1955. *The Religion of an Indian Tribe*, Bombay: Oxford University Press.

Erchak, Gerald M. 1972. Dusun Social and Symbolic Orders, *Sarawak Museum Journal* 20, 301-13.

Evans-Pritchard, E.E. 1956. *Nuer Religion*, Oxford: Clarendon Press.

... 1960. Introduction, *in* Hertz 1960.

... 1965. *Theories of Primitive Religion*, Oxford: Clarendon Press.

... 1973 [1953]. Nuer Spear Symbolism, *in* Needham (ed.) 1973.

Evens, T.M.S. 1982. Two Concepts of 'Society as Moral System': Evans-Pritchard's Heterodoxy, *Man* 17/2, 205-18.

Fabian, Johannes 1983. *Time and the Other: How Anthropology Makes its Object*, New York: Columbia University Press.

Faron, Louis C. 1973 [1962]. Symbolic Values and the Integration of Society among the Mapuche of Chile, *in* Needham (ed.) 1973.

Firth, Raymond 1970. Postures and Gestures of Respect, *in* J. Pouillon and P. Maranda (eds.), *Echanges et communications: mélanges offerts à Claude Lévi-Strauss*, Paris and The Hague: Mouton.

... 1971. *Elements of Social Organization*, London: Tavistock.

Forth, Gregory 1985. Right and Left as a Hierarchical Opposition: Reflections on Eastern Sumbanese Hairstyles, *in* R.H. Barnes, Daniel de Coppet and R.J. Parkin (eds.), *Contexts and Levels: Anthropological Essays on Hierarchy*, Oxford: JASO (JASO Occasional Papers 4).

Fournier, Marcel. 1994. *Marcel Mauss*, Paris: Fayard.

Fox, James J. 1988a. Chicken Bones and Buffalo Sinews: Verbal Frames and the Organization of Rotinese Mortuary Performances, *in* David S. Moyer and Henri J.M. Claessen (eds.), *Time Past, Time Present, Time Future: Essays in Honour of P.E. de Josselin de Jong*, Dordrecht and Providence (USA): Foris Publications.

... 1988b. Introduction, *in* James J. Fox (ed.), *To Speak in Pairs: Essays on the Ritual Languages of Eastern Indonesia*, Cambridge etc.: Cambridge University Press.

... 1989. Category and Complement: Binary Ideologies and the Organization of Dualism in Eastern Indonesia, *in* David Maybury-Lewis and Uri Almagor (eds.), *The Attraction of Opposites: Thought and Society in the Dualistic Mode*, Ann Arbor: The University of Michigan Press.

Friedberg, Claudine 1980. Boiled Woman and Broiled Man: Myths and Agricultural Rituals of the Bunaq of Central Timor, *in* James J. Fox (ed.), *The Flow of Life: Essays on Eastern Indonesia*, Cambridge, Mass.: Harvard University Press.

Fürer-Haimendorf, Christoph von 1967. *Morals and Merit: A Study of Values and Social Controls in South Asian Societies*, London: Weidenfeld & Nicholson.

... 1974. The Sense of Sin in Cross-cultural Perspective [Henry Myers Lecture 1974], *Man* 9/4, 539-56.

Gennep, Arnold van, 1960 [1909]. *The Rites of Passage*, London and Henley: Routledge & Kegan Paul.

Goody, Jack 1961. Religion and Ritual: The Definitional Problem, *British Journal of Sociology* 12, 142-64.

... 1962. *Death, Property and the Ancestors: A Study of the Mortuary Customs of the Lodagaa of West Africa*, Stanford: Stanford University Press.

... 1977. *The Domestication of the Savage Mind*, Cambridge: Cambridge University Press.

Granet, Marcel 1939. *Catégories matrimoniales et relations de proximité dans la Chine ancienne*, Paris: Félix Alcan (Annales Sociologique, Série B).

... 1973 [1933, 1953]. Right and Left in China, *in* Needham (ed.) 1973.

Gross, Daniel R. 1971. Ritual and Conformity: A Religious Pilgrimage to Northeastern Brazil, *Ethnology* 10/2, 129–48.

Halbwachs, Maurice 1928. Review of Hertz 1928, *Bulletin de la Faculté des Lettres de Strasbourg* 7, 200-1.

Hallpike, C.R. 1979. *The Foundations of Primitive Thought*, Oxford: Clarendon Press.

Harrisson, Tom 1962. Borneo Death, *Bijdragen tot de Taal-, Land- en Volkenkunde* 118/1, 1–41.

Heilbron, Johan 1983. Note sur l'Institut Française de Sociologie (1924-1962), *Etudes Durkheimiennes* 9, 9-14.

Hertz, Alice 1928. Préface, *in* Hertz 1928.

... [Mme Robert] and [Mme Louis] Trouillon 1920. *Du Grain de Blé Jusqu'au Pain: Plusieurs suites de causeries, travaux manuels, chants et jeux pour les enfants de 3 à 6 ans*, Paris: Librairie Classique Fernand Nathan.

Hicks, David 1976. *Tetum Ghosts and Kin: Fieldwork in an Indonesian Community*, Palo Alto (Calif.): Mayfield.

Hobart, Mark 1978. The Path of the Soul: The Legitimacy of Nature in Balinese Conceptions of Space, *in* G.B. Milner (ed.), *Natural Symbols in Southeast Asia*, London: School of Oriental and African Studies.

Hocart, A.M. 1914. Mana, *Man*, 46.

... 1954. *Social Origins*, London: Watts & Co.

... 1970 [1936]. *Kings and Councillors: An Essay in the Comparative Anatomy of Human Society*, Chicago: The University of Chicago Press.

Hockey, Jennifer Lorna 1990. *Experiences of Death: An Anthropological Account*, Edinburgh: Edinburgh University Press.

Holy, Ladislav, and Milan Stuchlik 1983. *Actions, Norms and Representations: Foundations of Anthropological Enquiry*, Cambridge: Cambridge University Press.

Howell, Signe 1985. Equality and Hierarchy in Chewong Classification, *in* R.H. Barnes, R.H., Daniel de Coppet and R.J. Parkin (eds.), *Contexts and Levels: Anthropological Essays on Hierarchy*, Oxford: JASO (JASO Occasional Papers 4).

... 1989 [1984]. *Society and Cosmos: Chewong of Peninsular Malaysia*, Singapore etc.: Oxford University Press.

Hubert, Henri 1901. Review of Alfred Berthollet, *Die Israelitischen Vorstellungen vom Zustand nach dem Tode*, *Année Sociologique* 4, 192-3.

... 1904. Introduction, *in* Chantepie de la Saussaye, *Manuel d'histoire des religions*, Paris: Colin.

... 1905. Etude sommaire de la représentation du temps dans la religion et la magie, *Annuaire de l'Ecole Pratique des Hautes Etudes, section des sciences religieuses* 1905, 1-39.

... 1950 [1932]. *Les celtes*, Paris: Michel (2 vols.).

... 1952. *Les germains*, Paris: Michel.

... 1979. Texte autobiographique, *Revue Française de Sociologie* 20/1, 205-7.

... and Marcel Mauss 1899. Essai sur la nature et la fonction sociale du sacrifice, *Année Sociologique* 2, 29-138.

... and Marcel Mauss 1904. Esquisse d'une théorie générale de la magie, *Année Sociologique* 7, 1-46.

Humphreys, S.C. 1981. Introduction: Comparative Perspectives on Death, *in* S.C. Humphreys and Helen King (eds.), *Mortality and Immortality: The Anthropology and Archaeology of Death*, London etc.: Academic Press.

Huntington, Richard 1973. Death and the Social Order: Bara Funeral Customs (Madagascar), *African Affairs* 32/1, 65–84.

... and Peter Metcalf 1979. *Celebrations of Death: The Anthropology of Mortuary Ritual*, Cambridge etc.: Cambridge University Press. (See Metcalf and Huntington 1991 for 2nd edition).

Isambert, Francois-André 1982. *Le sens du sacré: fête et religion populaire*, Paris: Editions de Minuit.

... 1983. At the Frontier of Folklore and Sociology: Hubert, Hertz and Czarnowski: Founders of a Sociology of Folk Religion, *in* Philippe Besnard (ed.), *The Sociological Domain: The Durkheimians and the Founding of French Sociology*, Cambridge and Paris; Cambridge University Press and Maison des Sciences de l'Homme.

Izikowitz, Karl Gustav 1951. *Lamet, Peasants of French Indo-China*, Goteborg: Etnologiska Studier 17.

James, Wendy, and Douglas Johnson (eds.) 1988. *Vernacular Christianity: Essays in the Social Anthropology of Religion Presented to Godfrey Lienhardt*, Oxford: JASO.

Jamin, Jean 1981. Quand le sacré devient gauche, *L'Ire des Vents* 3–4, 98–118.

... 1988. Introduction to Robert Hertz, *Le péché et l'expiation dans les sociétés primitives*, Paris: Michel Place.

... and François Lupu 1987. Introduction to Hertz 1987, *Gradhiva* 2, 42–4.

Jenner, Philip N. 1976. A Possible Case of Cosmological Gender in Khmer, *in* Philip N. Jenner, Laurence C. Thompson and Stanley Starostra (eds.), *Austroasiatic Studies*, Part II, Honolulu: The University Press of Hawaii.

Jones, Robert Alun 1977. On Understanding a Sociological Classic, *American Journal of Sociology* 83/2, 279–319.

... 1986. *Emile Durkheim: An Introduction to Four Major Works*, Beverly Hills etc.: Sage Publications.

Josselin de Jong, P.E. de, 1972. Marcel Mauss et les origines de l'anthropologie structurelle hollandaise, *L'Homme* 12/4, 62–84.

... 1976. Review of Needham (ed.) 1973, *Bijdragen tot de Taal-, Land- en Volkenkunde* 132/1, 171–4.

Karady, Victor 1979. Stratégies de réussite et modes de faire-valoir de la sociologie chez les durkheimiennes, *Revue Française de Sociologie* 20/1, 49–82.

... 1983. The Durkheimians in Academe: A Reconsideration, *in* Philippe Besnard (ed.), *The Sociological Domain: The Durkheimians and the Founding of French Sociology*, Cambridge and Paris; Cambridge University Press and Maison des Sciences de l'Homme.

Keesing, Roger M. 1984. Rethinking *Mana, Journal of Anthropological Research* 40, 137–56.

King, Victor 1980. Structural Analysis and Cognatic Societies: Some Borneo Examples, *Sociologus* 30/1, 1–28.

Kinietz, Vernon 1940. European Civilization as a Determinant of Native Indian Customs, *American Anthropologist* 42, 116–21.

Kligman, Gail 1988. *The Wedding of the Dead: Ritual, Poetics, and Popular Culture in Transylvania*, Berkeley etc.: University of California Press.

Kruyt, Alb. C. 1906. *Het Animisme in den Indischen Archipel*, The Hague: Nijhoff.

... 1973 [1941]. Right and Left in Central Celebes, *in* Needham (ed.) 1973.

La Flesche, Francis 1973 [1916]. Right and Left in Osage Ceremonies, *in* Needham (ed.) 1973.

Ladd, John 1957. *The Structure of a Moral Code: A Philosophical Analysis of Ethnical Discourse applied to the Ethics of the Navaho Indians*, Cambridge, Mass.: Harvard University Press.

Lapie, Paul 1898. *Civilisations tunisiennes, Musulmans, Israélites, Européens: Etudes de psychologie sociale*, Paris: Félix Alcan.

Leach, E.R. 1954. *Political Systems of Highland Burma: A Study of Kachin Social Structure*, London: Bell.

... 1961. Two Essays Concerning the Symbolic Representation of Time, *in* E.R. Leach, *Rethinking Anthropology*, New York: The Athlone Press.

... 1976. *Culture and Communication: The Logic by which Symbols are Connected*, Cambridge: Cambridge University Press.

Leacock, E. 1981. *Myths of Male Dominance*, New York: Monthly Review Press.

Leeuwen-Turnovcova, Girina van 1990. *Rechts und Links in Europa: ein Beitrag zur Semantik und Symbolik der Geschlechterpolarität*, Wiesbaden: Otto Harrassowitz.

Legendre, Maurice 1910. Review of Hertz 1910a, *Le Bulletin de la Semaine*, 23rd November 1910, pp. 583–4.

Leiris, Michel 1937. *Tauromachies*, Paris: GLM.

Lévi-Strauss, Claude 1950. Introduction à l'oeuvre de Marcel Mauss, *in* Mauss 1950.

... 1956. Les organizations dualistes, existent-ils?, *Bijdragen tot de Taal-, Land- en Volkenkunde* 112/2, 99–128.

... 1962. *Le totemisme aujourd'hui*, Paris: Presses Universitaires Françaises.

... 1967. The Story of Asdiwal, *in* Edmund Leach (ed.), *The Structural Study of Myth and Totemism*, London: Tavistock (ASA Monographs in Social Anthropology 4).

... 1984. *Paroles données*, Paris: Plon.

Lévy-Bruhl, Lucien 1922. *La mentalité primitive*, Paris: Félix Alcan.

... 1926 [1912]. *How Natives Think*, London: George Allen & Unwin.

Littlejohn, James 1973. Temne Right and Left: An Essay on the Choreography of Everyday Life, *in* Needham (ed.) 1973.

Llobera, Josep R. 1985. A Note on a Durkheimian Critic of Marx: The Case of Gaston Richard, *Journal of the Anthropological Society of Oxford* 16/1, 35–41.

Lukes, Steven 1973. *Émile Durkheim, His Life and Work: A Historical and Critical Study*, London: Allen Lane The Penguin Press.

MacClancy, Jeremy 1986. Mana: An Anthropological Metaphor for Island Melanesia, *Oceania* 57, 142–53.

... 1994. The Genealogy of Anthropology: Robert Hertz, Victor Turner, and the Study of Pilgrimage, *Journal of the Anthropological Society of Oxford* 25/1, 31–40 (Andrew Duff-Cooper Memorial Issue).

... and Parkin, Robert n.d. Revitalization or Continuity in European Ritual? The Case of San Bessu.

MacCormack C., and M. Strathern (eds.) 1980. *Nature, Culture and Gender*, Cambridge: Cambridge University Press.

Madan, T.N. 1981. Moral Choices: An Essay on the Unity of Asceticism and Eroticism, *in* Mayer (ed.) 1981.

... 1991. Auspiciousness and Purity: Some Reconsiderations, *Contributions to Indian Sociology* (n.s.) 25/2, 287–94.

Maître, Jacques 1966. La sociologie du catholicisme chez Czarnowski, Halbwachs, Hertz et van Gennep, *Archives de Sociologie des Religions* 21, 55–68.

Makarius, L.L. 1974. *Le sacré et la violation des interdits*, Paris: Payot.

... R. and L. 1973. *Structuralisme ou ethnologie: Pour une critique radicale de l'anthropologie de Lévi-Strauss*, Paris: Editions Anthropos.

Marcus, Julie 1984. Islam, Women and Pollution in Turkey, *Journal of the Anthropological Society of Oxford* 15/3, 204–18.

Matsunaga, Kazuto 1986. The Importance of the Left Hand in Two Types of Ritual Activity in a Japanese Village, *in* Joy Hendry and Jonathan Webber (eds.), *Interpreting Japanese Society: Anthropological Approaches*, Oxford: JASO (Occasional Papers, 5).

Mauss, Marcel 1907a. Review of Sir James Frazer, 'The Beginning of Religion and Totemism among the Australian Aborigines', *Année Sociologique* 10, 223–6.

... 1907b. Review of R.E. Dennett, *At the Back of the Black Man's Mind*, *Année Sociologique* 10, 305–11.

... 1910. Review of A.C. Kruijt, *Het Animisme in den Indischen Archipel*, *Année Sociologique* 11, 215–18.

... 1922. Note de l'editeur and Conclusion de l'editeur, *in* Hertz 1922.

... 1923. Intervention à la suite d'une communication de L. Lévy-Bruhl: 'La mentalité primitive', *Bulletin de la Société Française de Philosophie* 23, 24–8.

... 1925. In Memoriam, *L'Année Sociologique* n.s. 1, 7–29.

... 1927. Lucien Herr, *L'Année Sociologique* n.s. 2, 9.

... 1928. Alice Robert Hertz, *in* Hertz 1928.

... 1938. Une catégorie de l'esprit humain: La notion de personne, celle de 'moi' [Huxley Memorial Lecture 1938], *Journal of the Royal Anthropological Institute* 68, 263–81.

... 1950. *Sociologie et anthropologie*, Paris: Presses Universitaires Françaises.

... 1954 [1925]. *The Gift: Forms and Functions of Exchange in Archaic Societies*, London: Cohen & West.

... 1968, 1969. *Oeuvres*, Paris: Editions de Minuit (3 vols.).

... 1971 [1928]. Introduction, in Emile Durkheim, *Le Socialisme*, Paris: Presses Universitaires de France.

... 1983. An Intellectual Self-Portrait, *in* Philippe Besnard (ed.), *The Sociological Domain: The Durkheimians and the Founding of French Sociology*, Cambridge and Paris; Cambridge University Press and Maison des Sciences de l'Homme.

... 1994. Editor's Introduction and Conclusion, *in* Hertz 1994, 51–5, 111–19.

Mayer, Adrian C. (ed.) 1981. *Culture and Morality: Essays in Honour of Christoph von Fürer-Haimendorf*, Delhi etc.: Oxford University Press.

Meggitt M.J. 1964. Male–Female Relationships in the Highlands of Australian New Guinea, *American Anthropologist* 66 (Special Publication), 204–24.

Metcalf, Peter 1981. Meaning and Materialism: The Ritual Economy of Death, *Man* (n.s.) 16/4, 563–78.

... 1982. *A Borneo Journey into Death: Berawan Eschatology from its Rituals*, Philadelphia: The University of Pennsylvania Press.

... and Richard Huntington 1991. Introduction to *Celebrations of Death: The Anthropology of Mortuary Ritual*, Cambridge etc.: Cambridge University Press, 2nd edition. (See Huntington and Metcalf 1979 for 1st edition.)

Middleton, J. 1973. Some Categories of Dual Classification among the Lugbara of Uganda, *in* Needham (ed.) 1973.

Miles, Douglas 1965. Socio-economic Aspects of Secondary Burial, *Oceania* 35/3, 161–74.

Miller, Jay 1972. Priority of the Left, *Man* (n.s.) 7/4, 646–7.

Mimica, Jadran 1988. *Intimations of Infinity: The Cultural Meaning of the Iqwaye Counting System and Number*, Oxford etc.: Berg.

Mines, Diane Paull 1989. Hindu Periods of Death 'Impurity', *Contribution to Indian Sociology* 23/1, 103–130.

Moeran, Brian 1986. The Beauty of Violence: *Jidaigeki, Yakuza* and 'Eroduction' Films in Japanese Cinema, *in* David Riches (ed.), *The Anthropology of Violence*, Oxford: Basil Blackwell.

Moore, Sally Falk 1981. Chagga 'Customary' Law and the Property of the Dead, *in* S.C. Humphreys and Helen King (eds.), *Mortality and Immortality: The Anthropology and Archaeology of Death*, London etc.: Academic Press.

Morin, Edgar 1970. *L'Homme et la mort*, Paris: Seuil.

Morinis, E.A. 1984. *Pilgrimage in the Hindu Traditions: A Case Study of West Bengal*, Delhi: Oxford University Press.

Morris, Brian 1987. *Anthropological Studies of Religion: An Introductory Text*, Cambridge. Cambridge University Press.

Nandan, Yash 1977. *The Durkheimian School: A Systematic and Comprehensive Bibliography*, Westport, Ct., and London: Greenwood Press.

Needham, Rodney 1958. A Structural Analysis of Purum Society, *American Anthropologist* 60/1, 75-101.

... 1959. An Analytical Note on the Kom of Manipur, *Ethnos* 24/3-4, 121-35.

... 1960a. Alliance and Classification among the Lamet, *Sociologus* 10/2, 97-119.

... 1960b. A Structural Analysis of Aimol Society, *Bijdragen tot de Taal-, Land- en Volkenkunde* 116/1, 81-108.

... 1962a. *Structure and Sentiment: A Test Case in Social Anthropology*, Chicago and London: The University of Chicago Press.

... 1962b. Genealogy and Category in Wikmunkan Society, *Ethnology* 1/2, 223-64.

... 1963. Introduction to Durkheim and Mauss 1963 [1903].

... 1967. Terminology and Alliance: 2, Mapuche, Conclusions, *Sociologus* 17/1, 39-53.

... 1970. Introduction to Hocart 1970.

... 1972. *Belief, Language, and Experience*, Oxford: Basil Blackwell and Chicago: The University of Chicago Press.

... 1973a. Introduction, *in* Needham (ed.) 1973.

... 1973b [1960]. The Left Hand of the Mugwe: An Analytical Note on the Structure of Meru Symbolism, *in* Needham (ed.) 1973.

... 1973c [1967]. Right and Left in Nyoro Symbolic Classification, *in* Needham (ed.) 1973.

... 1976. Skulls and Causality, *Man* (n.s.) 11, 71-88.

... 1978. *Primordial Characters*, Charlottesville: University of Virginia Press.

... 1979a. *Symbolic Classification*, Santa Monica: Goodyear.

... 1979b. Hertz, Robert, *International Encyclopedia of the Social Sciences*, New York: The Free Press/London: Collier Macmillan (Bibliographical Supplement, Vol. 18, 295-7).

... 1980. *Reconnaissances*, Toronto: The University of Toronto Press.

... 1981. *Circumstantial Deliveries*, Berkeley etc.: University of California Press.

... 1985. *Exemplars*, Berkeley etc.: University of California Press.

... 1987. *Counterpoints*, Berkeley etc.: University of California Press.

Needham, Rodney (ed.) 1973. *Right & Left: Essays on Dual Symbolic Classification*, Chicago and London: The University of Chicago Press.

Nisbet, Robert A. 1975. *The Sociology of Emile Durkheim*, London: Heinemann.

Obeyesekere, Gananath 1968. Theodicy, Sin and Salvation in a Sociology of Buddhism, *in* E.R. Leach (ed.), *Dialectic in Practical Religion*, Cambridge: Cambridge University Press.

O'Flaherty, W.D. 1976. *The Origin of Evil in Hindu Mythology*, Berkeley: University of California Press.

Parkin, Robert 1988. Reincarnation and Alternating Generation Equivalence in Middle India. *Journal of Anthropological Research* 44/1, 1-20.

... 1992a. Asymétrie dualiste ou opposition hiérarchique? Le legs de Robert Hertz dans l'oeuvre de Rodney Needham et de Louis Dumont, *Recherches Sociologiques* 23/2, 43-68.

... 1992b. Robert Hertz: A Letter and a Bibliographical Update, *Durkheimian Studies/Etudes Durkheimiennes* 4 (Fall 1992), 21-4.

... 1992c. *The Munda of Central India: An Account of their Social Organization*, Delhi: Oxford University Press.

... 1994. Equality, Hierarchy and Temperament, *Journal of the Anthropological Society of Oxford* 25/1, 69-76 (Andrew Duff-Cooper Memorial Issue).

... forthcoming. From Science to Action: Durkheimians and the Groupe d'Etudes Socialistes, *Journal of the Anthropological Society of Oxford*.

Parry, Jonathan 1980. Ghosts, Greed and Sin: The Occupational Identity of the Benares Funeral Priests, *Man* 15/1, 88–111.

... 1985. Death and Digestion: The Symbolism of Food and Eating in North Indian Mortuary Rites, *Man* 20/4, 612–30.

... 1986. *The Gift*, the Indian Gift and the 'Indian Gift', *Man* 21/4, 453–73.

... 1991. The Hindu Lexicographer? A Note on Auspiciousness and Purity, *Contributions to Indian Sociology* (new series), 25/2, 267–85.

Pawlik, Jacek Jan 1990. *Expérience sociale de la mort: Etude des rites funéraires des Bassar du Nord-Togo*, Sankt Augustin: Editions Universitaires Fribourg Suisse.

Peel, J.D.Y. 1989. The Cultural Work of Yoruba Ethnogenesis, *in* Tonkin *et al.* (eds). 1989.

Perrin, Michael 1979. Il aura un bel enterrement: mort et funérailles guajiro, *in* Jean Guiart (ed.), *Les hommes et la mort: rituels funéraires à travers le monde*, Paris: Le Sycomore.

Pickering, W.S.F. 1984. *Durkheim's Sociology of Religion*, London etc.: Routledge & Kegan Paul.

Pina-Cabral, João de, 1980. Cults of Death in Northwestern Portugal, *Journal of the Anthropological Society of Oxford* 11/1, 1–14.

... 1986. *Sons of Adam, Daughters of Eve: The Peasant World-View of the Alto Minho*, Oxford: Clarendon Press.

... 1992. The Gods of the Gentiles are Demons: The Problem of Pagan Survivals in European Culture, *in* Kirsten Hastrup (ed.), *Other Histories*, London and New York: Routledge.

Platenkamp, J.D.M. 1990. 'The Severance of the Origin': A Ritual of the Tobelo of North Halmahera, *Bijdragen tot de Taal-, Land- en Volkenkunde* 146/1, 74–92.

Poppi, Cesare 1992. Building Difference: The Political Economy of Tradition in the Ladin Carnival of the Val di Fassa, *in* Boissevain (ed.) 1992.

Quaritch Wales, H.G. 1959. The Cosmological Aspect of Indonesian Religion, *Journal of the Royal Asiatic Society* 1959, 99–139.

Raheja, Gloria Goodwin 1988. *The Poison in the Gift: Ritual, Prestation, and the Dominant Caste in a North Indian Village*, Chicago: The University of Chicago Press.

... 1989. Centrality, Mutuality and Hierarchy: Shifting Aspects of Inter-caste Relationships in North India, *Contributions to Indian Sociology* n.s. 23/1, 79–101.

Rao, M.S.A. 1981. Changing Moral Values in the Context of Socio-Cultural Movements, *in* Mayer (ed.) 1981.

Rassers, W.H. 1959 [1922]. *Pañji, the Culture Hero: A Structural Study of Religion in Java*, The Hague: Martinus Nijhoff.

Rauh, Félix 1911. *Etudes de morale*, Paris: Félix Alcan.

Rigby, Peter 1973 [1966]. Dual Symbolic Classification among the Gogo of Central Tanzania, *in* Needham (ed.) 1973.

Rivers, W.H.R. 1926. *Psychology and Ethnology*, London: Kegan Paul, Trench, Trubner & Co. Ltd.

Riviere, Peter 1974. The Couvade: A Problem Reborn, *Man* 9, 423–35.

Rosaldo, M.Z., and J.M. Atkinson 1975. Man the Hunter: Metaphors for the Sexes in Ilongot Magical Spells, *in* Roy Willis (ed.), *The Interpretation of Symbolism*, London: Malaby Press (ASA Studies 3).

Roth, H. Ling 1896. *The Natives of Sarawak and British North Borneo*, London: Truslove & Hanson.

Sallnow, Michael 1981. Communitas Reconsidered: The Sociology of Andean Pilgrimage, *Man* (n.s.) 16/2, 163–83.

Sanchis, Pierre 1983. The Portuguese *romarias*, in Wilson ed. 1983.

Sax, William S. 1991. *Mountain Goddess: Gender and Politics in a Himalayan Pilgrimage*, New York: Oxford University Press.

Schärer, H. 1963 [1946]. *Ngaju Religion: The Conception of God Among a South Borneo People* (translated Rodney Needham), The Hague: Martinus Nijhoff.

Schulte Nordholt H.G. 1980. The Symbolic Classification of the Atoni of Timor, *in* James J. Fox (ed.), *The Flow of Life: Essays on Eastern Indonesia*, Cambridge, Mass.: Harvard University Press.

Schutte, G. 1980. Social Time and Biological Time: The Case of a Venda Child's Burial, *Anthropos* 75: 257-65.

Schwartz, Barry 1981. *Vertical Classification: A Study in Structuralism and the Sociology of Knowledge*, Chicago and London: The University of Chicago Press.

Sharma, Ursula 1973. Theodicy and the Doctrine of Karma, *Man* 8/3, 347-64.

Stanner, W.E.H. 1967. Reflections on Durkheim and Aboriginal Religion, *in* Maurice Freedman (ed.), *Social Organization: Essays Presented to Raymond Firth*, London: Frank Cass.

Steiner, Franz 1956. *Taboo*, Harmondsworth: Penguin.

Stephens, Meic 1978. *Linguistic Minorities in Europe*, Llandysul, Wales: Gomer Press.

Stöhr, Waldemar 1959. Das Totesritual der Dajak, *Ethnologica* (n.s.) 1, passim.

Strathern, Marilyn 1988. *The Gender of the Gift: Problems with Women and Problems with Society in Melanesia*, Berkeley etc.: The University of California Press.

Talbot Rice, Tamara 1987 [1967]. *Everyday Life in Byzantium*, New York: Dorset Press.

Tcherkézoff, Serge 1985. Black and White Dual Classification: Hierarchy and Ritual Logic in Nyamwezi Ideology, *in* R.H. Barnes, Daniel de Coppet and R.J. Parkin (eds.), *Contexts and Levels: Anthropological Essays on Hierarchy*, Oxford: JASO (JASO Occasional Papers 4).

... 1987 [1983]. *Dual Classification Reconsidered: Nyamwezi Sacred Kingship and Other Examples*, Cambridge: Cambridge University Press.

... 1994. On Hierarchical Reversals, Ten Years Later, *Journal of the Anthropological Society of Oxford* 25/2, 133-67; 25/3, forthcoming.

Thierry, Solange 1979. A Propos de l'étude de Robert Hertz: La représentation collective de la mort, *in* Jean Guiart (ed.), *Les hommes et la mort: rituels funéraires à travers le monde*, Paris: Le Sycomore.

Tonkin, E., M. McDonald and M. Chapman (eds.) 1989. *History and Ethnicity*, London and New York: Routledge (ASA Monographs, 27).

Traube, Elizabeth G. 1980a. Affines and the Dead: Mambai Rituals of Alliance, *Bijdragen tot de Taal-, Land- en Volkenkunde* 136/1, 90-115.

... 1980b. Mambai Rituals of Black and White, in James J. Fox (ed.), *The Flow of Life: Essays on Eastern Indonesia*, Cambridge, Mass.: Harvard University Press.

... 1986. *Cosmology and Social Life: Ritual Exchange among the Mambai of East Timor*, Chicago and London: The University of Chicago Press.

Turner, Terence 1984. Dual Opposition, Hierarchy, and Value: Moiety Structure and Symbolic Polarity in Central Brazil and Elsewhere, *in* Jean-Claude Galey (ed.), *Différences, valeurs, hiérarchie: textes offerts à Louis Dumont*, Paris: Editions de l'Ecole des Hautes Etudes en Sciences Sociales.

Turner, Victor 1966. Colour Classification in Ndembu Ritual, *in* Michael Banton (ed.), *Anthropological Approaches to the Study of Religion*. London: Tavistock Publications (ASA Monographs 3).

... 1974a. *Dramas, Fields, and Metaphors: Symbolic Action in Human Society*, Ithaca and London: Cornell University Press.

... 1974b. *The Ritual Process*, Harmondsworth: Penguin.

Vincent, Jeanne-Françoise 1978. Main gauche, main de l'homme: essai sur le symbolisme de la gauche et la droite chez les Mofu, in *Systèmes de signes: Hommage à G. Dieterlin*, Paris: Hermann.

Wadley, Susan S., and Bruce W. Derr 1989. Eating Sins in Karimpur, *Contributions to Indian Sociology* n.s. 23/1, 131–48.

Webb, Sidney, and Beatrice Webb 1911. *The Prevention of Destitution*, London: Longmans, Green & Co.

... 1912. *What Syndicalism Means*, London: The Crusader (Supplement).

Weiner, Annette 1980. Reproduction: A Replacement for Reciprocity, *American Ethnologist* 7/1, 71–85.

Weiner, James 1988. *The Heart of the Pearl Shell: The Mythological Dimension of Foi Sociality*, Berkeley etc.: University of California Press 1988.

Westermarck, Edward A. 1891. *The History of Human Marriage*, London: Macmillan (3 vols.).

White, John 1887-90. *Ancient History of the Maori: His Mythology and Traditions*, Wellington (6 vols.).

Wieschhoff, Heinz A. 1973 [1938]. Concepts of Right and Left in African Cultures, *in* Needham (ed.) 1973.

Wile, Ira S. 1934. *Handedness: Right and Left*, Boston, Mass.: Lothrop, Lee, & Shepard.

Wilken, G.A. 1884, 1885. Het Animisme bij de Volken van den Indischen Archipel, *Indische Gids* 1884/I, 925–1000; 1884/II, 19–100; 1985/I, 13–58, 191–242.

Wilson, Stephen 1983a. Introduction, *in* Wilson ed. 1983.

... 1983b. Cults of Saints in the Churches of Central Paris, *in* Wilson ed. 1983.

Wilson, Stephen (ed.) 1983. *Saints and their Cults: Studies in Religious Sociology, Folklore and History*, Cambridge etc.: Cambridge University Press.

Wouden, F.A.E. van, 1968 [1935]. *Types of Social Structure in Eastern Indonesia* (translated Rodney Needham), The Hague: Martinus Nijhoff.

Wright, Susan 1992. 'Heritage' and Critical History in the Reinvention of Mining Festivals in North-East England, *in* Boissevain (ed.) 1992.

Zeldin, Theodore 1973. *France 1848–1945, Volume One: Ambition, Love and Politics*, Oxford: Clarendon Press.

Zvelebil, K.V. 1988. *The Irulas of the Blue Mountains*, Syracuse, New York: Maxwell School of Citizenship and Public Affairs.

Subject Index

Name Index